HEGEMONY HOW-TO
A ROADMAP FOR RADICALS

by
Jonathan
Matthew
Smucker

MORE PRAISE FOR *HEGEMONY HOW-TO*

"Principles + Pragmatic Organizing = People Power. That's the pithiest summation of Jonathan Smucker's argument–but he's quick to show that radicals too often fetishize principle, disdain pragmatism, and eschew real power, and so never really change anything. Smucker wants to actively heal society; if that's you, too, study this fantastic book."

—**Ian Haney López**, author of *Dog Whistle Politics*

"One of the most creative organizers in the country has eloquently articulated the next generation's *Rules for Radicals*. A must read!"

—**Sally Kohn**, political commentator at CNN

"If Bernie Sanders' 2016 campaign showed anything, it's a broad appetite for deep change. But turning that hope into effective action will require thinking about social movements and how they work (and don't). There's much grist for the organizer's mill in these pages."

—**Bill McKibben**, author *Deep Economy*

"Jonathan Smucker gives a powerful and personal account of how the radical left often undermines its own political aims. But rather than just offering a critique, he also recommends practical and constructive ways forward... Written in an elegant, engaging style, Smucker's book is a must-read for all those seeking progress in our troubled world today."

—**Erica Chenoweth**, co-author of *Why Civil Resistance Works*

"Here are practical suggestions on how we build a mass movement to replace the dominant and debilitating individualism of the last forty years... Aspiring change-makers please take note."

—**Mark Rudd**, author of *Underground: My Life with SDS and the Weathermen*

"This is a valuable book for organizers for exactly this moment, when we need hope for the way ahead. Smucker provides so many important insights."

—**Heather Booth**, founding Director and President of the Midwest Academy

"Jonathan Smucker is a critical voice within an important emerging political project whose aim is to move the next left generation from symbolic and often self-marginalizing strategies toward approaches that can lead to effective main-stage intervention."

—**Max Elbaum**, author of *Revolution in the Air*

Hegemony How-To: A Roadmap for Radicals

© 2017 Jonathan Matthew Smucker

This edition © 2017 AK Press (Chico, Oakland, Edinburgh, Baltimore)

ISBN: 978-1-84935-254-3
E-ISBN: 978-1-84935-255-0
Library of Congress Control Number: 2016942001

AK Press	AK Press
370 Ryan Ave. #100	33 Tower St.
Chico, CA 95973	Edinburgh EH6 7BN
USA	Scotland
www.akpress.org	www.akuk.com
akpress@akpress.org	ak@akedin.demon.co.uk

The above addresses would be delighted to provide you with the latest AK Press distribution catalog, which features books, pamphlets, zines, and stylish apparel published and/or distributed by AK Press. Alternatively, visit our websites for the complete catalog, latest news, and secure ordering.

Hegemony How-To draws on writings that first appeared in the following publications: *Beautiful Trouble: A Toolbox for Revolution* (OR Books, 2012); *The Sociological Quarterly*, 54 no. 12; *The Berkeley Journal of Sociology*, 58; *n+1 Occupy! Gazette*, 5; and *We Are Many: Reflections on Strategy from Occupation to Liberation* (AK Press, 2012).

Cover design by Jonathan Matthew Smucker and Margaret Killjoy

Printed in the USA on acid free, recycled paper

We think radicals will gain a lot from Jonathan Smucker's arguments for a broad, inclusive movement that can take power away from capitalists and the politicians who do their bidding, in order to build a more free world. Our movements need to be investigated and critiqued. Smucker's personal politics sometimes include strategies for social change that AK Press doesn't advocate, but we think the ideas he presents will be useful to a range of strategic approaches, be they non-reformist reforms, revolutionary unionism, community syndicalism, prison abolition, or just about any radical attempt to reshape our society. We hope, dear reader, you'll enjoy this book in the spirit of critique and clarification—and may this roadmap assist as you chart your own journey and destination.

—The AK Press Collective

CONTENTS

FOREWORD

BY JANICE FINE

I have a good friend who is wary of social movements. He isn't a right-winger. He is a brilliant community organizer who has built major organizations in New York, New England, and the Midwest. Even when Occupy Wall Street was at its height, spreading from city to city, and attracting enormous media attention to the problem of economic inequality, my friend was unmoved. In his eyes, the encampment at Zuccotti Park was not an oasis, prefiguring a new society. It was a mirage, evocative of some of the worst pathologies of the American left and a distraction from the real work of organizing: recruiting a base, developing a strategy, formulating demands, expanding the scope of conflict, taking action...building power and lasting institutions.

As it turns out, my friend and Jonathan Smucker, a talented organizer who was a core participant in Occupy Wall Street, would have more to say to each other than I would have thought. Smucker has spent much of the past five years reflecting on the lessons of Occupy. *Hegemony How-To* is an insider's attempt to mine the sociological canon to wrestle with why Occupy sputtered and explore what it takes to more effectively organize and build power *with* the 99%. Smucker pays special attention to Occupy because it is emblematic of problems that he has experienced in his two decades of organizing work with a variety of social movements; the book is much more than a critique of this particular "movement moment." Through the questions he poses and the literatures he brings in, Smucker provides a fresh and insightful look at an old and vexing problem.

I particularly appreciate the book's deep examination of left "movement culture" and the light it shines on our tendency toward insularity and self-enclosure. Smucker observes that oppositional groups, as they struggle to create their own safe spaces, narratives, rituals, and distinctive communities, often have a penchant for developing in self-referential directions—sometimes coming to choose the comfort of their clubhouses over the scrum and the inevitable compromises of politics. Along these lines, he holds the emergent culture of Occupy responsible for its demise.

But Smucker's agenda isn't finger-pointing or blame. He urges us to take a hard look at patterns of internal dysfunction in order to better seize the abundant organizing and mobilizing opportunities before us today. Occupy's premature unraveling is a tragedy for Smucker precisely because of the radical potential its early success seemed to promise. Occupy wildly, thrillingly succeeded at "reframing a potent and popular class conscious narrative" and the mainstream media was shockingly open to carrying the message and covering the novel movement. But in its resistance to uniting with existing groups, social blocs, and institutions that were key to expansion, Occupy ultimately sabotaged itself. To partially explain the origins of these self-destructive inclinations, Smucker puts forward the notion of the *political identity paradox*: in order to succeed, social movements need to foster the deep group identity that leads a dedicated core to make extraordinary commitments of their energy and time, but this same strong internal cohesion can lead to isolation that will prevent organizations from acting effectively to achieve their political goals. I think he's spot on.

One of Smucker's most incisive observations about Occupy is that over time the rituals that grew up around the movement's process of decision-making came not to *facilitate* the development of strategy, but to *stand in* for strategy itself. While viewing the hyper-democratic General Assemblies at Zuccotti Park as brilliant theatre and an important part of the public message that "juxtaposed a visibly participatory people's movement against a rotted political system," Smucker nonetheless came to the conclusion that it was nearly impossible to get anything done through this forum. "Because they were so cumbersome and easily derailed, many of the most active Occupy organizers...eventually stopped attending with much frequency. We were too busy attending to tasks to be able to sit through hours upon hours of exasperating do-nothing meetings. Thus much of the real decision-making was pushed ... into underground centers of informal power." Anyone who has worked inside organizations, coalitions, or movements with hyper-democratic processes but no formal structures is sure to recognize the hard truth of Smucker's words.

In the existential and intellectual wrestling match between *movement* and *organization* that has been going on inside the American left for generations, this book reaches for synthesis. If our ambition is to be a hegemonic actor, Smucker argues that we should embrace the Gramscian concept of *articulation* where there is a fusion of the *institutional* contest —"the strategic capacity to maneuver through the minutia of political terrain to shape structures, laws, policies, distributions of wealth and relationships of power," which is the realm of organizing—with the *symbolic* contest—"the capacity to shape narrative, symbols, meaning, and common sense," which is the realm of movement. Our desire for such synthesis is the reason why the civil rights movement is every community organizer's favorite—because it was a movement that incorporated institutions while it also catalyzed challenger groups and included tactics and messages (e.g., lunch counter sit-ins, Freedom Rides, etc.) that compellingly prefigured the movement's vision of a more racially just society.

The subtitle for this book is "A Roadmap for Radicals." Smucker understands that to contest power, grassroots organizations and social movements must have more than a vision of a better world; they need some sense of *how* to get there. In his words, "knowledge of *what is wrong* with a social system and knowledge of *how to change* the system are two completely different categories of knowledge," and this book focuses first and foremost on the latter, thus serving as a twenty-first century organizer's toolbox for the day-to-day work of building and wielding collective power: how to build organizations, how to provide entry points and ladders of engagement, how to develop strategies calibrated to move more individuals and organizations from passive support into the active allies column, and how to put forth a set of ideas, narratives, and memes that are situated *within* American cultural tropes rather than outside of them.

I so appreciate Smucker's willingness to tell us what happened on the inside of Occupy, amongst other movements, from his perspective—to air his frustrations and mine the scholarly literature for insights into the predicaments, peccadillos, and contradictions of the US left. He says that when he first got involved in social movements, he felt like something of a "political orphan," not finding many mentors or resources to guide him toward thinking more strategically about social change. I hope that this book will find its way into the hands of many of the dedicated young people who may find themselves in a similar situation today. So much depends upon the new social movements that are emerging today to confront the multiple crises we presently face. In the right hands, this book might just contribute to these important movements' success.

Janice Fine is Associate Professor of Labor Studies and Employment Relations at the School of Management and Labor Relations, Rutgers University, Director of Research and Strategy at the Center for Innovation in Worker Organization (CIWO), and author of the book *Worker Centers: Organizing Communities at the Edge of the Dream* published by Cornell University Press and the Economic Policy Institute.

ACKNOWLEDGMENTS

There is a joke among organizers, that we ourselves are often quite disorganized. As someone who is surely guilty of this charge, I am certain that I will now forget some of the many people who have helped me with this book in so many ways. *Hegemony How-To* is the product of social movements. In contrast to academia, social movements tend to be spaces where individuals freely contribute ideas without much bother about proprietary questions concerning origins or credit. And the truth is that no book belongs to its author alone. While I take sole responsibility for the errors and shortcomings in this work, I am happy to share credit far and wide for anything the reader may find useful. I have wrestled with this work amidst constant dialogue and ongoing collaboration with several groups and countless individuals, over the course of many political struggles. I would like to express my deepest gratitude for the people who have helped me with this process.

First and foremost, I want to thank my partner in crime, Becca Rast, whose support throughout this long process has been so important to me, from providing invaluable feedback on draft chapters to tolerating my frequent antisocial retreats and solo all-nighters. I also want to thank Becca's and my families for all of their support along the way.

I would like to thank everyone in *Beyond the Choir* for workshopping sections of this book as part of our training curriculum: Ange Tran, Anika Fassia, Charon Hribar, Jose Vasquez, Judith

Leblanc, Michelle Crentsil, Scott Roberts, and Perry O'Brien. I especially want to thank Perry for providing elaborate feedback on the entire first draft of the book. Thanks also to Madeline Gardner, who helped to start Beyond the Choir as a humble side project over a decade ago, and whose intellectual collaboration set me on the path of developing the core ideas in *Hegemony How-To*.

Other movement groups and organizations that have helped to shape or support this book include *Beautiful Trouble* (especially Andrew Boyd, who deserves praise or blame for convincing all parties involved to keep the title; Andrew also provided me with volumes of helpful feedback); the *Center for Story-based Strategy*, whose narrative strategy tools have had a tremendous influence on my thinking (special thanks to Patrick Reinsborough and Doyle Canning); and the clandestine affinity group *The Recidivists* of Occupy Wall Street infamy (you know who you are).

I also want to thank all of my colleagues in the sociology department at UC Berkeley. I feel especially grateful for the wonderful and fun-loving members of my cohort, who, knowingly or not, helped me through our seminar discussions to work out many of the ideas in this book: Aya Fabros, David Showalter, Fatinha Santos, Ghaleb Attrache, Liz McKenna, Mark Quinn, Martin Eiermann, Ogi Radic, Phung Su, Robert Pickett, Santiago Molina, Seth Leibson, Steven Lauterwasser, Tom Gilbert, and Véronique Irwin. Faculty members who have been especially helpful in providing advice and feedback include Cihan Tuğal, Kim Voss, Loïc Wacquant, Margaret Weir, Marion Fourcade, and Michael Burawoy. Other colleagues at UC Berkeley (in or close to the sociology department) who workshopped chapters with me or who otherwise deserve credit: Alex Barnard, Ana Villarreal, Fidan Elcioglu, Gabriel Hetland, Rebecca Tarlau, as well as visiting scholars Marie Mourad and Simon Escoffier. Prior to my arrival at Berkeley, two of my advisors at Goddard College, Robert Buchanan and Eva Swidler, provided extensive feedback on early versions of chapters (in the form of assignments).

Other individuals who have provided me with thoughtful feedback on sections of the book, or who have provided helpful advice or much-appreciated support: Allyson Gross, Andrew Hsaio,

Astra Taylor, Austin Thompson, Beka Economopoulos, Brooke Lehman, Chandra Russo, Erik Olin Wright, Ernesto Laclau, Francesca Polletta, George Lakey, Guido Girgenti, Han Shan, Hannah Dunphy, Harmony Goldberg, Harriet Barlow, Holly Scott, James Jasper, Jane McAlevey, Janice Fine, Jason Haas-Hecker, John Neffinger, Kate Aronoff, Leah Hunt-Hendrix, Lina Blount, Mark Engler, Marshall Ganz, Max Berger, Max Elbaum, Meghna Chandra, Nelini Stamp, Nick Martin, Paul Engler, Richard Flacks, Richard Healey, Sara Blazevic, Waleed Shahid, Will Driscoll, Will Lawrence, William Gamson, and Zeynep Tufekci.

For two amazing month-long writing retreats, I am indebted to the Blue Mountain Center, whose coffee, cookies, and delicious cuisine made for the best writing fuel. And for a privately hosted month-long writing retreat in Arcata, California, I have to thank the Nasti Family: Hannah, James, Nyah, and Zae.

Finally, in writing this book, I stand on the shoulders of all those who have gone before, who number too many to even begin to list. But if I were to single out one specific person whose life and ideas contributed to this specific work, I would thank Antonio Gramsci—for his dedicated contribution to the social world from which he was banished. I wonder what he felt as he scribbled in fits and starts what we have come to know as the *Prison Notebooks*. I imagine that he must have tapped into some reserve whose source had to be somewhere far beyond the prison walls, whose truth was beyond the grasp of the fascist's censor. What is it that kept him at it, that kept him agonizing over how best to engage with this beautiful world, even as he had been sealed off from its wonders and beauty; over how best to engage power, even as power had confined him to a cell? What inspiration might we take today in our own struggles—personal and political—from such a persistent spirit who enjoins us to hold onto both a "pessimism of the intellect" and an "optimism of the will"?[1]

---

1   Antonio Gramsci, *Selections from the Prison Notebooks*, ed. and trans. Quentin Hoare and Geoffrey Nowell Smith (New York: International Publishers, 1971), 175.

POLITICAL ORPHANS

"My fellow radicals who were supposed to pass on the torch of experience and insights to a new generation just were not there."

—Saul Alinsky[1]

Late to the game

"Do you ever think we came to the game too late?"

Carmen Trotta has a heaviness about him. Burdened. He is also charming and always sincere, but he doesn't pose questions like this one for the sake of making conversation. He thought that there was a very good chance that we had literally been born too late to do anything to stop humanity from destroying itself completely.

Maybe the social movements of the 1960s, or those of the 1930s, could have corrected the course. Carmen wasn't about to argue that these movements had accomplished nothing important. But they had fallen short in important respects—and he wondered if the damage could be remedied at this point. A dozen years my senior, he had barely missed the wave of social movements—from civil rights to feminism, from student protests to anti-colonial revolutions—that had shaken the world, but that had by now, only about a quarter century later, become an almost unbelievable distant

---

1   Saul Alinsky, *Rules for Radicals* (New York: Vintage Books, 1971), xiii.

memory. Carmen came of age in the 1980s, an era that seemed to be inoculated against the memories and ideas of "the 60s."

Carmen, Jeremy Scahill, and I were discussing politics in a bar in New York City's Lower East Side, just two blocks from the Saint Joseph Catholic Worker house, where they both worked and lived. It was the spring of 1997. Bill Clinton had just been inaugurated for a second term and the Dow had just broken 7,000 points for the first time. At that point, Carmen had lived at the Worker for more than ten years—he still lives there today—splitting his time between serving meals to poor and homeless people, working on the Catholic Worker monthly newspaper (which still costs a penny a copy), and engaging in protest against social injustices—from opposing New York slumlords to US wars of empire. A practicing Catholic, Carmen found a political home in what remained of the Catholic left, taking action alongside people like Liz McAllister, Phil Berrigan, and Dan Berrigan (the ex-nun, ex-priest, and priest, respectively, who famously burned draft board files and broke into US military bases to hammer on weapons, "turning swords into plowshares").

Carmen's day-to-day routine of service and sacrifice points to an interesting thing about the question he posed: its answer didn't make a difference to how he lives his life. Whether or not there's any realistic reason for hope, he would continue to live with and serve the poor and to put his body on the line to oppose injustice— even if failure were assured—because it was the right thing to do. Carmen is one of those rare people who do not need hope in order to take costly moral political action. That did not mean, however, that outcomes were unimportant to him. He wanted to believe that our actions could make the world a better place. That is why he was asking us this question—he sincerely wanted to know what Jeremy and I thought about humanity's realistic prospects.

"Maybe it is too late," I answered soberly. "I really don't know."

We were living at "the end of history"[2]—the Cold War was over and capitalism had won, so the story went. Carmen, Jeremy,

---

2   Francis Fukuyama, *The End of History and the Last Man* (New York: Free Press, 1992).

and I certainly did not believe the claim that "There is no alternative,"[3] but neither did we see anything on the horizon resembling a threat to capitalism's hegemony, or a prospect for a world with more social justice. Those who had stayed active in the remnants of the movements of the long 1960s seemed to be perpetually up against the culture. Ronald Reagan's popularity—and all that went along with it—had a deeply demoralizing effect (not to mention the consequences of actual policies, from the PATCO[4] strike to intervention in Latin America). As the millennium came to an end, everything felt hopeless and apocalyptic for young social justice–oriented radicals like me, who were new to the scene.

Protest and politics were still so new for me then. I had met Jeremy in Cuba the summer before. He was as charismatic as he was politically astute, and I liked him immediately. He had just served a month in jail for civil disobedience at the Pentagon. I was inspired to meet someone who was willing to make sacrifices for what he believed—to put his money where his mouth was. We bonded by making wisecracks about all the Socialist Workers Party members who made up about a third of our youth delegation to Cuba. We viewed them as do-nothings who only wanted to sell their newspaper, *The Militant*—we called it *The Hesitant*—at the periphery of protests that other people organized. Upon our return to the States, Jeremy introduced me to Carmen, and soon the two of them were mentoring me as I organized a campaign against Walmart's grand opening in my hometown.

Righteousness and agency

My unlikely trip to Cuba, at age 18, had been made possible in large part by the fundraising efforts of the Philadelphia-based Cuba Support Coalition, and in part thanks to my parents' present

---

3   Margaret Thatcher, "Press Conference for American correspondents in London," Margaret Thatcher Foundation, June 25, 1980, http://www.margaretthatcher.org/Speeches/displaydocument.asp?docid=104389&doctype=1.

4   Professional Air Traffic Controllers Organization (trade union).

to me for (barely) graduating from high school. My parents' sponsorship of an illegal trip to Cuba may make me sound like a "red diaper baby," raised by radical communists. That's nowhere close to the truth. I grew up conservative and relatively sheltered. I was brought up Mennonite on a farm outside of the tiny town of Bird-In-Hand in Lancaster County, Pennsylvania. Bird-In-Hand's economy was based on agriculture and tourism. Tourists from New York City and around the world would come and stare from their cars at the Amish as the latter worked the land. The Amish were our neighbors, friends, and relatives, perfectly normal and boring—what was strange to us was why anyone would find them so interesting. As a Mennonite, my life revolved around church and family. I attended worship services at least twice a week, and attended Mennonite school, from Kindergarten onward.

Lancaster County was only a three-hour drive from that bar in the Lower East Side. Until only a few months prior I had lived my entire life in Lancaster. But now it seemed like a different universe and an eternity away. Though nowhere close to being a radical, my father had briefly flirted with the counter-culture at the tail end of the Vietnam War. The draft ended just one month before he would have come up for the lottery. When he was a high school senior, in 1971, he took an unauthorized "field trip" to Washington DC with his older brother for the May Day mass civil disobedience against the war. He and his brother even broke through a police line in order to avoid arrest. That was only seven years before I was born, the youngest of three children—but it probably seemed like an eternity away to my father by then. He and my mother, by age 25 and 23, respectively, had to provide for a family of five. Both of their families were poor, and neither of them had attended college. Economically, they had little choice but to settle down in their conservative community of origin and to forget about whatever alternative notions they may have briefly entertained. While they had no love for Ronald Reagan, they also hardly had a developed political analysis—or encouragement from anyone around them to pursue such a thing. My father took over managing a delicatessen stand at the Allentown Farmer's Market, and my mother worked various odd jobs. Whether or not he made a conscious decision to do so, Dad's social and economic survival strategy entailed shutting the hell up about his brief adventure in the counter-culture—so much so that all I ever caught wind of while growing up was seeing photos of him with long hair at age 19 working on a sail ship, and hearing a few stories about his hitchhiking adventures in Europe.

Indeed, the way I learned more about my father's short-lived radicalism was from my conservative uncles, who brought it up when I started inarticulately questioning the status quo myself. Their intention was not encouragement, but rather to dismiss my newfound politics as a passing phase.

"Yeah, your dad used to go to protests too. Don't worry, you'll grow out of it—just like he did."

I was afraid that time would prove them right. The truth was, other than the deep intuitive sense of social justice that I had acquired, I had no idea what I was doing. Only a few short years before, I had just been a more-or-less "normal" kid in rural America. I spent way too much time watching television and playing video games. I was always trying to make a few bucks selling contraband at school, like noisemakers and bubblegum. I was not scholastically inclined—a few times I had to take summer classes to not repeat a grade. I was not remotely well-read. I had a weak sense of history and politics, let alone cosmopolitan culture. Looking back, my "not knowing any better" sometimes played out in comical ways. I remember sitting in the back of the car listening to adults discussing poverty, when I was in sixth grade. A light bulb went on in my head and I butted in enthusiastically with my surely original idea:

"What if everyone just took everything that they made together and shared it?"

"There's a name for that!" my aunt snapped back at me, "It's called *communism!*"

I didn't know what that meant, but it seemed really bad. Two years later, after a childhood of Mennonite education in which I had to memorize assigned Bible verses every week, I started to read the Bible on my own—less selectively than how it had been taught to me up until then, it turned out. Very soon I discovered

that neither myself nor Karl Marx had invented the idea of sharing in common the product of everyone's labor; Jesus Christ had
spouted off about it two thousand years ago. And apparently it
got him killed.

I became disillusioned as I read the Bible and discovered that
the theology of individualistic salvation from eternal damnation
had little basis in the scriptures, while social and economic justice
was a central theme. I studied the gospels and the prophets and
began reading about the global economy at the same time, applying the message of the former to the contemporary world in which
I found myself awakening. I hadn't yet heard of *liberation theology,* but I was deeply inspired by the prophets and how they stood
up, sometimes all alone, on behalf of the poor and oppressed, to
admonish the rich and powerful—often at great personal cost. I
wanted to be like them. I felt myself called to the wilderness. At age
17 I told my parents that I was leaving home to follow that calling.

I left with $200, a backpack, and no plan other than to zeal-
ously seek whatever I might find. I hitchhiked from Pennsylvania up into New England, and then across the Midwest, camping
in fields and forests and relying on the generosity of strangers.
I prayed and fasted and read the Bible, while taking a month to
circle Lake Michigan. I didn't have any of the mystical visions
that I may have been hoping for. But I worked through a great
deal of fear. It wasn't hitchhiking or strangers or sleeping alone in
the woods that frightened me—all of these things delighted me.
What scared me to my core were the unsettling feelings I increasingly felt the more I learned about the structures of society, the
economy, and the United States government. This new knowledge defied the common sense that I had been learning over the
whole course of my childhood. I was deeply distressed that my
emerging beliefs seemed to contradict the version of Christianity
that I was raised to believe. Reading the gospels, I found a front-
and-center emphasis on social justice in the here and now, but
at church I heard mostly about individual salvation for a select
few in the hereafter. I experienced this as a profound break from
the *doxa* of the only community I had ever known—a community
that I loved. I wanted God to speak clearly and audibly to tell me

that my new and nascent beliefs were, in fact, *Truth*. If I could have absolute certainty about my beliefs, then I would be willing to do anything for them—to be ostracized, even to die. I prayed and prayed, asking for this certainty. And finally one day, alone in the American wilderness, in the silence, a strong sense suddenly came over me—a feeling that God was about to answer my prayer. There was no audible voice. There was only a thought, like a whisper:

"If I answer, you will stop asking."

In that moment it suddenly dawned on me that one should never know for certain that their partial truth was God's universal truth—or whether or not God was on their side. I thought of all the horrors that have been committed by people who entertained no doubts about the rightness of their actions, and I decided right then that I would always maintain a healthy measure of self-doubt. I would embrace a life in which questions were more important than definitive answers.

At the same time, however, I knew that a lack of certainty was no excuse for not taking decisive action on the moral issues of my time. I felt that I had to figure out a way to take bold action on the social justice issues that had captured my attention. I knew intuitively that there would be costs to speaking or acting upon my emerging convictions. I was quite familiar with the story of the righteous person who speaks truth to power. That story ended on a cross.

Like Carmen, I had come to the point where I did not need to believe that my efforts would achieve successful results in order to proceed. I returned home at the end of the summer in order to finish my last year of high school. This was the concession my parents had won from me when I left home, along with my promise to call twice a week—in exchange they had agreed not to report me as a runaway. Upon returning home, I knew what I had to do. At Lancaster Mennonite High School each day began with the approximately 800 students, plus faculty, gathering for chapel—a kind of mini-worship service. I signed up to lead one such service. I wrote myself a script. Half of it was scripture, the other half was information about the global economy: exploitation, sweatshops, union-busting, ecological destruction, death squads, imperialism, empire, and so on. We were all implicated, I argued, as complacent beneficiaries of an oppressive global order. I read verbatim the script I had written, my heart beating hard. Summarizing the Exodus story, a 17-year-old me, timid and shaking, said into the microphone to 800 fellow students: "A struggle is taking place; a struggle between the Egyptians and the Israelites; a struggle between oppressors and oppressed; a struggle between rich and poor. That's right, it's a class struggle. An economic class struggle is taking place. So it is no wonder that God sides with the Israelites. God always sides with the poor and oppressed, and is therefore against the rich oppressors."[5]

I could feel the disapproval of the Vice Principal, Mr. King, who sat on the bench on the stage behind me. Anticipating the possible content of my chapel, he had stopped me in the hall the afternoon before to advise, "You know, Jesus said that the poor will always be among us." As I read on, I kept wondering if he would interrupt me and put an end to my intervention. Silence in the auditorium. Except for my trembling voice. I looked up from my papers on the podium to see my dad at the back of the chapel, appearing to be following my words intently, deep in thought. He had come to see me speak, but he didn't know what I was going to say.[6] Then I saw Mike, who was both the student council president and my neighbor, rising from his seat and walking out defiantly. Several other students followed him. This was precisely the kind of thing I had been expecting. No normal classes would be held at LMH that day. Teachers had to facilitate heated discussions

---

5   I should make clear for any readers who may be unfamiliar with the Exodus story of the Bible—and how it is a staple text in *Liberation Theology*—that the "Egyptians" and "Israelites" describe a relationship of economic enslavement and oppression, and thus serve as homology. God being on the side of the Israelites, in the story, is about their position as the oppressed and enslaved people. *Egyptian* and *Israelite* here in no way reference any specific present-day nation or "people."

6   From that day forward, my father has been supportive of my political work, even if he was not ecstatic when I started getting arrested.

about my remarks the whole day long. In that sheltered environment, my message was the bombshell that I thought it would be. It was only a matter of time before I would be stoned to death or hanging on a cross, all alone.

What I had not anticipated was the number of students who would resonate with the message and who would want to find out more. They even wanted to do something about the situation I had spotlighted—to take some kind of action. Nor had I anticipated how many teachers and faculty members would agree with the social justice message. Teachers, it turned out, had to be careful to not appear too "liberal," lest they become the next victim of the periodic witch-hunts that conservative parents were known to take up. My act had given teachers cover to open up space in their classroom to candidly discuss social and economic justice issues, as they could not be accused of initiating the conversation. Starting the conversation was my part to play.

At the end of the school day, I went promptly to Mennonite Central Committee (MCC), an organization whose headquarters are in Lancaster County. It was at MCC's alternative resource library where I had first paged through publications like *New Internationalist, Multinational Monitor,* and *The Catholic Worker*—my initial sources for self-education about the global economy. This time I walked into the main office and I asked for help. I told the first folks I saw what I had done that morning. News travels fast in tight-knit Mennonite communities—they had already heard. I also told them about the response, especially the students who wanted to find out more. One of the two people I encountered there was Dave Schrock-Shenk, who just so happened to be working on a curriculum for a 30-day educational experiment for groups called *World of Enough.* It wasn't ready yet, but we soon made plans to pilot the draft curriculum with 70 interested students at Lancaster Mennonite.

This was my first small taste of political hope. I had psyched myself up to play my part in a *story of the righteous few.* I had expected that by speaking my truth, I would be rejected by everyone. It's not that there was nothing of value about the process I had gone through to psych myself up. After all, I had faced my deepest fears and overcome them. And I had found my voice—it was shaking, but it was audible and I could sense the power of saying aloud what I felt needed to be said. I wasn't totally off base in my prediction of the reaction: the social justice message was, indeed, rejected by many in the audience—violently so by a few folks later on. However, for others, the message had resonated and served as a spark.

In telling myself a story of the righteous few, I had assumed that *dominant* beliefs were held more enthusiastically by more people than was actually the case. Because I didn't see blatant, visible signs of a social justice paradigm, I assumed that meant that no one around me held these values. When I was a kid my mom was fond of saying, "It's not going to jump out and bite you!" whenever I was looking for something (like a missing toy) in a half-assed manner. She was teasing me for the ridiculousness of how I would impatiently glance around a room, not see the thing I wanted, and immediately give up. What I came to realize from the positive responses to my chapel talk—and from the 70 students who participated in the *World of Enough* campaign that followed—is that social justice values are always all around me, even if I can't see it at first glance, even if I have to dig around to uncover them. And my role isn't to mope about how I can't find what I'm looking for—let alone to condemn the whole scene, while fancying myself some kind of righteous prophet whom the world isn't ready for. There's nothing righteous about standing alone, impotently—at least not as long as I have other avenues to pursue. My role instead, I started to understand, was to dig in, to look under the surface, to find and to help cultivate and activate social justice values. I came to realize that dominant ideology is not believed by everyone—sometimes it is not even believed by the majority. Years later I came upon a passage by Brazilian educator Paulo Freire that nicely sums up my initial error: "Sometimes, in our uncritical understanding of the nature of the struggle, we can be led to believe that all the everyday life of the people is a mere reproduction of the dominant ideology. But it is not. There will always be something of the dominant ideology in the cultural expressions of the people, but there is also in contradiction to it

the signs of resistance—in the language, in music, in food prefer-
ences, in popular religion, in their understanding of the world."[7]

My experience of connecting with others on social justice
values and then of figuring out together a way to take collective
action produced in me a feeling of efficacy—like I could help to
make a change in the world.

Immersion

At the same time, I also felt exhausted. In Lancaster I was something like a "political orphan," making it up as I went.[8] Jeremy and
Carmen were my only mentors, and they lived in New York. After
the Walmart campaign in Lancaster, I decided to move to the
Dorothy Day Catholic Worker in Washington DC—just for a little
while, I thought, to learn and to rejuvenate. I was so happy to find
a deep sense of community there and to be able to protest alongside people who already "got it"—folks who I didn't have to organize to get them to come to the protest. We protested sweatshops
in Haiti, oil drilling in Nigeria and Colombia, US sanctions and
escalation against Iraq, human rights abuses around the world,
the death penalty, the drug war, the military industrial complex,
imperialism, racism, sexism, bigotry, and on and on. I spent two
years at the Catholic Worker. Each protest and campaign led to
the next. In no time I was fully plugged into the radical subculture. By the end of the 1990s—after just a few years—I had been
involved in numerous campaigns and had been arrested 20 times
for protest and civil disobedience.

I had acquired an empowering sense of agency through the
experience of taking action and seeing directly how my actions
made an impact. However, that impact seemed to be limited to
the level of mobilization itself. In other words, I could get people
to come to actions, and I was becoming adept at action logistics,
but our actions seemed to consistently fall short of influencing

---

7   Paulo Freire, Ana Maria Araujo Freire, and Donaldo P. Macedo, *The
     Paulo Freire Reader* (New York: Continuum, 1998), 212.

8   I first heard this phrase from my friend and comrade Max Berger.

political outcomes. In Lancaster I had stirred things up, but I hadn't come even close to stopping Walmart or effecting any changes in the government policies and corporate practices I protested. My sense of agency in local mobilization and logistics was at odds with the deep resignation I felt in the face of a very bleak larger political reality. Carmen's question of whether it was too late for us to make a difference weighed heavily on me.

I felt a deep sense of fulfillment in joining with others to put our bodies on the line and speak truth to power. Power, however, did not seem overly concerned with our truth. Power is concerned with power. And we didn't seem to have very much of it. Over time I started to understand that a "slogan doesn't threaten anyone"[9]; that those of us who wish to "speak truth to power" have to arm our truth with power too; that "truth" and social justice, in the world of politics, are only particular agendas in a sea of possible outcomes. The universe was not somehow bent toward their eventual automatic realization. We would have to fight.

That much was already obvious. We *were* fighting. The problem was that our fighting seemed hopeless; our resistance, futile. Our opponents seemed to hold all of the advantages. At most, we might be capable of being a nuisance. All the evidence pointed toward the harsh reality that idealistic social justice-oriented young people like me had indeed arrived "too late to the game." We were up against the culture itself, it seemed, swimming feebly against a powerful tide.

This is what troubled Carmen so deeply: the idea that he could devote his whole life to an activity that, in the end, might make no difference at all—like Sisyphus, condemned to push a boulder up a hill only to see it roll back down, time and time again. Yet Carmen wouldn't live his life any other way. He couldn't look away from the suffering of the poor and oppressed. He couldn't carve out a comfortable niche for himself within a system that caused so much suffering and injustice. And it's not as if such a life was

---

9   Tariq Ali, "Venezuela: Changing the World by Taking Power," Venezue-
     lAnalysis.com, interviewed by Jardim, Claudia and Jonah Gindin, July
     22, 2004, http://venezuelanalysis.com/analysis/598.

all doom and gloom. There was tremendous joy to be found in the struggle. There was a depth of community and meaning that seemed to be in short supply in contemporary American society. Sure, people like Carmen and Liz and Phil would sacrifice and risk a great deal for the sake of the struggle, but they would be the first to tell you that the life they chose was abundantly full of joy. I felt the same way. One night, following an especially spirited protest, I wrote in my journal, "I have found my church. I have found my family." Carmen, Jeremy and I went back and forth at that bar about the potential for long-term, large-scale political opportunities—grand recalibrations—but, for ourselves, we knew that we would keep on keeping on either way. This is how, despite a bleak assessment of the prospects of social justice movements, I stuck with it. I plodded on in the small and marginal social movement groups that I had stumbled upon in my neck of the United States in the 1990s. In a moment that felt hopeless, I was able to find others who held out hope—or who at least acted, even without hope. I realized, however, that we would have to figure out some as yet unknown game-changing intervention, if we were ever to shift the odds in our favor.

A taste of potency

Then one day it happened.

On the morning of November 30, 1999, heads of state, trade ministers, and official delegates from around the world gathered in Seattle, Washington for the ministerial meeting of the World Trade Organization. More accurately, these delegates *attempted* to gather. They were greeted instead by ten thousand people—mostly young—who had successfully blockaded all the intersections leading to the convention center where the meetings were to be held. This was a major tactical coup that no one in power had expected. Groups I'd been involved with in the two years prior, like the Direct Action Network, The Ruckus Society, and Art & Revolution had been working in the months leading up to Seattle to train people in the use of lock boxes for "hard" blockades (where blockaders locked their arms into hardware, like chains and welded-together metal apparatuses, to make it very difficult for police to disperse them). These direct action–oriented organizations created a plan wherein specific *affinity groups* took over each of the intersections and entry points.

The affinity groups were trained not only to erect blockades, but also to respond to the contingencies that would follow. How do you de-escalate a charged situation with police or with hot-tempered vigilantes? How do you stay calm so that you can think clearly? What will you do if the police start pepper-spraying people or using pain-compliance holds? How do you alleviate the painful sting of pepper spray and teargas after the fact? What will you do—and who in the group has relevant expertise—if there is a medical emergency? Who in the group will talk to reporters if they approach? Who will explain the reasons for the protest to passersby? Who will keep track of folks who get arrested, and provide support from the outside? How will the group make the kind of quick decisions that are often necessary in street scenarios? The affinity groups were prepared. The police and city government of Seattle were not.

As the hours passed on that fateful morning, the police escalated. They used teargas, pepper spray, pain compliance, and other aggressive tactics. Donning gas masks and riot gear, they looked like Imperial stormtroopers. The governor declared martial law and deployed the National Guard. As news spread of what was going down, the affinity groups were joined by tens of thousands of unionists who had also turned out in larger-than-expected numbers for a permitted rally against the WTO. Thousands of Seattle residents also joined the fray spontaneously—outraged that their city had suddenly been turned into a police state.

The next day the delegates were able to convene. But no regular business could be conducted. What had happened the day before was on the front page of every major newspaper around the world. The images clearly depicted a strong mobilized opposition in the streets of a major US city. The images showed peaceful civilians engulfed in clouds of teargas and a melee of rubber bullets, concussion grenades, and unrestrained police batons. The world was both shocked at the sight of the "gloves coming off" in America, and inspired that people in the United States were visibly joining with movements in the Global South that had been protesting against neoliberal policies for decades. Inside the convention center, official delegates from Global South nations seized the platform that this dramatic intervention had provided them. They spoke against the brutal treatment of nonviolent protesters and against the WTO and neoliberal policies that benefited the few against the interests of the many. The ministerial meetings collapsed and were declared a total failure. The WTO, which most Americans had never heard of before November 30th, suddenly became a household name. Most Americans might have had only a very vague idea what it was, but the optics of the situation provided a strong impression that, whatever the hell it was, it wasn't very democratic.

For young radicals in the United States at the turn of the century, Seattle was our "coming out party." We were "coming out" not only to the nation and to the world, but also to ourselves— realizing our own existence as a *force*. Overnight, the game had changed. Margaret Thatcher's claim that *There is no alternative* had suddenly been replaced by the new slogan of the global justice movement: *Another world is possible.*

I threw myself into the new global justice movement with a renewed spirit. I got myself to Washington DC in early 2000, two months before the meetings of the International Monetary Fund and World Bank—which would serve as the site of our next battle against neoliberalism and the global capitalist elite. For two months I worked with Nadine Bloch and Madeline Gardner in a hole-in-the-wall office that Greenpeace had graciously lent to the effort. I dove headlong into a half-dozen working groups, especially the direct action, training, and public relations working groups. Considering myself an anarchist at the time, I also did a great deal of informal diplomacy between fellow anarchists and more established organizations, like labor unions and environmental organizations. On April 16 and 17 we pulled off another strong mobilization of tens of thousands of people, drawing public scrutiny to global financial institutions that had managed to operate behind the scenes for decades. After that, we targeted the national conventions of both political parties, the Republicans in Philadelphia and the Democrats in Los Angeles. Then there was the Free Trade Area of the Americas meeting in Quebec City. There was the G8 meeting in Genoa, Italy. The list goes on. Each city provided a site for dramatic skirmishes between protesters and police at the perimeters of the secured fortresses of the global elite.

We were never able to repeat the incredible tactical success of Seattle. And there were all sorts of problems along the way, including the diminishing returns on our tactical repetition. The media called us "summit hoppers"—as if the same exact group of people descended upon each city. And the negative optics of "protesters vs. police" was eclipsing the much more advantageous juxtaposition of "the people vs. the global elite." These problems aside, the approximately two-year window of the global justice movement provided an amazing shot in the arm. I was thrilled by our success. By subjecting global elite institutions like ...e WTO, IMF and World Bank to public scrutiny, the movement was able to set some measurable limits on their policies and their agenda. Many of the changes were rhetorical, where the institutions started to emphasize fighting poverty and so on. But a rhetorical shift is a start; it sets the stage for potential policy and structural changes.

During these years I put a lot of intention and effort into building up my grassroots organizing experience and skill set. I wanted to learn as much as possible, so I could be as effective as possible—and to try to help this budding movement to be as effective as possible. While Seattle and the burst of momentum that followed felt amazing, I viewed our tactical maneuver of actually shutting down the WTO ministerial meeting as an anomaly and thought that we had to get more creative than simple repetition. Moreover, I saw the value of our intervention in Seattle as mostly symbolic and believed we would need to increase the capacity of our operation many times over if we were to ever achieve any political outcomes worth writing home about.[10] But Seattle provid-

---

10   By suggesting that the value of an action is mostly *symbolic* I do not
      mean that it is therefore unimportant. Symbolic contests are indispens-

ed the all-important taste of victory that made such a trajectory seem possible. I committed to developing my own political skill set, and to doing what I could to spread organizing, mobilizing, and campaigning skills among my fellow movement participants.

Second break

    In addition to leading skills trainings, I kept finding myself in communications-related roles—in the global justice movement, with various local organizing efforts, and then later in the post-9/11 antiwar movement.[11] Roughly half of this communication work was directed *externally*, i.e., "public relations": developing campaign messages, writing press releases, training spokespeople, and so on. This would remain one of the ways I would contribute to movements and campaigns for years to come—up through the present—from serving as communications director of School of the Americas Watch, to managing the PR operation for the Chelsea Manning Support Network, to plugging into the PR working groups of mobilizations like Occupy Wall Street. The other half of my communication-related work was *internally* directed, and it often took priority. It turns out that contentious movements can be internally contentious as well. I spent a great deal of my energy attempting to build consensus. Sometimes this required delicate diplomacy between coalition partners, sometimes strong facilitation of heated meetings, sometimes long one-on-one conversations over coffee, and sometimes more formal mediation processes. The

---

    able to changing structures and relationships of power and winning measurable gains. I will explore this theme in depth later in the book.

11   While I do lead some trainings on my own, I have mostly worked collaboratively with co-trainers through training organizations or campaigning organizations, including The Ruckus Society, Center for Story-based Strategy, School of the Americas Watch, War Resisters League, MoveOn.org, and many other local campaigns and *ad hoc* mobilization training working groups. Today my training work is through Beyond the Choir (see http://beyondthechoir.org).

role became something of a niche for me, and I found it fulfilling in a number of organizing contexts. I was good at helping people to understand each other better—to make peace and play nice with each other. I had had to do so much "translation" work in the first place, for myself, in order to transition from a rural conservative religious working-class background and assimilate into social movements that often drew participants from more educated, affluent, secular, and liberal-leaning backgrounds. Perhaps as a result, I tended to hear all of the movement messages from several standpoints at once, often thinking about whether and how a message could be made to connect with the values of "unlikely allies," like I myself had been.

And perhaps that's also why the internal consensus-building role I played sometimes bothered me. It felt like navel-gazing. My diplomatic efforts were not in the service of bridging across great divides, but rather across marginal distinctions between individuals and groups that all scored well above the ninetieth percentile on the lefty-land spectrum. On the one hand, I felt myself effective at building working consensus. I could facilitate marathon meetings—often eight, ten, or twelve hours long—and my patient touch sometimes seemed to do the trick in moving different factions forward in a common direction. I got a lot of positive feedback, and that felt really good. At that point in my life the discovery that I had something useful to contribute was important for my own development and self-worth. Not very much time had passed since I had nearly flunked out of high school—with a Grade Point Average so low that college would not even become an option, had I been interested, until several years later. So that all felt positive. On the other hand, over time I started to think that the decisions we arrived at were often not very good decisions. The heated disagreements seemed self-referential and far removed from my sense of what might reach broader audiences or measurably impact the issues we cared about. The groups that I was working hard to get to play nice with each other were often very small, lacking a social base. I wondered what difference it made if they worked together or not. It felt like the difference between one or two drops in an otherwise empty bucket. After the fleeting moment that was the global justice movement had passed, we had again become so small. Even at the apogee of the global justice movement, we were really only at the point of "getting started"—in terms of the numbers needed to actually make a substantial impact on political outcomes. Without a growth trajectory, I did not see how we would attain the collective power needed to make the changes we imagined.

Rather than strategize together about how we might tap into a broader social base of power, we would waste enormous amounts of time in esoteric debates. During the lead-up to the IMF and World Bank protests in DC, I remember the Direct Action working group spending more than half of our meeting time—for five consecutive weeks—debating the wording of the mobilization's mission statement.[12] It wasn't that a mission statement was totally unimportant to me, but there was an enormous amount of practical work that still had to be done—first to mobilize people to come to DC, and then to work out the overwhelming logistics (e.g., housing, food, training, meeting spaces, and legal support) for when they would arrive by the thousands. Critical tasks were being sidelined because of an excruciating collective editing process of text that had probably been good enough the first time around. Besides, there were so many ways that we were getting our messages out daily that were far more impactful than a one-paragraph mission statement that would be posted on our website. We wheat-pasted posters all around DC, mailed an informational broadsheet to hundreds of organizers and organizations across the country, and held press conferences and countless interviews with reporters in the lead-up. Our press work was reaching millions of people. So why all the fuss about a damned mission statement?!

Then one day an explanation suddenly dawned on me. The mission statement was contentious because it was an expression of our *identity*. It was about who we were as people—what we stood for and believed and how we expressed ourselves—much

---

12   I mean here the mission statement for the larger effort, which was dubbed the *Mobilization for Global Justice*.

more than it was about our instrumental purpose and political goals as a mobilization. Our debate about the mission statement was qualitatively different than navigating and negotiating legitimate disagreements over political goals or strategies and tactics for their achievement. This was about how we conceived of ourselves and projected our identities. That made compromise very difficult.

This epiphany provided a new lens through which I could examine a lot of behaviors in the groups I was part of, including my own actions. How many times, I wondered, had I favored a particular action or tactic because I really thought it was likely to change a decision-maker's position or win over key allies, as opposed to gravitating toward an action because it expressed my activist identity and self-conception? How concerned were we really, in our practice, with political outcomes? We often seemed more preoccupied with the purity of our political expression than with how to move from Point A to Point B. It felt as if *having the right line* about everything was more important than *making measurable progress* on anything.

I took to questioning more and more, not only the injustices of "the system" and the status quo, but also myself and the righteous social justice movements to which I felt a profound sense of loyalty and belonging. Looking back at my brief time organizing in Lancaster County at age 17–18, before I really even had a concept of what *organizing* meant, it struck me that in important ways I had been better at it back then, before I assimilated into radical subcultures. Back then I wasn't living in a magical universe composed mostly of ideologically driven self-selectors. I was engaging the people in my day-to-day life. It was really challenging, but I was oriented to persuade the people around me—to find words that would connect with their values and reference points. This was my orientation during the campaign I had organized to oppose Walmart's arrival in Lancaster County. The campaign generated a lot of involvement from people who had no prior experience with collective action, and it generated a lot of negative media coverage for Walmart. Sure, we lost the campaign, but I was only 18 years old—I was just getting started!

I thought back on how when I moved into the Catholic Worker I had intended for it to be a temporary move—eventually I would return to where I was from, rejuvenated and more experienced, and I would make change there. Instead the Catholic Worker had served as a diving board into the deep waters of subculture. Somewhere along the way I had lost myself to a subculture whose first point of reference often seemed to be itself. I suddenly felt as if I had checked my own good sense at the door. And for what? I knew that it was because I longed to belong in a community that centered explicitly around social justice values. That was an understandable and worthy goal. But now I felt like I had carved out this identity at a cost of connecting with everyday people—"non-activists"—which also meant a severe cost in political impact.

During my initial politicization in high school, I had experienced a jarring break with the *doxa* of my community of origin. I had become disillusioned as I began to detect a gap between my community's stated beliefs and the economic structures that shaped our objective relationship to other people in the world. As I developed this political analysis, I found others who shared it, and soon I dove headlong into subcultures whose bases were (varieties of) this analysis. But now I was experiencing a second break. I was starting to see how the subcultures I was part of were maintaining their own kind of *doxa*. We were righteously narrating our actions and intentions in ways that hid—mostly from ourselves—the ways that social, identity, community, and ego motivations were driving much of our behavior. It's not that these motivations are inherently bad. Building community, for example, is a worthy pursuit. But these motivations become a problem when they trump our motivation to accomplish our ostensible political goals. The gap between what we said we were trying to do and the likelihood that our actions would produce such an outcome became glaringly apparent to me.

This second break felt in many ways just as jarring as the first. I questioned and shattered the assumptions I had been working under, one after another, until my own identity seemed to me like the dissected frog from high school biology lab, mercilessly cut open, pulled apart, pinned down and labeled. With my overlapping and competing motivations unearthed, I found myself unable to fulfill some requirements of membership in the radical groups and subcultures in which I had been submerged. I felt conflicted about playing my part in maintaining the group narrative. I stopped ignoring my own better judgment. Now I could see how the flyer decrying US imperialism—with its raised fist and edgy font—was designed to reflect our narrative and identity back to us, not to reach beyond our small insular circle. Our tactics were not really tactics, in the sense that a tactic is one step to move forward a strategy to achieve a measurable goal. More so, our actions were collectively performed rituals to express our values and ourselves. I remembered how I had written in my journal that I had "found my church." Yes, the movement reminded me a lot of church. Going to a protest felt a lot like a worship service. Getting arrested for civil disobedience was something like baptism; a rite of passage; an assertion of one's rightful place in the group. And, similar to my childhood experience of indoctrination in a conservative version of Christianity, some information was emphasized and spotlighted, while other information was downplayed, ignored, or attacked. The narrative acted as a powerful meaning-making filter. The same way a stained glass window depicts a static story at the cost of preventing parishioners from seeing outside, our narrative filter prevented us from accurately assessing reality.

We would all refer to "the movement." We were all part of the movement. I started asking, *Where?* Where is there a *movement?* Show me something that fits the minimum requirements of what most people mean by the term *movement*. Where were there masses of people in motion to advance any of our causes? The moment of the global justice movement had passed. In the peace movement, I did not see the depth or breadth of a movement, aside from the brief window leading up to the 2003 military invasion of Iraq. I have given years of my life to this cause, and those who have stuck it out through decades when the whole culture seemed against them include some of the most dedicated people I have ever known. But the perseverance of a righteous few does not a movement make. What we had was not a movement. Perhaps it could have constituted itself as the *core* of a movement, but, as it was, it seemed more like residue from when there had been a movement, once upon a time. It often felt like we were gathering to perform historical re-enactments of scenes from an era we wished had not ended.

I wondered why I had devoted so much time to such small and insular circles of people. Was it simply because they were the ones waving the banner of radical change most visibly? Dedicated as we were, I started to see our grip on that banner as a kind of disadvantageous monopoly. Somehow in our society, the project of grassroots collective action had been transformed from a means toward social and political change into a negatively branded niche identity called "activism" that most of the public was effectively inoculated against. Many people in society, including people who were sympathetic on the issues, seemed to view this enterprise—to which I was devoting my whole life—as a foolhardy phase that college students pass through before they grow up.

The relatively recent invention of activism

This was one young radical's experience coming of age in the lonely decades of a weak and fragmented political left in the United States at the turn of the 21st century. It is this experience with political challenger groups and social movements that serves as the basis for the reflections, concepts, and syntheses that fill the pages that follow.

My organizing and campaigning experience over the past two decades spans many issues, including economic justice (global, national, and local), racial justice, indigenous rights, labor, environmental and climate justice, human rights, US foreign policy, veterans' issues, and health care; and I have been an active supporter and occasional collaborator on many other issues, including feminist causes and reproductive rights, immigrant rights, prison abolition, and student organizing. I have felt both proud and humbled to work alongside so many dedicated people from so many walks of life, to try to make the world a better place. It is a tricky thing to critique projects that one is part of—perhaps especially in written form. It's not hard for me to critique my political opponents—I have much more difficulty critiquing things that I love. In this work, my critiques may at times seem harsh, but I hope readers will see this more as self-critique than finger pointing. I hope readers will see that these reflections come from a place of love. I use the pronoun "we" without hesitation throughout the book, to refer to groups and movements of which I am a part, and also to refer to a far larger "we": the project of society itself.

A central argument of this book is that the larger social world (i.e., society) must always be our starting place and our touchstone. We have to meet people where they are at. The other side of this coin is that underdog groups have to vigilantly resist the tendency of insularity and self-enclosure. There are many factors that contribute to political groups constructing barriers between themselves and society (patterns that I explore at length in the first part of this book). One important contributing factor that has emerged in the United States over just the past few decades is the construction of a new category called *activism*. You read that right.

Over the years, people have constantly introduced me to others as an "activist." And let me tell you what a *buzzkill* dropping that label can be! Of course *some* people are glad to meet a real live activist, or a "fellow activist." Such sympathetic or curious persons have asked me countless times over the years *how I became an activist*. The question of how individuals *as individuals* become *activists*, fascinating as it may seem, carries equally fascinating assumptions about *activism* itself. It tends to imply a voluntary and self-selecting enterprise, an extracurricular activity, a realm of subculture, and a generic differentiating label; that an *activist* is a *particular kind of person*. When people refer to me as an activist, I have taken to correcting them: "I dislike the label activist," I politely explain, "It lets everyone else off the hook!"

The label *activist* marks a content-less distinction between the active social change participant and the society. It gets in the way, while adding zero value. Moreover, people haven't always used this word as they do today. Indeed, until half a century ago, people didn't use it at all. *Activism* is a surprisingly new word and a new social category. It is tempting to look back at past movements like the abolitionists, suffragettes, or union movement and think of the participants as *activists*, but the words *activism* and *activist* did not even exist during the time of these movements. The word first appeared about a century ago. It had an entirely different meaning for its first couple of decades.[13] With (at least elements of) its current meaning, the term only really started to enter into the English lexicon in the 1960s. It hit a plateau at a relatively low level in the 1970s, and then it resumed its ascent in the 1980s and 1990s.

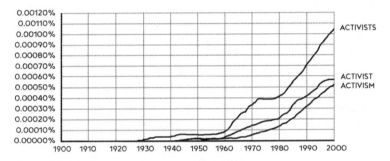

Figure 1: Google Ngram Viewer search of "activists, activist, activism" 1900-2000.[14]

So what? Weren't there other words that were more or less equivalent? Isn't *activism* just a relatively new label that describes old phenomena? While this is true to an extent—i.e., some characteristics of what is today called *activism* were certainly present in collective action that predated the existence of the word—there

---

13   At first *activist* was used to describe people in Sweden who advocated getting involved in World War I; it was intended as a counter to the label *pacifist*.

14   Google Ngram Viewer is a corpus tool that charts the frequency of words and phrases in books published from 1800–2012 (to date).

is a great deal of evidence that suggests the word *activism* also carries important new meanings that were absent in earlier manifestations of collective action. I believe many of these new meanings are detrimental.

Labels are certainly not new to collective political action, but classifications like *abolitionist, populist, suffragette, unionist*, or *socialist* all referenced specific contents. These labels were often polarizing, but each polarization constituted its own contest of meaning in the popular imagination. *Activist*, on the other hand, is an apparently "content-less" label that now traverses political issues and social movements. Negative general stereotypes about *activists* deter popular support for particular political projects and can even negatively impact people's opinions about a given political issue once it has been associated with generic "activists."[15] The *activist strawman* repels many people, cognitively blocking their entry into collective action.

Yet some are attracted to activism as such. Privy to a particular constellation of shared radical meanings and reference points, many activists take pride in activism partly because of their willingness to do something that is unpopular; some come to see their own marginalization as a badge of honor, as they carve out a radical oppositional niche identity. My own story provides texture to this "temptation"—this social pattern— which I had to develop a conscious awareness about in order to not succumb to it.

The likeminded clustering of activists fits into a broader trend in advanced capitalist nations: individual self-selection into values-homogenous communities, especially apparent within the expanded middle class of post-WWII American society.[16] Thus, it is a relatively recent phenomenon, partly the re-

---

15   Nadia Bashir, Penelope Lockwood, Alison Chasteen, Daniel Nadolny, and Indra Noyes, "The Ironic Impact of Activists: Negative Stereotypes Reduce Social Change Influence," *European Journal of Social Psychology* 43, no. 7 (2013): 614–626.

16   Bill Bishop and Robert G. Cushing, *The Big Sort: Why the Clustering of Like-minded America Is Tearing Us Apart* (Boston: Houghton Mif-

sult of tectonic cultural shifts in patterns of identity and social organization over the past half-century (atop major structural and economic shifts). In broad strokes, society has become more individualistic and self-expressive,[17] as civic involvement has declined.[18] With this backdrop, it is as if activism has morphed into a specific identity that centers on a hobby—something akin to being a skier or a "theater person"—rather than a civic or political responsibility that necessarily traverses groups and interests. In a society that is self-selecting into ever more specific micro-aggregations, it makes sense that activism itself could become one such little niche; that *activism* would become its own particular community of interest, which self-selecting individual activists join. The problem is that, when it comes to challenging entrenched power, we need more than little niches and self-selectors. We need much larger swaths of society to get involved.

A fledgling movement that attempts to attract only individuals as individuals, one at a time, will never grow fast enough to effect big systemic change. Powerful political challengers have never built their operations entirely from scratch, but rather by means of politicizing, activating, and aligning existing social blocs and institutions. Participation in the civil rights movement, for example, was hardly an individual matter; it tended to arise in relation to already established membership in communities and institutions—especially membership in black churches, historically black colleges, and chapters of the NAACP. This is the basic "formula" for how movements gain the kind of leverage they need to contend politically. In the 1980s Ralph Reed and other leaders of the emergent so-called Christian right studied the civil rights movement and emulated components of its approach, as they organized whole

---

flin, 2008).

17   Ronald Inglehart, *The Silent Revolution: Changing Values and Political Styles among Western Publics* (Princeton, N.J.: Princeton University Press, 1977).

18   Robert D. Putnam, *Bowling Alone: The Collapse and Revival of American Community* (New York: Simon & Schuster, 2000).

congregations and denominations—far more effective than waiting for individual self-selectors to join a movement because they
happened to see a flyer. In this way, conservative congregations,
especially in white suburban areas, became a major base of power
that has been profoundly important for establishing and maintaining the hegemony of a conservative alignment (of Wall Street and
social conservatives, in broad strokes) for the last few decades. The
right seems to have learned more lessons of political strategy from
the civil rights movement than the left has. While some important left campaigns did engage progressive religious congregations
(e.g., the Central America solidarity movement), overall the left
did not do anything comparable in the 1980s that was remotely
at this scale. Instead the liberal left professionalized, producing a
plethora of single-issue non-profit organizations (501-c3s), whose
memberships were, by and large, passive—useful mostly for dona-
tions—if the organizations even had members at all, let alone local
chapters that met face to face.[19] At the same time, the radical left
dramatically imploded and contracted. Many movement veterans
were understandably traumatized by the repression and intensity
of the 1960s and 70s. The active remnant narrated a common radical constellation of shared meanings and reference points. Newcomers would then orient themselves toward the center of the radical constellation, learning the radical lingo, which was profoundly
out of touch with the language, worldview, and social practice of
most Americans. Over time, this alienation and marginality vis-à-
vis American society became deeply internalized in the practices
and psychology of many radicals.

Both the liberal professionalization track and the radical
alienation track are part of the story of the relatively recent invention and emergence of *activism* as a label and social category.[20]
Idealistic social justice–oriented young people today tend to take
for granted that activism as such has always existed—that it is

---

19   Theda Skocpol, *Diminished Democracy: From Membership to Man-
      agement in American Civic Life* (University of Oklahoma Press: Nor-
      man, 2003).

20   The rise of neoliberalism is an important backdrop to both tracks.

the category they must step into in order to take collective action. Not understanding the history and structures that constructed activism, most "activists" do not question how this construction might constrain their actions and options.

When activists enter a special cultural space where activism takes place among likeminded activists, what happens is that some of the most idealistic and collectively minded young people in society remove themselves voluntarily from the institutions and social networks that they were organically positioned to influence and contest. While most activists may not fully extricate themselves from "non-activist" spheres of their lives (e.g., family, workplace, etc.), still the framework that activism occupies a special space unto itself—that it is an activity disembedded from the day-to-day lives, cultural spaces, and workplaces of most people in society—encourages activists to check their activism at the door when entering "non-activist" spheres. Alternatively, they may proudly and defiantly wear their activism on their sleeve, but more as self-expressive fashion that distinguishes them from the group—and likely inoculates others against taking them seriously—than as part of a genuine attempt at strategic political engagement.

The spheres of everyday life are certainly not easy to engage politically, let alone to organize into a political force. There are plenty of legitimate and understandable reasons why many social justice-oriented people gravitate towards spaces where we feel more understood, and why we choose the path of least resistance in other spheres of our lives. However, the slow work of contesting and transforming such messy everyday spaces is the *essence* of grassroots political organizing. When we do not contest the cultures, beliefs, symbols, narratives, and common sense of—and from within—the existing institutions and social networks that we are part of, we also walk away from the resources and latent power embedded within them. This is not a winning trajectory. In exchange for our own shabby little activist clubhouse, we give away the farm. We let our opponents have everything.

Should we then abandon the "activist" label? A better question would be: Is there any compelling reason to persist in using a label that inoculates so many people against us and our messages? If this word effectively functions as a cognitive road-block that prevents most people from considering anything we do or say, while also excusing sympathizers (who don't consider themselves "activists") from joining us, then inertia is not a good enough reason to hold onto such a disadvantageous label.

Just abandoning the label will only get us so far, though. It is much more important that we break out of the contained cultural niche that the label has prescribed; that we also abandon a make-believe world of activism in favor of strategically engaging in the terrain of politics. Our work is not to build from scratch a special sphere that houses our socially enlightened identities (and delusions). Our work is, rather, to contribute to the politicization of presently de-politicized everyday spaces; to weave politics and collective action into the fabric of society.[21]

A caveat is important here. The category of activism is a product of social, political, structural, cultural, and linguistic processes. It's not the activists' own original invention. The critique of the category is not about hippie-punching. It is all too easy to parrot negative stereotypes about "activists" and "protesters" and to attribute blame only to the aspiring change agents for what they fail to accomplish. This principle extends beyond just the category of activism. It extends to social movements generally, in relation to their milieus. It is hardly fair to place all the blame for internal movement problems upon the movements themselves. Movements must be conceptualized in relation to the societies they spring from. If a society lacks social movements that are strong enough and strategic enough to function as drivers of meaningful political change, then culpability and responsibility for that lack is shared to some extent across the society. How absurd would it be to only scrutinize those who are visibly attempting remedial collective action when so much of the problem often has to do with those groups and members of society who make no such attempt, or who get in the way? Challenger movements are not

---

21   I am borrowing language here from my friend and comrade, Beka Economopoulos, who I once heard advocate, informally at a meeting, that we must "weave ourselves into the fabric of society."

conjured out of thin air. They emerge organically within larger social realms, in relation to and in tension with status quo structures, cultures, norms, and policies. Changes and developments in the larger social realm shape the character and content of emerging challenger movements. The same is true for the constraints that movements face, including constraints internal to movements' cultures. Social movements are not fully autonomous subjective actors, neatly separable from the status quo they challenge. If a certain strategic error or pitfall is found to be recurring within challenger movements of a particular era, then we may be able to reasonably theorize a relationship between the common error and larger sociological patterns. To understand social movements' internal challenges, we also have to study the broader social, economic, and political context in which they are situated.

On the other hand, because progressive social movements occupy such a unique symbolic place in the larger public imagination, and because they have played such an indispensable role in effecting historic progressive changes, it behooves us to focus a significant portion of our attention on their internal dynamics, in order to make the movements of our time as effective as possible, both as catalyzing symbols and as instruments of change. This is why I dedicate so much effort in this book to examining the interior of political challenger movements. It is not about blame. It is not about posturing. It is certainly not about making them more pure. The purpose of such an examination is to gain clearer understandings of our constraints, external and internal, structural, cultural, and even psychological, so that we might better navigate them.

Ultimately, it's about taking responsibility for our future. Frederick Douglass famously said that "power concedes nothing without a demand."[22] We can righteously shout slogans at the halls of power until we're blue in the face, but in the long run we have to take responsibility for constructing the collective power

---

22 Frederick Douglass, *Frederick Douglass on Slavery and the Civil War: Selections from His Writings* (Mineola, NY: Dover Publications, Inc., 2003 [1857]), 42.

needed to make our demands potent. Social movements in the United States today do not have anywhere close to the capacity needed to mount sustained challenges to the entrenched power structures that we are up against, at least when it comes to issues for which change would threaten capital and the increasingly plutocratic order (e.g., progressive taxation, public education, universal public health care, cutting military spending, public elections, corporate personhood, financial regulation, or combating climate change). Given our weak state of popular organization over the past few decades, the emergence of Occupy Wall Street was a beacon of hope for many in the United States, as it provided a powerful, popular counter-hegemonic narrative that aligned overnight a hitherto fragmented left and created a political opening to connect to far more popular audiences and broader social bases than we had had access to in decades. However, as we have seen, momentarily seizing the national narrative did not send bankers and Wall Street executives packing. A much more massive movement is needed if we are to actually challenge the formidable power of capital. Fortunately for us, we know from history that such challenges are possible. Tremendously difficult, but not unprecedented. Possible, when enough segments of society can be mobilized as bases of power.

So how do we build such a movement? Digging into this question is the central purpose of this book. *Hegemony How-To* is an invitation to imagine a reality in which values of social justice do not need to be defensively guarded by a righteous few—because these values have been woven into the fabric of society itself. This book is an invitation to strategize together about how to make it so. I should qualify the word "roadmap" in the subtitle though: Even if someone managed to draw up the perfect "roadmap" or to write the perfect field manual for social movements, it would be outdated as soon as any politically active person read it—because changes in the strategic knowledge within a terrain will alter the terrain itself. There is no universal manual for such complex social problems. There is no silver bullet solution, no perfect formula, no tactic that works the same exact way twice, and no universal tool suitable for every particular problem. Does this mean that there is no useful knowledge that might help to prepare us for more effective engagement in political struggle? Of course not. We just need to be careful to always recognize our strategic knowledge as limited and as valid only insofar as its utility is empirically demonstrated on the ground, in real-life contexts. Useful knowledge of strategy, technique, and terrain does exist—and, to be clear, this book is filled with specific "tips and tricks"—but because the political terrain is constantly shifting under our feet, and with it the utility of any given technique or tactic, the most important thing becomes our ability to "think on our feet." More than specific techniques, my focus is on conceptual structures that can help to clarify our thinking and action.

Right does not equal might

Today we face mounting social and economic problems, and a formidable ecological crisis to boot. These crises have common roots, and they also compound one another. The ecological crisis is already disproportionately damning the poor. And as class stratification increases, the potency of racism is renewed in important ways: e.g., the policing of poor and working class communities of color becomes a deadly line of scrimmage in a deepening but misrecognized class conflict. Add to the mix the alarmingly fast rise of right-wing authoritarian movements and political parties over the past five years, and it should be clear that we are seeing serious signs of trouble all around us. How do we begin to approach these daunting predicaments?

Analysts, pundits, and academics who approach facets of these problems often work with an unstated assumption that solutions will come from more accurate understanding. Global warming, for example, is often treated as more of a problem of information, facts, and beliefs, than of power and economics. In a way, this is a problem of "Enlightenment thinking"—the assumption that we live in a rational society whose "marketplace of ideas" will enable the best ideas to prevail by way of persuasion through rational and, one assumes, symmetrical debate. This belief is rarely acknowledged explicitly, as it stands so feebly against conscious scrutiny, but it functions nonetheless as a detrimental unexamined idea. With the problem framed as a lack of good ideas, the solution that arises intuitively is to focus our efforts on coming up with and educating people about better ideas—as if it were only ignorance, and not a profound power imbalance, that constrains us. Adding to and incentivizing this implicit naiveté is the academic orientation of so many intellectuals, which, in the words of Pierre Bourdieu, causes them to "uncritically attribute political efficacy to textual critique."[23] When asked for prescriptions that pertain to *political terrain*—e.g., the audience member's question, "What can *I* do about the problem?"—they cannot help themselves from offering, authoritatively, an answer that, more often than not, is well beyond the scope of their competence. They thereby extend the authority they have derived from their advanced knowledge of a particular issue into an entirely different realm—one that has little to nothing to do with their area of expertise: namely, political terrain. In other words, there is no reason to assume that an individual who possesses pertinent insights that could inform sound policy *also* has a clue about how to navigate the realm of *policymaking* itself (or the realm of building and wielding a collective force with enough power to intervene in policymaking and politics).

It is of course critical that scientists and scholars study and understand the details of complex problems like global warming. However, this expertise gets us nowhere if we fail to see that our central problem is one of power and will. Truth, unfortunately, is not its own arbiter. Here we have to invert the maxim that *Might does not equal right*. For our purposes it matters just as much that *Right does not equal might*. Of course it is important to continue refining our scientific understanding of global warming, but the pressing task at hand is to build a new alignment of power that can counter the entrenched power of the fossil fuel industries. In the case of economic inequality, we could certainly use a few more left-leaning economists, but, much more so, we need to

---

23   Pierre Bourdieu, *Pascalian Meditations* (Stanford, CA: Stanford University Press., 1997), 108.

construct a broad-based political alignment that has capacity to throw down in a protracted struggle.

Here we are making explicit a conceptual distinction that is as basic as it is elusive: that knowledge of *what is wrong* with a social system and knowledge of *how to change* the system are two completely different categories of knowledge. For shorthand, we might refer to these two types as *knowledge of grievances* (i.e., what's wrong) and *knowledge of political strategy* (i.e., how to make change by political means). Too many critics fail to grasp that having the former does not automatically confer them with the latter.

The book that you hold in your hands is my attempt to give attention to knowledge of political strategy and the terrain of power, because I believe that such knowledge is immensely powerful. It creates the possibility that people who today hold very little power might tomorrow, with a lot of labor and a little luck, cohere into a force strong enough to threaten and reshape the established order. For elites to maintain possession of a vastly disproportionate share of wealth, power, and privilege, they must also hoard this knowledge of political strategy and the terrain of power. Functionally, such hoarding has much more to do with asymmetries between different social classes' dispositions and educational access than calculated conspiracy.[24] Power tends to appear magical to those who have less of it, and mechanical to those who are accustomed to wielding it instrumentally. This is why elites are sometimes incredulous—even morally indignant!— when challengers break "the taboo of making things explicit"[25] by pulling back the curtain and sharing this knowledge with people who just might use it to effectively upset the order. From Machiavelli to Gramsci to Alinsky, this "pulling back the curtain" has never been merely a matter of exposing the crooked plots of the powerful—as if exposure ever accomplished anything on its own.

---

24 This is not to suggest that elites never conspire to maintain and expand their powers, privileges, and profits. Of course they do.

25 Pierre Bourdieu, *Practical Reason* (Stanford, CA: Stanford University Press., 1998), 96.

Revelations of misdeeds of the powerful induce only popular resignation if there is no viable counter-power to seize the opening. The threat comes when, at a politically ripe moment, the terrain of power itself is revealed—when knowledge concerning how to contend effectively is made accessible to "the wrong people" at "the wrong time."[26]

My hope for this book is that it might make even a very small contribution to this long-haul project of revelation. My focus throughout this work is on facets of the knowledge of political strategy and terrain, within the particular historical context in which I find myself. While I have no shortage of political opinions, this is not a book about issues and opinions per se. This is a book about how to join with others to act effectively upon your political opinions. Of course, I am not shy about sharing my own political positions. The stories and anecdotes woven into the pages that follow are of organizers, groups, and movements that are working to advance particular goals and political agendas with which I am politically aligned—whether to halt foreclosures, change immigration policy, end wars, oppose racist policing, fund education, or win a living wage. Yet, this is not a book that does much to elaborate those particular issues. The particulars of different issues and social systems become relevant for the purposes of this book insofar as these particulars show up on the terrain of power as constraints or opportunities. Capitalism, for example, is relevant here inasmuch as concentrations of wealth can stack the deck against political challengers by rigging the political system and by out-resourcing them in the fight. Racism, ethnocentrism, xenophobia, patriarchy, homophobia, and other social systems of privileges and exclusion are relevant here inasmuch as they hinder the solidarity that social justice movements need to cultivate in order to mobilize. I have strong opinions on all of these issues, and I make no effort to mask them, but the purpose of this book is not to comprehensively explicate any issue or social system of oppression. I am glad that there are many fine authors who engage in the hard work of researching for and writing such books.

---

26   "Wrong" from the vantage point of elites, of course.

However, this work in your hands is not such a book. It is not intended for explaining why to care about any particular issue or why to hold any particular political opinion. This book is for people who already have a pretty good idea about *why*, to explore *how* and *what holds us back*.

As such, *Hegemony How-To* is also intended as an apologia for leadership, organization, and collective power, a moral argument for its cultivation, and a strategic discussion of dilemmas that challenger movements must navigate in order to succeed. I believe that such an apologia is profoundly necessary today. This work is situated a few years into a "moment" of global uprising, in which an anarchistic self-expressive "prefigurative politics" has emerged, initially at least, as predominant (dare I say *hegemonic* within many of the movements). The historical actor of Occupy Wall Street—within which this author was a core participant—performed an impressive intervention that shifted the common sense in the United States in a class-conscious direction. But Occupy was also a high-momentum mess that ultimately proved incapable of mobilizing beyond a low plateau of usual suspects. We were not merely *lacking* in our ability to *lead* the promising social justice alignment that our audacious occupation kicked off; many of the loudest voices were openly hostile toward the very existence of leadership, along with organization, resources, engagement with the mainstream media, forging broad alliances, and many other necessary operations that reek of the scent of political power. Having spent years submerged within anarchist currents of the contemporary US left, I am speaking to—and from—the best intentions of the anti-authoritarian impulse. I believe, however, that such a humanistic ambivalence toward power must mature; that its adherents must learn nuance and appreciation for the details of context and terrain—if we are to develop something that can accurately be called a *political force*.

If we fail to build such a force, then history—if there is anyone to tell it—may well conclude that our generation did, indeed, come to the game too late. I take no solace in the prospect of history listing me among the righteous few who denounced the captain of a ship that sank. We can and we must aspire to more than this. We must conspire to take the helm. This book is an invitation to join such a conspiracy.

Overview

I want to make transparent to readers the challenge that I have had in the *writing* of this book, which I conceive of as two interlocking challenges: that of pedagogy and of style. In terms of style, this is a highly conceptual work that relies heavily on story, anecdote, parable, and metaphor. Throughout the book I oscillate between a plainspoken story-telling voice and a more detached theorization, which seeks to generalize, abstract, and distill lessons from experience, observation, and history. Add to this that *Hegemony How-To* is also something of a moral apologia for collective power, and this presented me with another stylistic element to have to weave into the work, all while attempting to minimize visible seams. Most authors, in my experience, make a choice between these stylistic options, and it is perhaps wise of them to do so. A book may be narrative-driven, and the concepts, "lessons," or "point" remain under-developed and ambiguous, open to different readers' interpretations. On the other end, a book may be highly theoretical, where the elaboration and specification of concepts is its purpose. The former option tends to be more readable and accessible, while the latter tends to be more dense, typically requiring of readers a prerequisite specialized vocabulary. For better or for worse, I have ambitiously attempted to merge these styles, and my reasons have to do with pedagogy. For the past several years, I have had a recurrent interaction with editors (usually of magazines), where they tell me that they themselves love my submission, but they hesitate because they think it's too much "inside baseball" for their readership. They push me to "dumb down" the theory, and I push back to keep it in. The times when I have prevailed in the back-and-forth (to keep the heart of the theoretical argument intact, while gratefully accepting other edits), editors have been consistently pleasantly surprised by how much play these kinds of pieces get (usually measured in terms of traffic to the web page). It is my experience that there are many readers who want to know more than the specifics of the given issue; they want to gain a better understanding of the political "inside baseball" that can help to determine the outcome. This is the pedagogic project that I have been attempting with my writing and my training work in relation to the workings of collective action and social movements for the past decade. The reality is that all fields develop specialized or technical language in large part because they are dealing with more things than outsiders need to bother themselves about. It is enough for me to understand that my car has an engine; my mechanic had better have a more precise understanding of the component parts and how they interact. Unlike the field of automobile maintenance and repair, however, we as a society cannot afford to leave the workings of the political field to the specialists. Responsible citizenship requires some understanding of this field. More precise understandings often require more precise words. This is hardly a tragedy. Words are lovely and powerful things, and we should not be upset about having to learn new ones and new uses of them in order to gain a better understanding of something that concerns us. Nor should we assume that because a work engages with Gramsci or Habermas that a less formally educated reader (who is interested in the subject matter) will inevitably "get lost." I myself nearly flunked out of high school and did not attend college until my mid-30s, and I hope this experience helps me to stay oriented both to making my language accessible *and* to not underestimating the intelligence of readers (e.g., readers who are, like myself, from working class backgrounds and interested in the subject matter). So, this is my pedagogic and stylistic challenge: I believe that a somewhat specialized theoretical vocabulary can help us to understand the "field" of social movements and political struggle, but I am committed to introducing and explaining terms; to building the theoretical apparatus from "the ground floor up."

As for the progression of the book, this opening chapter partly serves to introduce myself to you the reader, and to situate myself and my work in relation to the concepts and frameworks that follow. While my own stories appear throughout the work, this chapter contains much more memoir than the rest of the book— which also includes anecdotes from other organizers, collected through interviews.

In chapter two I discuss the importance and the symbolic structure of Occupy Wall Street's dramatic intervention, as well as its shortcomings and internal problems. This discussion sets up chapter three, where I focus on the interior and the social and psychological micro-dynamics of political groups and social movements. I examine what I call the *life of the group*, a term that includes a group's internal workings, but especially speaks to its culture and motivational structure. I explore how the logic of the *life of the group* operates in tension with the logic of political instrumentality (i.e., the group's potential accomplishments beyond its own existence), and the creeping tendency of self-referential formulas and fetishes to stand in for strategic action. I discuss the *story of the righteous few*, wherein some individuals and groups become invested in their own marginality vis-à-vis society, and how this story has gotten mixed up with the story of what it means to be "radical." I then discuss a *political identity paradox* that challenger groups have to navigate: on the one hand, they have to cultivate a strong identity in order to mobilize in the first place; on the other hand, they have to be on guard against how strong identity can also create walls between them and potential allies—too much cohesion can lead them down a dead-end path of insularity.

In chapters four and five I dig into the deep ambivalence toward power that thrives in many pockets of the social justice left in the United States (and elsewhere) today. I look at contemporary movements through a lens of an *ethic of responsibility* versus an *ethic of ultimate ends*, as elaborated by sociologist Max Weber. While acknowledging the abundant good reasons for critiquing power, I discuss how the wholesale rejection of engagement in the terrain of political power is especially concentrated in advanced capitalist nations and correlates with relative economic privilege—and how it is, ironically, a product of neoliberalism. I discuss at length how these dynamics played out over the course of Occupy Wall Street's brief run, where the dominant tendency within Occupy's core rejected all forms of power and leadership, at least rhetorically, but another tendency struggled, with limited success, to build leadership skills and to develop clearer political goals and strategies. I make both a moral and a strategic case for why challenger movements must engage conscientiously in the terrain of power, by building and wielding a collective force. I argue that to eschew political power is to commit political suicide and to abdicate responsibility.

While chapters 1–5 deals as much with "how *not* to" (i.e., internal patterns that are presently holding us back) as with "how *to*," in chapters 6–8 I explore the operations of a political challenger force that embraces the morality and the necessity of engaging in the terrain of power. In chapter six I explore the necessary growth trajectories of nascent political operations and social movements, discussing movements' *kinetic* versus their *potential* force. In chapter seven, I look at how organizations, movements, and campaigns have to learn how to speak the language of the people they're seeking to organize or mobilize. In chapter eight I examine how underdog challengers have to articulate a compelling "we" to serve as the basis of political alignment.

Throughout this book I discuss constraints and openings that are sometimes particular to the contemporary context in the United States, but that may nonetheless be of interest to readers in other parts of the world; given the current reality of American economic, political, and military hegemony across the globe, I think it is safe to assume that sympathetic readers all around the world will share an interest in the US social justice left figuring out how to pick up our game a few notches. I conclude with a discussion of what a new political zeitgeist—one in which radicals embrace a moral and strategic imperative to contend in the terrain of politics and power—might look like.

Already now there are signs that such a zeitgeist may be coming into view. Indeed, this book is positioned within what I see as an emerging tendency within the contemporary US left; a tendency whose strong moral sense is also oriented toward understanding, mapping, and effectively intervening in the messy terrain of political power. My hope is that some readers may wish to be part of this tendency, and to help it to mature and grow.

THE 99%: THE SYMBOL AND THE AGENT

In this chapter I take a brief first look at Occupy Wall Street, a key "case study" that I will keep coming back to throughout the book. Occupy succeeded in introducing a popularly resonant populist narrative about economic inequality and a rigged political system. How it did so is instructive and foreshadows key concepts that I will keep building upon in later chapters. However, Occupy also offers us lessons about what not to do; I will examine how Occupy turned inward in ways that severely limited its ability to take the popular outrage it had stirred up and mobilize it into a political force.

"The years in which the hegemony of neoliberalism was unchallenged have fortunately come to a close."

–Chantal Mouffe[1]

November 15, 2011, 1:36 a.m. EST

A massive police force is presently evicting Liberty Square, home of Occupy Wall Street for the past two months and birthplace of the 99% movement that has spread across the country.

The raid started just after 1:00am. Supporters and allies are mobilizing throughout the city, presently converging at Foley

---

1   Chantal Mouffe, *Agonistics: Thinking the World Politically* (London & New York: Verso, 2013), 65.

Square. Supporters are also planning public actions for the coming days, including occupation actions.

Two months ago a few hundred New Yorkers set up an encampment at the doorstep of Wall Street. Since then, Occupy Wall Street has become a national and even international symbol—with similarly styled occupations popping up in cities and towns across America and around the world. The Occupy movement was inspired by similar occupations and uprisings such as those during Arab Spring, and in Spain, Greece, Italy, France, and the UK.

A growing popular movement has significantly altered the national narrative about our economy, our democracy, and our future. Americans are talking about the consolidation of wealth and power in our society, and the stranglehold that the top 1% have over our political system. More and more Americans are seeing the crises of our economy and our democracy as systemic problems that require collective action to remedy. More and more Americans are identifying as part of the 99%, and saying "enough!"

This burgeoning movement is more than a protest, more than an occupation, and more than any tactic. The "us" in the movement is far broader than those who are able to participate in physical occupation. The movement is everyone who sends supplies, everyone who talks to their friends and families about the underlying issues, everyone who takes some form of action to get involved in this civic process.

This moment is nothing short of America rediscovering the strength we hold when we come together as citizens to take action to address crises that impact us all.

Such a movement cannot be evicted. Some politicians may physically remove us from public spaces—our spaces—and, physically, they may succeed. But we are engaged in a battle over ideas. Our idea is that our political structures should serve us, the people—all of us, not just those who have amassed great wealth and power. We believe that is a highly popular idea, and that is why so many people have come so quickly to identify with Occupy Wall Street and the 99% movement. **You cannot evict an idea whose time has come.**

Most of us had been anticipating an imminent police raid of Zuccotti Park (a.k.a. Liberty Square), so I wrote the first draft of the above press statement about ten days before the eviction. Initially, the draft was received less than enthusiastically by some of my colleagues in the OWS Public Relations working group, so I decided to abandon it and repurpose some of the language for another article.[2] However, as the eviction unfolded in the middle of that November night, members of the PR team asked me to adapt the draft as quickly as possible and post it to OccupyWallSt.org and blast it to the press.[3] I raced over to Patrick Bruener's apartment, we gave it a final look-over, and we hit "send."[4]

Beyond the radical fringe

Two months earlier, I was living in Providence, Rhode Island, and I was quite skeptical about Occupy Wall Street. When I first read *Adbusters* magazine's call for a Tahrir Square–style uprising in New York City's financial district, the lack of appreciation for context annoyed me.[5] Wall Street is not Tahrir Square. And though I was inspired by the Arab Spring, I didn't think

---

2   Jonathan M. Smucker, "The Tactic of Occupation and the Movement of the 99%," *BeyondtheChoir.org,* November 10, 2011, https://jonathansmucker.org/2011/11/10/the-tactic-of-occupation-the-movement-of-the-99/.

3   OccupyWallSt, "You can't evict an idea whose time has come," *OccupyWallSt.org,* November 17, 2011, http://occupywallst.org/article/you-cant-evict-idea-whose-time-has-come/.

4   Immediately following the eviction and the release of this statement, the phrase "You cannot evict an idea whose time has come" went viral and was seen on signs (and painted on tents) at occupations and solidarity rallies across the globe, instantly becoming one of Occupy's signature slogans. It's a play on Victor Hugo's phrase "Nothing is stronger than an idea whose time has come."

5   *Adbusters,* "#OCCUPYWALLST," *Adbusters.org,* 2011, https://www.adbusters.org/blogs/adbusters-blog/occupywallstreet.html.

you could neatly transplant its tactics. Moreover, as Occupy Wall Street kicked off, it looked to me like the brave radicals initiating it were making the classic mistake of putting their counter-cultural foot forward first, thereby dooming the action to be locked onto a predictably lonely path where so many Americans who agreed with their populist sentiments would be inoculated against them as the messengers. It seemed to me to fit a pattern I had long been critical of, where self-selecting "activists" connect with each other at the expense of connecting with the broader society. A week into Occupy Wall Street, I even wrote a post for my blog with this critique titled, *Occupy Wall Street: Small Convergence of a Radical Fringe.*[6]

That was the experienced grassroots organizer in me. That's the thing about experience. When you hear about an idea, you can instantly foresee a million things that could go wrong. And when your concerns repeatedly play out, it is easy to grow a little cynical and even a little bitter. It is easy to forget that revolutionary moments require an ingredient that you may now be running low on: a drive that once consumed you, but now pulses through the veins and brains of people younger than yourself, whom you are tempted to condescendingly dismiss as politically naïve. Can't they see that to mobilize masses of people, you need more than a militant call to action and a Twitter account? Sure, just about everyone was furious with Wall Street, but turning latent discontent into coordinated collective action requires strategies to organize people and build alliances, and an appreciation for context.

Sometimes what you really want is to be proven wrong. That is how I started to feel when the occupation of Zuccotti Park persisted and the story started to significantly break into the mainstream media cycle; when labor unions and longstanding community organizations started to endorse and to plan actions

---

6   Jonathan M. Smucker, "Occupy Wall Street: Small Convergence of a Radical Fringe," *BeyondtheChoir.org*, September 26, 2011, https:// beyondthechoir.org/diary/99/occupy-wall-street-small-convergence -of-a-radical-fringe.

under the new frameworks of "occupy" and "we are the 99%"; when GOP strategist Frank Luntz said he was "frightened to death"[7] of the effort and House Majority Leader Eric Cantor decried the "growing mob"[8] of Wall Street protesters, while House Minority Leader Nancy Pelosi expressed her support,[9] and the *New York Times* also endorsed the protest.[10]

Overnight, it seemed, a new political force had emerged; one that had the potential to frame the national debate and finally create popular pressure—a counterforce to the formidable power of capital. Despite my doubts, the thing had started to go big.

Grassroots movements for change are more often than not rife with all kinds of clumsy missteps. Thankfully the concerns that I was stuck on were not enough to stop the rapid growth of this audacious new movement. I realized that I myself had to get unstuck. If I were to wait for the perfect movement—one that I had no critiques of—I would wait forever. History would pass me by.

I heard that my friends Beka Economopoulos, Brooke Lehman, and Han Shan were involved, and I called them up. Then I freed up ten days from my schedule and took the train from Providence to New York City.

Ten days turned into the better part of a year.

7   Said Jilani, "Top GOP Strategist Admits He's 'Scared' Of Occupy Wall Street Because It's 'Having An Impact,'" *Think Progress*, December 1, 2011, http://thinkprogress.org/special/2011/12/01/379365/frank-luntz -occupy-wall-street/.

8   Michael O'Brien and Carrie Dann, "Cantor says he's concerned by 'mobs' at 'Occupy Wall Street,'" *NBC News*, October 7, 2011, http:// firstread.nbcnews.com/_news/2011/10/07/8206043-cantor-says-hes -concerned-by-mobs-at-occupy-wall-street.

9   Jessica Desvarieux, "Pelosi Supports Occupy Wall Street Movement," *ABC News*, October 9, 2011, http://abcnews.go.com/Politics/pelosi -supports-occupy-wall-street-movement/story?id=14696893.

10   The New York Times, "Protesters Against Wall Street," *The New York Times*, October 9, 2011, http://www.nytimes.com/2011/10/09/opinion /sunday/protesters-against-wall-street.html.

Occupation as tactic and as symbol

By the time I arrived, Occupy Wall Street had already broken into the mainstream media and was profoundly changing the national narrative about wealth, power, and democracy in the United States. Occupy's initial success in recalibrating the mainstream discourse about politics and the economy is remarkable. It was as if a 30-year spell had suddenly been lifted, as a new "common sense" was unveiled about what is at stake and who is to blame. It behooves us to retrospectively examine why this particular tactic of occupation struck such a nerve with so many Americans and became such a powerful catalyzing symbol. To do so, we have to make a distinction between Occupy's broad audience and its core actors, and between the meanings that resonated popularly and the meanings that the physical occupation held for the dedicated people who were on the ground occupying. Zuccotti Park was home to a thriving civic space, with ongoing dialogues and debates, a public library, a kitchen, live music, General Assemblies, more meetings than you can imagine, and all varieties of high-energy, creative activities. In this sense, *occupation* was more than just a tactic. Many participants were consciously *prefiguring* the kind of society they wanted to live in.[11]

But it was also a tactic. A tactic is basically an action taken with the intention of achieving a particular goal, or at least moving toward it. In a long-term struggle, a tactic is better understood as one move among many in an epic game of chess (with the caveat that the powerful and the challengers are in no sense evenly matched). A successful tactic is one that sets us up to eventually achieve gains that we are not presently positioned to win. As Brazilian educator Paulo Freire asked, "What can we do now in order to be able to do tomorrow what we are unable to do today?"[12] Thus, a tactic is a kind of stepping stone.

---

11   I discuss this idea of "prefigurative politics" in depth in chapter four.

12   Paulo Freire, *Pedagogy of Hope: Reliving Pedagogy of the Oppressed*, trans. Robert R. Barr (London and New York: Bloomsbury Publishing Plc, 2014[1992]), 115.

By this definition, the primary tactic of Occupy Wall Street (physical occupation of public space) could be considered enormously successful. We subverted the decades-old hegemonic conservative narrative about our economy and our democracy with a different moral narrative about social justice and real democratic participation. As a result, we are arguably better positioned than before to make bold demands, as we can now credibly claim that our values are popular—even that they are *common sense*—and connected to a substantial social base. With a new broadly resonant vocabulary, we are now better positioned to organize popular social bases to take more powerful political action. Such a shift in the constellation of popular meanings is among the central operations required in a long-term hegemonic struggle.

I want to suggest that the primary reason the tactic of occupation resonated so far and wide is because it served as a symbol about standing up to powerful elites on their own doorstep. To most sympathizers, the "occupy" in "Occupy Wall Street" essentially stood in for the F word. Millions of Americans had been waiting for *someone or something* to stand up to Wall Street, the big banks, the mega-corporations, and the political elite. Then one day, a relatively small crew of audacious and persistent New Yorkers became the catalyzing symbol of defiance we had been waiting for.

Thus, Occupy Wall Street served as something of a *floating signifier*, amorphous enough for many different kinds of people to connect with and to see their values and hopes within the symbol.[13] Such ambiguous symbols are characteristic of popular challenger alignments. Many objects can serve as the catalyzing symbol, including actions (e.g., the occupation of Tahrir Square or of the Wisconsin State Capitol), individual politicians

---

13   Ernesto Laclau, *On Populist Reason* (London & New York: Verso, 2005); Claude Lévi-Strauss, *Introduction to the Work of Marcel Mauss* (London: Routledge & Kegan Paul Ltd., 1987); Jonathan Matthew Smucker, Andrew Boyd, and Dave Oswald Mitchell, "Floating Signifier," in *Beautiful Trouble: A Toolbox for Revolution*, ed. Andrew Boyd and Dave Oswald Mitchell (New York and London: OR Books, 2012), 234; Smucker, "The Tactic of Occupation."

(quintessentially Juan Perón in Argentina), or even constructed brands (e.g., the "Tea Party"). As these examples suggest, this phenomenon can be seen in all kinds of political alignments, across the ideological spectrum. In all cases though, a good degree of ambiguity is necessary if the symbol is to catalyze a broad alignment. If the symbol's meaning becomes too *particular*—too associated with any one current or group within the alignment— it risks losing its powerfully broad appeal.

It is important to note that although the signifier is *floating* (i.e., not peg-able), it is not *empty* of content. First of all, it has to feel meaningful enough to resonate. Furthermore, different symbols tend to pull in different directions (depending partly on the strength of the organization and "ground game" of those who are pushing or pulling them). Candidate Barack Obama as floating signifier, for example, pulled a lot of grassroots energy into what has in many ways turned out to be an establishment-reinforcing direction. Occupy Wall Street as floating signifier, on the other hand, pulled—at least initially—both popular and some establishment forces in the direction of the fired-up, social justice-oriented grassroots movement, intent on systemic change.[14]

When a challenger social movement hits upon such a catalyzing symbol, it's like striking gold. One might even argue that broad political alignments are constituted in the act of finding their *floating signifier*. Hitherto disparate groups suddenly congeal into a powerful aligned force. Momentum is on their side and things that seemed impossible only yesterday become visible on the horizon.

It is important to recognize a few things, then, about our relationship to the *tactic of physical occupation* during Occupy Wall Street's brief run:

1. It accomplished more than any of us really imagined it would have.

---

14   Five years later, at the time of this writing, Bernie Sanders has picked up the torch, filling the role of floating signifier of a still-emerging alignment of progressive social forces.

2. A significant part of the tactic's political value was in serving as a popular defiant symbol that shifted prevailing meanings in the culture.
3. It was incredibly resource-intensive to maintain.
4. The tactic was not going to serve us forever. Indeed, its utility was waning prior to our eviction.
5. Moving forward in the years ahead, we will have to come up with other popular expressions of the values and hopes that OWS brought to the surface.

Here it becomes important to distinguish between our *tactics*, our *message*, and our *movement*. Of these three, our *tactics* should be the thing we are *least* attached to. In oppositional struggle, it is critical to maintain the initiative; to keep one's opponents in a reactive state. This is not accomplished by growing overly attached to any particular tactic—no matter how well it worked the first time—and thereby doing exactly what our opponents expect us to do. Of course, it is a lot easier to conceptualize the need to be innovative and to keep our opponents on their toes than to actually come up with the right thing at the ripe moment to make it so. Moreover, it is wrongheaded to get caught up in the elusive search for the perfect silver bullet tactic. Movements are, more than anything else, about people. To build a movement is to listen to people, to read the moment well, and to navigate a course that over time inspires whole swaths of society to identify with the aims of the movement, to buy in, and to take collective action.

The "Occupy" in Occupy Wall Street was the tactic that launched a movement for social justice and real democracy onto center stage in the United States, even if ephemerally. It served as the initial catalyzing symbol. Hopefully ten or twenty years from now, when we look back at all we have accomplished together, we will credit this mobilization as a critical *moment* that helped to spark and then build a longer-term *movement*. However, when we fail to find other successful tactics—and other popular expressions of the movement's values—we are pronounced dead as soon as the initial tactic fades. Of course, most successful movements are first pronounced dead many times over. Still, this challenge of *popular mobilization* remains looming before us. Fortunately, Occupy Wall Street—and the *tactic* of occupation—was neither the primary *message* nor the *movement* itself.

And, fortunately, we do not have to reinvent the movement's message from scratch, come the next rounds. What emerged in tandem with the deployment of the captivating tactic of occupation was the compelling message that "We are the 99%!" We might well consider this among our core messages in a new movement era. The framework of *the 99%* accomplishes a number of important feats that it is important to explicitly note:

- *The 99%* frames the consolidation of wealth and political power in our society—the central grievance of the Occupy movement and a central crisis of our times.
- *The 99%* frames a class struggle in a way that puts "the one percent" on the defensive (whereas the common accusation of "class warfare" had somehow tended to put a lot of people in the middle on the defensive).
- *The 99%* casts an extraordinarily broad net for who is invited to join the movement. Most everyone is encouraged to see their aspirations tied to a much bigger public. Thus it frames a nearly limitless growth trajectory for the movement.

The meme of the *99%* is a real winner. Its message and framework may prove better at helping us "weather the winter" than any single tactic could. It points the way towards a necessary expansion. It encourages us to not just act on behalf of, but along-side, "the 99%"; to look beyond the forces already in motion, to activate potential energy, to articulate a moral political narrative, and to claim and contest our culture and our future.

Of course, many critics from the left and from the academy have taken issue with the meme of the *99%*, arguing that it poses a false unity that obfuscates important heterogeneity and power concentrations within an absurdly broad category. Analytically, they are of course correct, but these critics neglect to consider this framing as a *power move*—what Pierre Bourdieu might call a "worldmaking" operation. Here again is a classic example of the academic error of "uncritically attribut[ing] political efficacy to textual critique."[15] While we often think of elites and the already powerful as the forces that construct and wield "universality" as a tool in service of their (particular) power and privilege, I will argue throughout this book that it is just as necessary for underdog challengers to articulate differently framed "universalities," even if such operations are rife with additional moral and strategic dilemmas. As such, I embrace "the 99%" for strategic reasons and assert that its ambiguity is necessary for the construction of an alternative hegemonic alignment. That the scope of such universalizing rhetorical moves can be expanded by subsequent movements (notably Black Lives Matter) does not negate the political value of the former move.

Five years after the gathering at Zuccotti Park was disbanded, it is abundantly clear that a still-emerging progressive political alignment has indeed taken the core of its populist language from Occupy Wall Street. The unexpected popularity of self-identified democratic socialist Bernie Sanders—unexpected by the punditry, but also by many in the left—in his campaign for the presidency is at this point probably the most notable next manifestation of the nascent alignment.

Holding up a mirror

"As we see our face, figure, and dress in the glass... so in imagination we perceive in another's mind some thought of our appearance, manners, aims, deeds, character, friends, and so on, and are variously affected by it. A self-idea of this sort seems to have three principal elements: the imagination of our appearance to the other person; the imagination of his judgment of that appearance, and some sort of self-feeling, such as pride or mortification...The thing that moves us to pride or shame is not the mere mechanical reflection

---

15   Bourdieu, *Pascalian Meditations*, 108.

of ourselves, but an imputed sentiment, the imagined
effect of this reflection upon another's mind."
                        —Charles Cooley, The Looking Glass Self[16]

Let us imagine a particular group imagining itself through the
reflection of the perceptions of other groups or of the larger society—through the others' impressions, associated meanings, and
stereotypes about the particular group. We can also imagine the
reverse: the larger society glimpsing something of itself in the reflection of a particular group (that is contained within itself). In
this way, we can conceive of a powerful challenger movement as
"holding up a mirror" in which society recognizes its own reflection. Society sees parts of itself that had escaped its conscious
gaze, and, thereby, society re-imagines itself.

Sociologist George Mead discussed how particular "individuals stand out as symbolic. They represent, in their personal relationships, a new order, and then become representative of the
community as it might exist if it were fully developed along the
lines that they had started."[17] If we substitute Mead's "individual"
with an *individuated collective actor*, and substitute "the community" with *society*, we can conceptualize how Occupy Wall
Street became symbolically representative of society "as it might
exist if it were fully developed along the lines" that Occupy started. Thus, Occupy Wall Street held up a mirror and we recognized
ourselves in the reflection—not just *we* the self-selecting individuals who physically took the park and the streets in New York's
financial district; "America" itself saw itself in this mirror, saw its
own condition: saw the level of economic inequality and political
disenfranchisement it had come to tolerate. We might compare it
to waking up ten years after a traumatizing disaster, catching a
glimpse of oneself in the mirror, and finally seeing oneself clearly

16   Charles Horton Cooley, "The Looking-Glass Self," in *Social Theory: The
      Multicultural Readings*, ed. C. Lemert (Philadelphia: Westview Press,
      2010 [1902]), 189.

17   George H. Mead, *Mind, Self and Society* (Chicago & London: The Uni-
      versity of Chicago Press, 1962 [1934]), 217.

again; reconnecting with the hint of one's precious long-lost soul in a glimmer in one's own eyes, after having identified for so long with the shell one had become; like a feeling of returned wholeness after years of fragmentation and anomie.[18] In that reflection were Wall Street and capitalism and the power they had attained over our material and moral universe. In that reflection were the failures of our political representatives to represent public interests and even, in their dominant discourse, to represent a recognizable picture of most people's reality. In that reflection was a lack of popular collective power. And in that reflection was an intuitive ringing truth; that, *yes, we are the 99%*, a re-imagined public ready to unify and claim our share.

In a sense then, Occupy Wall Street provided the mirror for a new unification to recognize itself as a "community" with shared interests, as a revived public. At the center of that reflection of a broader community, there was the *core*, which we might call *Occupy Proper*: those who were most active, explicitly as part of OWS, and who therefore felt intense ownership and identification with the named group. Occupy Proper operated as a symbol and the signifier of the very existence of the larger unification, the newly re-imagined community. The imagined community, however, was far larger than Occupy Proper.[19] Its projection in-

---

18 Many of the movement's participants and sympathizers have remarked upon how Occupy Wall Street launched almost exactly ten years after the 9/11 terrorist attacks, and only blocks from Ground Zero. The global justice movement (aka alter-globalization movement), whose window of opportunity opened up dramatically on November 30, 1999 in the streets of Seattle, closed just as quickly less than two years later on September 11, 2001. Many veterans of the global justice movement, including this author, saw Occupy Wall Street as a kind of post–Bush-years "resurrection" of a popularly resonant economic justice movement and message.

19 I borrow the term "imagined community" from Benedict Anderson and use it somewhat interchangeably with "social unification," even if these two terms emphasize different aspects of the same essential thing: a premise for common identification for a "group" that is so large that

cluded, in a sense, all of America—even the "one percent," insofar as Occupy's signature slogan, "We are the 99%!" was a new
class-conscious framing of the *whole* national public, including
the class antagonism within it.

However, Occupy Proper also saw itself distinctly *individuated* in the mirror. And it sometimes mistook itself and its
bounds for the whole community of concern, rather than seeing
itself as a *symbol* and special *agent* in the service of a much larger
social unification. This smaller individuated core, in this narrower reading of the mirror, was comprised of those who physically
occupied and participated in the occupations' recognized upkeep
and projects. If the boundaries of such a core were to become too
clearly delineated, it would lose its ability to activate and influence the direction of a larger movement. To go in this self-enclosing direction, its growth trajectory would have to rely only
on bringing more people into the core itself, through inspiration,
self-selection, and replication (i.e., occupying more public parks).
More and more individuals would join Occupy—and assimilate
into its distinctive subculture—until it somehow reached a critical mass. Many occupiers implicitly believed this to be the path
to scaled growth. America could join Occupy Proper, but only entirely on the latter's own terms.

The problem with this smaller reading of the mirror is that
as soon as the symbol circumscribes itself as a neatly bounded
object unto itself, it ceases to be the signifier of a larger unification. It loses its magical properties and its symbolic power.
It shrinks and is distorted into an *other*. As an *other*, it loses its
power to name and catalyze the larger unification. The social
fragments that were in the process of becoming an ascendant
political unification instead become inoculated against the initial catalyzing agent, Occupy Proper (i.e., those dirty hippies
in the park who won't stop drumming). The mirror that the

---

it not actually experienceable by those who identify with it; it can only
be imagined, but as such it is still powerful. Anderson used this term
especially to describe nations and national publics. Benedict Anderson,
Imagined Communities (London & New York: Verso, 1983).

nascent unification caught a glimpse of itself in becomes a picture of a stranger.

The moment the newly framed unification caught a glimpse of itself in the mirror was the same moment that constituted Occupy Wall Street's initial success. At this moment, the core of the embryonic movement faced its first test of maturity. For a fleeting moment—perhaps two months—it seemed as if sun, moon, and stars orbited around the movement and its intervention. Incredible attention focused on the *individuals* who occupied—i.e., Occupy Proper. Paradoxically, to succeed politically, we had to use the attention directed at us to shift attention to a broader public, i.e., to our new and prescient articulation of unification: a public-as-protagonist in an unfolding epoch. We had to avoid staring too much at our own narrow reflection in the mirror—the trap of narcissism—and becoming unwitting accomplices to our opponents' playbook one-two punch: first, to brand us as *special* (i.e., as a *particular*; an *other*) and then as especially malignant, thereby hindering our ability to catalyze a larger force, by inoculating enough of the public against us.

The movement's active core had to remain in the story, but as a popular symbol of the values and aspirations of many different sorts of people. Like a guest at a party who suddenly finds herself at the center of everyone's attention and praise, a nascent movement has to resist talking on and on about herself or allowing the conversation to stay focused on her personally. Her presence may be captivating and novel at first, but soon the other guests will grow bored. Instead, she uses her soapbox to strategically draw attention to other situations, stories, and symbols; situations, stories, and symbols that draw additional scrutiny to her opponents and to the crises she has eloquently named. She speaks not about herself but directly to the identification her audience feels with her cause. She invites that grain of awakening identification to grow. She invites her audience to become the historical actor, the protagonist. She seeks to invent new flashpoints, new moments, featuring new (aligned) actors stepping into history. She lowers the bar for entry and builds many on-ramps. If she is very good, her audience will have taken its

first step forward without even realizing, in order to lean in to
hear her.

Otherization

Immediately following Occupy Wall Street's inauguration, its opponents mounted a public relations offensive to negatively brand
the burgeoning movement. They attempted to individuate, carica-
turize, and otherize the visible actors—the occupiers—in order to
inoculate more Americans against identifying with a larger unification—the 99%—and keep them from joining or aligning with the
movement. We had to counter this attempt by projecting ourselves
as symbolic of a larger unification. Occupy Wall Street served as a
powerful floating signifier of a newly imagined unification, and so
its opponents predictably sought to nail down the signifier; to fill
its positive ambiguous contents with negative stereotypes about an
otherized Occupy Proper (i.e., stinky counter-cultural types who
drummed all night and defecated on neighbors' doorsteps).

When Mayor Bloomberg attempted to "clean Zuccotti Park"
on October 14, 2011, he was making the first move in what became a ceaseless character assassination campaign. Bloomberg's
talk of "cleaning" was an attempt to frame occupiers as dirty and
to use sanitation as a ruse to evict us from Zuccotti Park for seemingly non-political reasons. However, in a jujitsu move, we used
the mayor's ploy to catalyze the broadest visible political support
the movement had seen to date. Recognizing Bloomberg's cleaning attempt for the threat of eviction it was, local and national
allied organizations called upon their members to flood the park.
By six o'clock on the morning of the attempted cleaning/eviction,
the crowd had swelled to several thousand. By 6:30am the deputy
mayor had announced that the "cleanup" was off. The whole epi-
sode served as free publicity for a rally at Times Square that had
already been planned for the next day (as part of a Global Day of
Action). There, tens of thousands of New Yorkers joined together
for one of Occupy Wall Street's largest public actions.

Bloomberg and other opponents sought to portray the movement as *a particular kind of person doing a particular thing* (e.g.,

"dirty hippies"), rather than a popular response to a common crisis. To counter this strategy, movement organizers sought to bring *more kinds of people*, visibly engaged in more kinds of things, into the movement. We sought to make and portray the nascent movement as more than a protest, more than an occupation, more than any particular tactic, and more than any one particular type of person. Within its first few months, the movement did indeed become far broader than those who were able to participate in physical occupation. Occupy Wall Street included people like Elora and Monte in rural West Virginia who sent hand-knit hats to occupiers at Zuccotti. It was 69-year-old retired Iowa public school teacher Judy Lonning who attended weekly Saturday marches in Des Moines. It was Nellie Bailey, who helped to organize the Occupy Harlem Mobilization. It was Michael Ellick and other religious leaders who brought Occupy Faith to their congregations. It was Selena Coppa and Joe Carter, who marched in formation to the New York Stock Exchange with 40 fellow "Veterans of the 99%." The boundaries of Occupy Wall Street were intentionally expanded and blurred. Occupy was everyone who took some kind of action to confront the democratic and economic crises initially named by a few hundred defiant occupiers in New York City's financial district.

Thus, the needed expansion that Occupy was criticized for lacking was not entirely absent—not even close. But it is certainly the case that not enough of Occupy's core was oriented toward the task of scaling up these fits and starts.

Occupy fashion

Those of us who worked intentionally to make Occupy Wall Street represent a broader unification had to navigate more than just our opponents' efforts to otherize the movement; we also had to navigate the movement's own internal tendencies toward self-enclosure. I have referred to Occupy Proper, which until now has been my own private moniker for the tendency amongst a core of participants to own, protect, and clearly delineate Occupy's boundaries. This tendency wrapped itself in ideological rationales, especially the imperative to keep "liberal reformists" from co-opting the radical movement. My intent here is not to dismiss wariness of the possibility of such cooption outright, but instead to assert that, regardless of the merit of such rationales, another force drove this wariness as well: the force of *individuation* itself. To apprehend how this force or pattern played out in Occupy Wall Street, let us momentarily suspend judgment about Occupy's ideological content and look at the movement through a lens of *fashion*. Many of the movement's core participants signaled belonging in the new group by simultaneously signaling difference, defection, disobedience, or rebellion from aspects of the status quo. It may be useful to consider such signaling behaviors as analogous, at least, to how fashion functions. Fashion's usefulness as a lens is evidenced by the fact that such signaling often manifested most visibly in the literal form of fashion—i.e., clothing, styles, and other external adornment—which any casual visitor to Zuccotti Park could corroborate.

It is hardly novel for political expression and fashion to blend together. Georg Simmel spoke of an "increased power of fashion" that "has overstepped the bounds of its original domain, which comprised only personal externals, and has acquired an increasing influence over taste, over theoretical convictions, and even over the moral foundations of life."[20] One might object that Occupy Wall Street was attempting to do the opposite of what fashion does; that fashion gravitates toward that which is considered elegant or refined, in constant imitation of the upper strata of society, while Occupy was oriented in the opposite direction.[21] Occupy's oppositional orientation may have, indeed, changed the content and kinds of expressions of fashion, but it does not negate that the same essential form or pattern of fashion was at work. Simmel's description of "club-haters organiz[ing] themselves into a club" is apt:

---

20   Georg Simmel, *On Individuality and Social Forms* (Chicago & London: The University of Chicago Press, 1971), 303.

21   Norbert Elias et al., *The Civilizing Process: Sociogenetic and Psychogenetic Investigations* (Oxford, UK; Malden, MA: Blackwell Publishers, 2000); Pierre Bourdieu, *Distinction: A Social Critique of the Judgement of Taste* (Cambridge, MA: Harvard University Press, 1984).

...it becomes evident that the same combination which extreme obedience to fashion acquires can be won also by opposition to it... If obedience to fashion consists in imitation of such an example, conscious neglect of fashion represents similar imitation, but under an inverse sign... Indeed, it occasionally happens that it becomes fashionable in whole bodies of a large class to depart altogether from the standards set by fashion. This constitutes a most curious social-psychological complication, in which the tendency towards individual conspicuousness primarily rests content with a mere inversion of the social imitation and secondly draws in strength from approximation to a similarly characterized narrower circle.[22]

With fashion we are essentially describing the same pattern of group delineation already discussed. Yet the lens of fashion adds texture and may aid in understanding Occupy Proper. If we conceive of fashion as a social mechanism whose essential function is individuation (or distinction), we may better understand why and how many occupiers seemed to jealously guard ideas that one might suppose—looking through a lens of political strategy—they would want to spread. "As soon as an example has been universally adopted, that is, as soon as anything that was originally done only by a few has really come to be practiced by all—as in the case of certain portions of our apparel and in various forms of social conduct—we no longer speak of fashion. As fashion spreads, it gradually goes to its doom."[23] Thus, there was a social incentive for many movement participants to attempt to prevent "universal adoption" of the movement's symbols and messages. When pop star Miley Cyrus made a music video lauding movement participants for "standing up for what they believe in," a prominent occupier publicly snubbed Cyrus's support, saying, "I double dog dare [her] to fight on the front line of economic civil rights... Revolutionaries occupy, Ms. Cyrus."[24] When civil rights

---

22 Simmel, *On Individuality and Social Forms*, 306.

23 Ibid., 302.

24 Aly Semigran, "Miley Cyrus' supposed Occupy Wall Street support song

icon Rep. John Lewis visited Occupy Atlanta, participants denied him the opportunity to publicly voice his support.[25] These are two of the more notable examples among countless others where some vocal occupiers turned away or denounced more mainstream support. Looking through a lens of (the social function of) fashion can help us understand this protectionist disposition.

It is my opinion that this disposition deserves a large share of blame for why Occupy Wall Street, while succeeding in reframing a potent and popular class-conscious narrative, ultimately failed to arm its critique with political power. Every time a prominent supporter was snubbed, a message was sent to all *potential* supporters: "Your support is not wanted. This thing is *ours*." Successful social movements characteristically put great effort into actively courting influential supporters, in order to set more social forces into aligned motion. Occupy Wall Street had an incredible opportunity to do this—indeed, many influential supporters were *courting us*—but too often we did precisely the opposite.

While Occupy Wall Street may have taken this protectionist, self-expressive, self-enclosing tendency to impressive "new heights," it was certainly not the first movement to struggle with the tendency. As we will see in the next chapter, the "life of the oppositional group" tends to develop in a self-referential direction, unless mechanisms are devised to check such an insular trajectory.

---

and video stirs up mixed opinions," *Entertainment Weekly*, November 30, 2011, http://popwatch.ew.com/2011/11/30/miley-cyrus-occupy-wall-street/.

25   Jim Galloway, "Your morning jolt: An 'Occupy Atlanta' dissing of John Lewis." *Atlanta Journal Constitution*, October 10, 2011, http://blogs.ajc.com/political-insider-jimgalloway/2011/10/10/your-morning-jolt-an-%E2%80%98occupy-atlanta%E2%80%99-dissing-of-john-lewis/.

3

LIFE OF THE OPPOSITIONAL GROUP

Building on the discussion of Occupy's tendency toward insularity, I now dive deeper into the internal life of social movement groups. I examine micro-dynamics and group behavioral tendencies, while I also position these patterns in relation to social and economic structures. Here I see the social psychological layer of mobilization as one that any practical political organizer has to concern herself with—if she wants to successfully navigate it and engage effectively in a larger political contest. I introduce conceptual frameworks and principles that can help leaders to navigate the dynamic "life of the oppositional group."

"Intuitively speaking, not all social groups involve the current pursuit of a goal or end, in spite of the impression given by some writers."

—Margaret Gilbert[1]

"Thus the other-directed child is taught at school to take his place in a society where the concern of the group is less with what it produces than with its internal group relations, its morale."

—David Riesman[2]

---

1   Margaret Gilbert, *On Social Facts* (Princeton, NJ: Princeton University Press, 1989), 18.

2   David Riesman, *The Lonely Crowd: A Study of the Changing American Character* (New Haven & London: Yale University Press, 1950), 65.

The personal is political

When Carol Hanisch published her classic essay "The Personal is Political" in 1969, she was pushing back against critics who had been dismissing women's caucuses and discussion circles as being merely "therapeutic."[3] The essential argument of the criticism—which was coming from *within* social justice movements—was that women were indulging in "navel-gazing" retreats to talk about their "personal problems," distracting themselves and others from the "real work" of challenging systems and structures (like capitalism). If a woman was doing too much of the cleaning, cooking, or childcare at home, or if she was dealing with an abusive husband or boyfriend, the problem was a personal one, for her to either get out of or to figure out how to deal with. Maybe she should just be more assertive. Hanisch rejected this view. She argued that while individual women were facing innumerable everyday forms of oppression on their own, isolated from one another, this oppression was *structured* and *common* across a category (i.e., women). Hanisch asserted that to address these problems women needed to come together *as women*—as a group—in order to articulate their grievances together and ultimately to enter into the political field with enough force to make structural changes: "One of the first things we discover in these groups is that personal problems are political problems. There are no personal solutions at this time. There is only collective action for a collective solution."[4]

Thus, the phrase *the personal is political* was originally intended to mean that the oppression you experience as an individual is patterned—that there are structural factors underlying your experience, and so there are probably others experiencing similar things. *The personal is political* encouraged individuals who were experiencing oppressive situations—a woman abused by her husband, or a worker exploited by her employer—to view these situations not as

---

3   Carol Hanisch, "The Personal Is Political," *Notes from the Second Year: Women's Liberation* (1970).

4   Ibid.

personal problems, but as political problems, and to realize that remedial action requires coming together with others to address the issue in the public sphere. It is no small irony that the phrase *the personal is political* is now often used to mean something almost opposite of its original meaning. While it once meant that personal problems are not really personal, inasmuch as they are *structural* problems and collective action is required to address them, now people use the phrase to advocate uncoordinated individual action (e.g., buying organic shampoo) as somehow constituting a political intervention. This morphing of meaning may say something about the rise of individualism in the culture—even within social movements—as the tendrils of neoliberalism penetrate more and more of social life and its individualist logic makes the logic of collective action less and less intuitive (a theme I will continue to explore in this and other chapters).

But with its original meaning, the phrase *the personal is political* spoke to the process of fragmented and isolated individuals coming to identify as a group with common—or *political*—grievances and goals, rather than merely personal problems or shortcomings. This is the process of *politicization* in a nutshell. Articulating such a basis for common identity is precisely what Antonio Gramsci meant by the word *articulation.*[5]

Recently, such a process has been unfolding across the United States as police killings of our black and brown brothers and sisters are now being articulated popularly as a pattern, a structural problem, and a political problem—recognized as such by more and more people. Of course some voices have been saying this for decades and organizing consistently around these issues, but only recently has this analysis and mobilizaton broken through into a nationally recognized movement. This means that each needless death and each instance of excessive force is now understood as part of a bigger moral narrative. Victims' families and communities no longer have to struggle on their own, isolated from each other. There is now a stronger sense, at least, that "you are not alone." This articulation of a common story about

---

5   I will elaborate on this concept in chapter eight.

structural racism and economic inequality in relation to America's police departments provides a stronger basis for the collective mobilization it will take to change this intolerable situation.

However, it is not easy to get people to recognize as a political problem what the prevailing common sense has told them to see as a personal shortcoming. Struggling homeowners in the wake of the 2008 financial crisis, for example, tended to struggle in isolation. In the American Dream narrative, homeownership is a source of individual pride. Foreclosure and underwater mortgages have thus been implicitly, and sometimes explicitly, framed as personal problems and even reason for shame. Thus, struggling homeowners often worked extra jobs to make payments on underwater mortgages, or they went quietly when facing foreclosure and eviction. However, as the banks got bailed out to the tune of a trillion dollars, but no relief was extended to struggling homeowners—and as banks' predatory lending practices started to face scrutiny—the political nature of the housing market crash began to come into focus. At the height of Occupy Wall Street, Monique White went to the public park where Occupy Minnesota had set up and asked the occupiers to help her fight to save her home. By joining with others to take collective action, she was able to fight the bank and eventually save her home. In similar fashion, Occupy Homes campaigns kicked off all across the country, successfully saving many homes along the way. Still, most homeowners who joined the effort did not start out as ready as Monique White. Tim Franzen, an organizer with Occupy Homes Atlanta explained how "The biggest barrier was getting homeowners to fight—to believe that it was right and just for them to fight, instead of just suffering alone in the shadows." Individual homeowners had to confront the intuitive shame they often felt—a product of seeing their situation as their own personal problem or shortcoming—in order for the personal to become political.

Belonging and "therapy"

Jose Vasquez served fourteen years in the United States Army. As he watched the George W. Bush Administration exploit the political capital it had been awarded following September 11 to launch a war of choice in Iraq, Jose became disillusioned. Eventually he successfully petitioned to become a conscientious objector. Exiting the army, he hit the ground running by joining Iraq Veterans Against the War (IVAW), where over the past decade he has served in several leadership roles, including President of the IVAW NYC Chapter, Co-chair of the national board, and Executive Director of the organization. I first met Jose in the office of the War Resisters League (WRL) on Lafayette Avenue in Manhattan's Lower East Side, when I started working for WRL as their national field organizer.[6]

Jose described to me how he had met a fellow veteran at a public event that IVAW NYC had organized. The veteran, who would soon join up to become an IVAW member, had found out about the event from a professor at his college.

> The event was actually Iraq vets reading from their memoirs, so it was people telling their stories...
>
> Then he came out and hung out with us afterwards and was just really excited and animated and said, "Man, I've been kind of like holed up in my apartment for the last six months." He literally said, "It's so fucking good to meet you guys. I just thought I was, like, going crazy. I thought I was the only one who thought the whole war was fucked."
>
> So yeah, I think it's empowering to identify with other people, to find like-minded individuals, to have that outlet, to do things with others—sort of taking that negative energy and turning it into something positive. A lot of people come home from war with their whole worldview shattered and it leaves them in a very fragmented place, but being able to talk things through... it's *therapeutic* to just be able to tell your own story and not be judged. And I think people begin to then rebuild a new worldview for themselves... They start to then *take their own very individualized experience of combat and place it in*

---

6   Jose and I now work together at Beyond the Choir, especially on the Veterans Organizing Institute.

the larger context, and then bounce it off of other people's...
"Oh, yeah, this happened to me over here. I was in Fallujah. I
was in Ramadi." And so they understand that like, "holy shit,
this kind of stuff was happening all over the place!"[7]

Jose provides us with yet another powerful example where
what felt like personal and isolated experiences were discovered
to be widespread phenomena, and thus articulated as *political*
matters. Yet Jose sees this realization as not only politically necessary (in order to organize a force to pressure a change in US
foreign policy), but also as *therapeutic.* For him the two purposes get mixed up with each other. There's no clear line separating
them and there's no reason to diminish the one in order to elevate
the other. On another occasion, Jose went into even more detail
about the therapeutic aspect of IVAW members' organizing work
together: "The camaraderie is a huge asset. It's probably saved a
couple of people's lives actually—people on the verge of suicide.
They meet up with other IVAW members and realize, 'I'm not
alone. It's okay for me to be against what I just did.' That's enormous for some people."[8]

How are we to square this with Carol Hanisch's pushback,
four decades earlier, against the charge that women's groups were
merely indulging in personal therapy? Hanisch's important and
necessary intervention has to be interpreted partly in relation to
the narratives she was pushing against. She never argued against
the value of individuals finding in each other's company a sense of
belonging and a space for healing. Rather, she rejected the notion
of stopping there.

It is important that we recognize the necessary therapeutic
subtext that is always operative in social justice struggles. Yes,
we come together with others because there is political strength
in numbers, and we are aiming to accomplish instrumental goals.
But we also come together with others because it feels good to do

---

7   Jose Vasquez, interviewed by the author in January 2015. My emphasis.

8   Jose Vasquez, interviewed by the author in December 2007 as part of
     the War Resisters League's listening process.

so—because we find a deep sense of community and belonging that accomplishes what could be described as "therapeutic" purposes.

In modern US society, many of us suffer from a lack of adequate community in our daily lives. Indeed, social alienation and psychological strain seem to be endemic to late-stage capitalist societies. As such, we are both psychologically and politically motivated to participate in protest and collective action. In other words, the social, economic, and political structures that are the source of our political grievances are also a major cause of psychological strain. Why then should we count psychological motivation as something that is not *political*? If psychological strain is produced by an alienating underlying social structure, then psychological and political motivations can be one and the same (which is not to say that they will never operate in tension with each other).

Add to this the particular sense of alienation that can accompany political radicalization. We who hold progressive or radical values often feel an acute lack of representation, if not outright repression, of these values in the dominant culture. Many of us, during the process of our politicization, come to feel isolated within our communities of origin, and often for good reasons. As I came of age in rural Lancaster County, Pennsylvania, I encountered resistance to my newfound radical notions of social justice, and I felt isolated. So I went out looking for like-minded people. Finding them and communing with them has been and continues to be both inspirational and therapeutic. It contributes to my well-being.

When we look at the state of the world we may understandably feel frustrated, angry, and heartbroken. Besieged by a dominant culture in which destructive values and politics seem to reign supreme, we may feel isolated. We can find community—a sense of sanity and belonging—by coming together with like-minded people to express our alternative values boldly, loudly, and, most importantly, collectively. The explicit purpose of coming together with like-minded people is to effect change, more effectively by joining together in greater numbers. A second, less explicit purpose is to surround ourselves with community and also with reflections of the values that we hold dear. Together we create projects, spaces, culture, and ritual that cultivate a strong *life of the group*.

Collective ritual and strategic engagement

As we have seen, achieving our political goals and fulfilling our psychological needs can be mutually reinforcing and positive processes. Unfortunately, this is not always the case. These two purposes can also operate in tension, and can even undermine one another. While the "therapeutic" motivation may be an inherent and even necessary part of social change work, it is also deeply connected to self-defeating patterns that can undermine our political efficacy.

Before proceeding, a clarification of the term "therapy" must be raised, as the term can conjure a picture of individuals pursuing their own psychological health *as individuals*, often in order to personally adjust themselves to the structural causes of psychological strain, as opposed to joining with others to confront these causes. The form of "therapy" that I have been discussing here is fundamentally a *group* process, essentially about community and belonging. The longing for meaningful community—which, unfulfilled, is indeed a major source of psychological strain for many—can be fulfilled in social movements through the *life of the group* (a term I will use throughout this book). Motivations that pertain to the life of the group overlap substantially with what are often referred to in the academic social movement literature as *expressive* motivations. I prefer the term *life of the group*, because *expressive* can imply an individualistic *self*-expressive motivation. My view is that a collective dynamic is the main driver of the patterns I have observed, which I hope to illuminate here.

The life of the group is cultivated through *collective ritual*. By collective ritual I mean collaborative expressions of shared values that serve to further a sense of community and belonging. *Ritual* can describe acts that affirm our sense of community, our collective narratives, and the values contained therein. In Christianity, collective ritual may include church attendance, group singing, and Eucharist, but it can also be found in far subtler aspects of everyday life. In social change groups and subcultures collective ritual may include protests, events, gathering places, music, fashion, publications, specialized vocabulary, and much more. Collective ritual is hardly distinct from culture itself. We can find a layer of collective ritual in any word or deed that affirms the group or subcultural identity and narrative. This is not to say that a protest has no *instrumental* political purpose other than affirming a group's identity—or an individual's sense of belonging to the group—but rather that this affirmation is *always part* of what motivates protest participants. And without conscious awareness of this layer of motivation we run a greater risk of our protests and collective action truly having no instrumental value; that it will accomplish nothing other than making us feel good.

Ritual is important—vitally so for collective action and social movements. Our rituals partly represent the survival of alternative values within a dominant culture that under-represents and represses such values. Through collective ritual we gather strength and build solidarity by surrounding ourselves with reflections of our alternative values and visions. However, expressing values and living principles is not the same as strategically engaging society and political structures in order to win systemic change. Even though these *expressive* and *instrumental* aspects intermingle in messy reality, it is nonetheless important to draw a conceptual distinction between collective ritual and strategic political engagement—between the *life of the group* and what the group accomplishes beyond its own existence (i.e., the work of engaging with social and political structures in order to effect change). Strategic engagement overlaps with collective ritual, but the two are conceptually distinct, and it is advantageous to develop a consciousness about when and how we utilize one or the other or both. Both agendas are essential, and social change movements suffer when either is neglected. Collective ritual serves as a remedy to the paralysis caused by isolation. It provides connection, community, a sense of belonging—and there can be no politics without this collective sense. However, strategic thinking and action in social movements is hampered when participants pursue insular ritual at the neglect of broader strategic engagement.

Author and grassroots organizer Mark Andersen describes the distinction in terms of *subjective* and *objective*:

...if we are to really contribute to change, much less revolution, we must distinguish between the "subjective" (internal: seeking personal identity, meaning, purpose) and the "objective" (external: actually helping to change power relations, structures, and values that uphold oppression of the many by the few) aspects of our activism. ...Both the subjective and the objective are critical, at different times and in different ways. They are even interconnected—i.e., I begin to feel personal power, which enables me to take actions that might help striking workers get better pay and working conditions or, more fundamentally, help to build power to alter social structures. However, the two are not the same.[9]

While both are important, these two motivations for participation in social change efforts often operate in tension with each other. A group that focuses only on instrumental goals and neglects the well-being of its members will likely burn out its core while repelling potential newcomers. The opposite problem is when groups become content to functionally operate as little more than therapy, losing interest in questions of political efficacy and strategy.

I have seen the latter situation play out an embarrassing number of times. Let's be frank. I suspect that anyone who has meaningfully participated in contemporary social movements in the United States would have a hard time denying that movements often attract some very alienated individuals who sometimes arrive with overwhelming psychological needs. There is even a logic to the pattern: by publicly challenging aspects of the status quo, movements may unsurprisingly become a kind of "magnet" that attracts people who feel especially alienated from that status quo. And movements often provide a space where such individuals can meaningfully participate and feel empowered. It can be highly problematic to psychologize the motivations of individual participants in political movements, but given that we have to practically navigate—toward *political ends*—the consequential social psychological level within social movements, it behooves us to

9   Mark Andersen, *All the Power*. (New York: Punk Planet Books/Akashic Books, 2004), 22.

candidly assess this level, including the pathologies.[10] We might lean toward structuralist explanations for social, economic, and political problems, but if we want to build functional political vehicles run by actual human beings, we cannot afford to be disinterested in the psychological level of collective action. This level is an important part of the terrain that we have to learn to navigate.

By understanding our own psychological motivations and how they are connected to our political grievances, we will be better equipped to act effectively on both. And by developing an analysis of how collective ritual and strategic engagement often operate in tension, we might get better at making sure they operate symbiotically instead. We can become more discerning about when and how we fulfill each purpose. We can act more effectively, while also building a beloved community together.

Integration and insularity

While in Argentina in 2004, I interviewed Maba and Valde, siblings from MTD Solano, one of the Movements of Unemployed Workers (movimiento de trabajadores desocupados; MTD) groups. In the wake of Argentina's economic and political collapse three years prior, MTDs like Solano were an important movement organizational form that rapidly spread across the country. Interviewing the siblings separately, I asked them what they value most about their work with the MTD. Both answered that they value how *integrated* their lives are now. Maba said that while many join MTDs out of necessity, she joined by election, because her life felt too fragmented before. Now nearly everything she does is related to MTD Solano: her work at a collectively run cafe, a children's workshop she organizes, her neighborhood, her family, etc. All of her activities share a singular meaning and purpose and relate to one group identity.

---

10   To be clear, pathology is only a very small part of a discussion of the social-psychological level of social movements. And again, while there are certainly pathological manifestations related to social alienation, there is also an undeniably political aspect and structural foundation.

Political scientist Emily Stoper describes a similar cohesion experienced by members of Student Nonviolent Coordinating Committee (SNCC) during the civil rights movement: "Many [SNCC] members report that before 1964, they often experienced a sense of harmony and certainty that is rarely felt by other Americans. Their lives were not fragmented. Instead of filling a series of largely unrelated roles (parent, employee, citizen), they filled only one role: SNCC worker. Instead of balancing in their heads a multiplicity of values, all of them tentative, they had one certain, absolute set of beliefs. The group provided a world order that is far more complete and stable than any that individuals could assemble for themselves."[11]

Stoper's description also reminds me of the intense sense of harmony that I felt during the Minnehaha Free State campaign and land occupation in Minneapolis in the late 1990s. There our political aim was to stop the controversial rerouting of a highway through a neighborhood, parkland, and sacred sites to the Mendota Mdewakanton Dakota Community and the American Indian Movement. For sixteen months we did everything together: cooking, eating, cleaning, building tree stands and barricades, meeting, working security shifts, singing, sitting around the campfire, even getting arrested or roughed up by the police. When I would leave camp, it was to produce or distribute flyers for events related to the campaign, or to meet with allied organizations. We regularly remarked at the profound sense of community that we felt together.

While this sense of harmony and integration can be deeply fulfilling to those experiencing it, it can also be alienating to those on the outside. Unchecked, the distinctiveness of a political group's subculture can become self-referential to the point of being incoherent to outsiders—even sympathetic outsiders. Furthermore, group members may even lose the inclination to connect with others beyond the bounds of the group. In his examination of the implosion of Students for a Democratic Society

---

11   Emily Stoker, "The Student Nonviolent Coordinating Committee: Rise and Fall of a Redemptive Organization," *Journal of Black Studies* 8, no. 1 (1977): 30.

(SDS) and the emergence of the Weather Underground, Frederick D. Miller describes the phenomenon of *encapsulation*:

> Encapsulation occurs when a movement organization develops an ideology or structure that interferes with efforts to recruit members or raise demands. ...members may develop such strong cohesion among themselves that outsiders become unwelcome. In prolonged interaction, a group may develop an ideology that is internally coherent but virtually unintelligible to recruits and outsiders who do not share all of the members' assumptions. Such groups are not uncommon in movements; they constitute the fringe of organizations that appears strange to outsiders. An encapsulated organization may find it easy to maintain its dedicated core of members, whose identities are linked to the group and who may have few outside contacts, but such groups have little chance of growing or increasing their influence. Most strikingly, they may lose interest in such things, contenting themselves with maintaining their encapsulated existence.[12]

Insularity—and ultimately, encapsulation—can happen for very understandable reasons. Alienated by the dominant culture, many people seek to live a different story, an alternative narrative, or simply to find a community to which they feel they *belong*. Participation in a collective struggle can be a deeply fulfilling and integrating way of accomplishing this. However, because social movements' alternative narratives exist in opposition to the status quo, they often create or deepen barriers between the participants and the broader society. Collective ritual that furthers the alternative narrative often builds group cohesion by drawing attention to how the group is different from the status quo. Unchecked, this can easily come to mean different *generally from everyone else*. The further developed an oppositional group's

---

12   Frederick D. Miller, "The End of SDS and the Emergence of the Weatherman: Demise through Success," in *Waves of Protest: Social Movements Since the Sixties*, ed. Jo Freeman and Victoria Johnson (Langham, Maryland & Oxford: Rowman and Littlefield, 1999), 307.

alternative narrative—the longer it has been alive within a particular group or series of groups—the more it will tend toward
insularity and encapsulation, unless specific mechanisms or intention prevents this from happening.

Full-scale encapsulation did not occur in the context of the
Minnehaha occupation for the same reasons that it did not occur
with SNCC or SDS—at first. These were political movements and
campaigns, which required regular interaction with allied groups
and a larger public. Still, in each of these cases a core group developed a strong cohesion that, at least at times, tended toward
insularity, which is the path to encapsulation. We might think of
encapsulation as an extreme form of insularity—unmitigated and
consolidated. In the case of SDS many core members broke with
public organizing to form the Weather Underground, which had
virtually no dialogical interaction with any broader constituency.[13]

How prevalent is this phenomenon within social movements?
Full-blown encapsulation is relatively rare, but the tendency of social change agents to create identities that distinguish them from
others, and to become self-referential and insular, is quite common. The negative impact of encapsulation is disproportionately
harmful to social movements, because it occurs especially within
the core of the most active and dedicated participants—people
who give all or nearly all their time and energy to the movement,
and who are often ready to sacrifice even more. Social movements need these people in order to be successful. That is, movements need some people who are heart-and-soul dedicated to the
cause, flexible and free from other commitments or distractions.
Yet, critical as these people are, they comprise a very small percentage of any successful social movement. To be successful, most

---

13   It should be noted that WU members were situated in a context where
      global revolution seemed to them to be just around the corner. Their
      reference groups were armed revolutionaries from other parts of the
      world. They worked under a theoretical framework that seemed com-
      pelling, at the time. On the other hand, it's not only history that judges
      their errors harshly; many dedicated leaders at the time made repeated
      attempts to persuade WU that their approach was suicidal.

movements (at a national scale) need tens of thousands—if not hundreds of thousands or even millions—of people who are willing to give *something* of themselves. To get plugged into movements in ways that contribute to organizational capacity, these folks generally need, first, to feel welcomed by, and then, given some direction from, the more involved core movement participants. Encapsulation and the general tendency of radical groups to self-isolate prevents this needed relationship, creating an unbridgeable chasm where there should be a continuum of levels of involvement—as well as levels of political analysis—and leaving dedicated radicals vulnerable as they are cut off from a broader movement.

To prevent insularity and encapsulation in our social movements and organizations, core members have to take responsibility for ensuring that collective rituals and alternative narratives are oriented to connect with broader bases of society. There's nothing wrong with creating social movement spaces where we speak some of our own internal jargon, but, if we want to build a truly mass movement for social justice—one capable of making the kinds of changes worth writing home about—we must also orient ourselves to speak the language of the people who are all around us. The starting place of the movement must always be *society*—rather than the movement's core itself. When our subcultures become too self-referential and incoherent to outsiders, then our words and actions may come to function as repellants to others—even to our allies and people who agree with us on the issues. Needless to say, this profoundly limits our potential power. People who may be aligned with our vision may refrain from joining us because they are not interested in assimilating into—or being identified with—a self-marginalizing fringe subculture, or because they see a lack of strategy.

The power of jargon

I remember a planning meeting I attended years ago when I was living in Minneapolis. We were planning for a protest to target a biotech industry meeting. While the goals and strategy of our action were never clear to me, we were at least discussing how to turn out more people for the protest; how to reach beyond the "usual suspects." In the midst of a discussion about how to get families with children to join us, one woman suggested that we might add a legally permitted component to the otherwise un-permitted protest—in order to make it clear that there would be a relatively safe place for people who wanted to join the protest, but who did not want to risk getting arrested in order to do so (e.g., families with children). Others immediately derided the woman's suggestion as a *liberal* idea. This was not a case of conservatives deriding liberals. Rather, this was a group of radicals—to the left of liberals—and a culture had been established within the group wherein the suggestion of a permitted component to the protests could not even be considered for its tactical or strategic merit, but was instead summarily dismissed, because of the association of permits with the label of *liberal* and, more importantly, the cluster of particular meanings that this label conjured for the group. *Liberal*, for this group, meant less than radical, less than militant, less than revolutionary; a naïve, misguided approach to social change that, at best, achieves piecemeal reforms while strengthening the system and selling out the true radicals.

Within this group the word *liberal* referred to and carried this story without having to actually spell it out. Francesca Polletta uses the trope of *metonymy* to elucidate this phenomenon. A metonym is a figure of speech where something related to a thing—an aspect, attribute, or associated object—stands in for the thing itself. Examples of metonymy include *hand* referring to help (e.g., "Can you give me a hand?"); *suits* referring to business people; *crown* referring to a king; *brass* referring to military offi-cers. Groups and subcultures develop their own particular meton-ymies: words that stand in for whole stories and clusters of asso-ciated meanings. In the example above, *liberal* stood in for a story about a kind of person and a tendency that the group rejected.

Polletta illustrates the concept with a story about union of-ficials in the farm workers' movement initially dismissing the idea of boycotts and marches because these tactics were "not the union way": "'Union way' stood metonymically for a variety of things: political secularism; an unwillingness to engage in moral and emotional appeals; most importantly, an approach that was not that of the civil rights movement or a religious campaign."[14] These negative associations within the given union culture foreclosed potentially advantageous tactical options.

Polletta elaborates on how this pattern can play out socially and psychologically in the life of a group: "Activists count themselves in the know because they recognize the cluster of meanings associated with the term used. Such meanings are unrecognizable to those outside the group. The more the metonymic relation is referred to, the more conventional it becomes. Note, again, that the metonymy signals a cluster of terms and also that the relations among the terms are never specified. The relations are assumed to be obvious but that assumption discourages activists from considering whether the implied relations are empirically accurate."[15]

Returning to my example of the discussion about how to get people with children to turn out for a protest; the group's tactical options were constrained by the metonymic association of permits with the group's story of the *naïve liberal*. Getting a permit might concretely help the group realize their tactical objective of attracting target demographics (i.e., families with children) to the protest, but this could not even be considered. To even suggest applying for a permit meant that you did not "get it"; you did not understand the problem of liberals and of "playing by the rules." Perhaps you did not really belong in the group.

The group may very well have had a valid political critique of liberalism, piecemeal reformism, and so on. The legitimacy of that critique is not the point. What matters strategically is 1) how

---

14   Francesca Polletta, "Three Mechanisms by Which Culture Shapes Movement Strategy: Repertoires, Institutional Norms, and Metonymy," in *Strategies for Social Change*, ed. Gregory M. Maney, Rachel V. Kutz-Flamenbaum, Deana A. Rohlinger, and Jeff Goodwin (Minneapolis & London: University of Minnesota Press, 2012), 52.

15   Francesca Polletta, *It Was Like a Fever: Storytelling in Protest and Politics* (Chicago, IL: University Of Chicago Press, 2006), 60.

the association of that vague critique with certain tactics foreclosed the group's options, and 2) how risky it was, socially, for individual members of the group to question the validity of that association. Polletta continues: "As a kind of shorthand, metonymies both assume the existence of a group for whom the shorthand makes sense, and they signal membership in the group. *That makes them difficult to challenge because to do so can be interpreted as a sign of one's ignorance and possibly one's insecure place in the group.* It is always possible to think outside canonical narratives and the tropes on which they rest. To articulate those alternatives is risky, whether in a congressional hearing or in a group of like-minded activists."[16]

Questioning—or even explicitly naming—certain assumptions can call one's own belonging in the group into question. Such an *in the know* dynamic promotes an unnamable culture of conformity that inhibits strategic innovation and flexibility. This pattern of group behavior can limit a group's tactical options, as well as group members' ability to evaluate the strategic value of tactics. It is yet another mechanism that can privilege the internal life of the group over the group's external accomplishments.

Ironically, the same group that so adamantly dismissed the idea of obtaining a permit, also argued for a "diversity of tactics" and to use "every tool in the toolbox." These phrases were less than genuine. They were not meant to be taken literally. Rather these phrases—like the word *liberal*—stood in for bigger stories. What was meant, in effect, is that everyone should unquestioningly accept a few participants' use of a particular style of tactics, regardless of how, when, where, or to what effect these tactics were employed. When it came down to it, the group was unwilling to consider at least one "tool in the toolbox"—obtaining a permit—even if it may have been the most suitable means of achieving a clear shared objective. Indeed, disparaging such tactics and the groups that used them was a regular conversation topic within this circle. As was extolling militant tactics for the sake, it would seem, of militancy itself. Both the praise and disdain for these

---

16   Polletta, "Three Mechanisms," 52. My emphasis.

respective tactics occurred absent any discussion of how specifically the tactics may or may not contribute to a strategy to bring the group closer to achieving any political goals.

Sacrifice

Sacrifice is a collective value often esteemed in social movements. Personal sacrifice for a greater good can be a dramatic expression of positive collective values, such as sharing, solidarity, and mutual aid. A movement participant's willingness to make a personal sacrifice or take a risk speaks profoundly to the world she is trying to build—one in which individuals are willing to give of themselves for the good of the whole. And the value of sacrifice is not only "prefigurative" and expressive of values. It is also a practical necessity for groups engaged in social change. To succeed, movements need *people power*, which means a lot of time and energy. We need folks who are willing to give up or put on hold other parts of their lives—and to sometimes endure hardship or take risks—if we are to build our collective capacity for a long-term struggle.

There are clear downsides to sacrifice, however. Half of the concept of sacrifice is cost; the other half is some greater benefit (e.g., group benefit or future benefit). Sacrifice for its own sake can hardly be counted as a good. I would assert the same about sacrifice that only expresses and reinforces the group culture, without benefit to the group's goals (or to its capacity to achieve future goals). Giving up one's time, safety, or freedom for a cause should be tied to at least an educated bet that the sacrifice will help the cause to succeed.

During my time with the Catholic Worker, soon after high school, I was part of a network that gathered several times a year for reflection and protest against militarism and other social injustices. This group was part of what is known as the *plowshares* movement: activists who hammer on military machinery (missile silos, fighter jets, etc.) to symbolically convert "swords into plowshares," as referred to by the prophet Isaiah in the Bible. The first plowshares action was in 1980 in King of Prussia, Pennsylvania, where eight activists—including Daniel and Philip Berrigan, the radical Catholic priest brothers who raided draft boards, burning the files in the late 1960s—entered General Electric with household hammers to destroy nosecones for nuclear weapons. This action happened in the context of numerous anti-nuclear campaigns and a growing anti-nuclear consciousness in the United States. Since then, many plowshares actions have been carried out around the world, but mostly in the United States. Cumulatively, plowshares activists have served decades of prison time, with individual sentences ranging from probation to over ten years' imprisonment. This is a group for which sacrifice and risk clearly play a big part in the life of the group.

I got involved in this network the summer after I graduated from high school. I was deeply inspired by participants' commitment and willingness to put their lives on the line. By the end of the year I moved into a Catholic Worker intentional community in Washington DC that was part of the network's core. Soon I started getting arrested at demonstrations, and before long I was facing criminal charges for my part in a higher-risk nonviolent action at the Pentagon. I was seriously contemplating joining a plowshares action when a friend pointed out an interesting social dynamic within this network I had become immersed in. There was an arbitrary hierarchy of tactics, my friend observed. Not entirely arbitrary though; it corresponded to levels of risk, and perhaps also to how dramatic the action seemed. Coming to a protest was good. Taking an arrest was better. But the pinnacle of resistance was to physically hammer on part of the arsenal of empire. I reflected on how some people granted me more respect and attention—almost certainly unconsciously—the further I traveled down this established tactical path. The effect was that newcomers were socially encouraged to imitate rather than to innovate or be critical. No one was talking about strategy or the achievement of concrete political goals.

Two years later I began recognizing this same dynamic endemic in the anarchist circles that I had joined following my time at the Catholic Worker. Taking the streets was good—as long as you didn't have a permit! "Direct action" was better. And "fucking shit up"—an ambiguous phrase that implied property destruction, usually directed at a large corporation—was the pinnacle of resistance. People often seemed "cool" to the extent that they embraced "hardcore" tactics, and were definitely uncool, even "liberal," if they were passé enough to suggest that the group consider applying for a permit or refraining from certain tactics in certain situations. Little if any time was spent discussing strategy and concrete goals.[17]

Such tactical hierarchies are implicit doctrine within these subcultures.[18] They serve as subcultural rites of passage. In both examples, the tactics were endorsed because of their reflection of the group's values and their service to the life of the group, rather than for their strategic utility. The black bloc tactic (wearing all black and masking up in a group during protests; highly associated with anarchists), for example, was ostensibly, on the tactical level, about anonymity and camouflage as a means of self-protection, but in reality participants who donned this uniform were targeted by police much more frequently and severely than other participants during protests. The supposed "tactic" was really more of a *signal*; it was about signaling belonging, commitment, and willingness to take risks in, and on behalf of, the group.

Engaging in higher-risk actions is exalted partly because the dramatic expression captured in these actions punctuates the collective narrative of the group, and partly for the sacrifice, heroism, and "hardcore-ism" involved. Smashing a bank window or breaking into a military base symbolically disrupts representations of the dominant culture, replacing them for a moment with components of the alternative narrative of the given group. As such, a dramatic action can function as a kind of shortcut to symbolically subvert the dominant culture's hegemony—a momentary seizing of the cultural stage. In this regard, dramatic

---

17   The examples provided in this section may seem extreme to some readers, and perhaps they are. In order to illuminate patterns that often play out in very subtle ways it can be useful to examine more extreme manifestations of the pattern.

18   Indeed, it can be very difficult for an individual to explicitly critique this group pattern from inside the group.

actions can be strategically useful—at least in theory. However, to our detriment we often fail to ask essential strategic questions: Who will see the action? What will the action communicate? To whom? And for what purpose?

The plowshares movement, while regularly engaging in highly dramatic direct actions, has too often not bothered to put much effort into strategically messaging or publicizing its actions. Often the only people who learn of the actions are a small number of military personnel and the small, already sympathetic readership of these communities' newsletters and websites. When this is the case—and there have been important exceptions—these dramatic and temporary disruptions of the dominant culture's representations (e.g., symbolically pouring blood on a B52 bomber), are reflected back almost exclusively to the actors themselves. This may be enough to further their own collective narrative and identity, but it falls short of strategically engaging the broader society or the power structure. Similarly, some black bloc groups have engaged in property destruction actions that have generated a great deal of media coverage, but these groups typically put little care into the message they are communicating through the combination of their tactics, appearances, and words (or lack thereof).[19] Their dramatic and temporary disruptions of the dominant culture's representations (e.g., smashing up a business district) have sometimes been reflected back to millions of people through the mass media, but the public's perceived meaning of the action differs severely from the actors' intended or self-understood meaning.

Such actions feed the actors. To be clear, feeding the actors is a necessary component of political action. As I have discussed at length in this chapter, finding a beloved community in a political group can be a critical source of motivation. However, we have a responsibility to push ourselves to act strategically, especially when we are considering substantial risk and sacrifice. Our time and energy—as well as our freedom and our very lives—are important, and we have a responsibility to calculate our risks

---

19   It should be noted that not all black blocs engage in property destruction.

(including how the risks we take might impact others, especially our political allies).

Sacrifice can serve as both a beautiful reinforcement of our collective values and a clear asset in our groups' abilities to function with capacity. It is good to appreciate that which each of us is willing to give of ourselves. By maintaining a consciousness of the appropriate role of sacrifice in our groups, we can appreciate it while not letting it lead us to the risk-for-the-sake-of-risk mentality, which is characteristic of a martyr mindset. We have to choose the risks we take and the sacrifices we make based on strategic factors; not because the act of taking risks asserts our place in the group and reinforces our sense of a righteous identity.

The story of the righteous few

Radicals tend to *become radicals* when we become disillusioned with aspects of the dominant culture. When we become aware of the destructive impacts of capitalism, racism, sexism, and other social systems that we see perpetuating oppression, we do not want to be part of it. We feel a moral repugnance and a desire to not cooperate with injustice.

However, the desire to separate ourselves from injustice can easily morph into a tendency to set ourselves apart from society in general. In other words, when we see the dominant culture as a perpetrator of injustice, and we see society as the storehouse of the dominant culture, then our desire to separate ourselves from injustice can easily develop into a mentality of separating ourselves from the larger society. With the mainstream seen as bad, we begin to look for ways to distinguish ourselves and our groups from anything that seems mainstream. We begin to notice, highlight, and exaggerate distinctions between ourselves and the mainstream, because these distinctions reinforce our radical identity. This tendency toward differentiation can go well beyond abstention from those aspects of the dominant culture that we find offensive. Radicals may start to adorn themselves with distinguishing features to express separation from society, and also to signal affinity with other radicals.

Writer and community organizer Mark Andersen discusses how this pattern plays out in radical punk subculture, which has many of the hallmarks of a tribe: "...piercings, tattoos, more. These markers, also including hairstyle, dress, music form, even slang, help to demark the boundaries of the group, to set it off from the larger populace. In this way, appearance can even be a form of dissent, a strikingly visual way to say, 'I am not a part of your corrupt world.'"[20]

The signifiers of distinction in punk subculture may be especially conspicuous, but many radical subcultures display versions of the same underlying pattern (as we saw in the previous chapter's examination of Occupy Wall Street through a fashion lens). Too often, radical subcultures caught in this pattern of emphasizing how different they are start to even prize their own marginalization. If society is unjust, then our justice-oriented identity may be reaffirmed when we are rejected by society. If society is bad, then marginalization within society must be good. We may tell each other stories of how we were ostracized from this or that group, how we are the outcast in our family, how we were the only radical in a group of compromising reformists, and so on. We begin to swim in our own marginalization. We begin to act out the *story of the righteous few.*

In the story of the righteous few, success itself becomes suspect. If, for example, a political group or message is embraced by a significant enough portion of society, it must be because it is not truly revolutionary or because it has been watered down. This mindset can lead us to publicly diss our allies when they succeed—to be oriented to look for and exaggerate their flaws, and to posture as more radical than them. It can seriously mess with radicals' heads when some of our ideas start to become popular! We are so accustomed to being the most radical kid on the block, and suddenly people whom we have never met are coming out of the woodwork, marching in the streets with us, and spouting some of the lines that we have been saying for years. It can lead to something of an identity crisis.

---

20   Andersen, *All the Power*, 46.

Here we see the importance of checking our narratives for faulty components. When we allow the story of the righteous few to have a place in our narrative about social change, we will always be hindered by the urge to separate ourselves from society and to retreat from success. To organize effectively, this mentality has to turn 180 degrees. We have to orient ourselves to connect with others, to notice commonalities, and to embrace being embraced by society. For many radicals, this may require a big shift in the way we see ourselves and our society.

The good news is that we have before us an opportunity to make a profound paradigm shift. Occupy Wall Street, in highlighting economic inequality in the United States, popularized the concept of *the one percent* and, more importantly, *the 99%*. The latter frames an alignment of our vision of justice and equality with a supermajority. It encourages us to think of almost everyone as a potential ally. Over the past four decades, it often felt like radical social justice movements in the United States were up against the whole culture. Radicals clustered into increasingly insular circles, looking to each other for connection, as if to hold onto our sanity in a world gone mad. It was easy to feel powerless in the face of "free trade," austerity, raging wars of aggression, ecological devastation, attacks on gains made by earlier social justice movements, and many other setbacks.

Frameworks like "We are the 99%!" can help to pull us out of a *counter-cultural* mentality and orient us to claim and contest the culture—*our* culture—rather than denounce, abandon, and distinguish ourselves from it. *We are the 99%. We are the true moral majority.* Of course, no slogan will do all the work for us. While we challenge the dominant story, we must also examine our relationship as radicals to the broader society. To win, we have to scrap the chapter of the righteous few, and replace it with a story about huge swaths of society building a movement together. The underlying socioeconomic conditions are politicizing more and more people, creating greater potential for the emergence of a broad-based movement than we have seen in decades. And for this we need radicals, without whom, such a movement could lose its fire and settle too soon for too little.

Must our radical identity confine us to being eternally ostracized? That is the story of the righteous few. The powerful are always ready to tell that story, and we must not be a predictable character in their script. Serious radicals must dispense with that martyr mentality. Serious radicals must aim to succeed. Taking on an advantaged opponent without any intention or strategy for success is not so much fighting as it is coping. The tendency of the outgunned resister to run headlong, kamikaze-style, into enemy lines is the tendency of someone who wants to be righteous—not of someone who seeks to actually change the world. We must ask ourselves if our intention is to bring about meaningful change, or if it is simply to act out righteous narratives.

Political identity paradox

In critiquing the danger of insularity and self-involvement, we have to be careful to not let the pendulum swing too far in the other direction. The internal life and morale of the group is critically important to the group's external political achievements. Developing a strong core—i.e., very active participants and leadership—is essential for any social movement or political project, and such a core requires strong morale and a thriving internal life. Indeed, there can be no serious social movement—the kind that challenges the powerful and privileged—without a corresponding serious group identity; a sense of solidarity and cohesion that encourages a core of members to contribute an exceptional level of commitment, sacrifice, and heroics over the course of prolonged struggle.

However, as we have seen in this chapter, strong group identity is a double-edged sword. The stronger the identity and cohesion of the group, the more likely its members are to become alienated from other groups, and from society as a whole. I call this dilemma the *political identity paradox*. This paradox suggests that while political groups require a strong internal identity to foster the commitment needed for effective political struggle, this same cohesion tends to isolate the group. And isolated groups are hard-pressed to achieve political goals.

Strong bonding *within* a group tends to create distinctions *between* groups. This is true to an extent for all kinds of groups, but it tends to have particular consequences for groups involved in oppositional political struggle. Consider a sports team that defines its group identity partly in distinction from rival teams. The team may very well play all the harder against rivals as a result of the distinction. A group engaged in challenging entrenched power, on the other hand, has to contend with far more powerful opponents in incredibly lopsided political contests. Such a group, therefore, has not only to foster a strong internal identity; it also has to win allies beyond the bounds of that identity, if it is to build the collective power it needs to move any serious political goals forward. To extend the sports metaphor: if a movement group wants to score any goals, it has to see and value *other groups* as players on the same team, moving the ball in the same general direction.

On top of this challenge, the dynamics of *oppositional* political struggle can quickly escalate the tendency toward isolation. Oppositional struggle can trigger an oppositional psychology in the minds of core participants, and this can do a real number on a group. Movements that meet the kind of brutal repression that the civil rights movement endured, for example, have an exceptional balancing act to perform. On the one hand, participants need to turn inward toward each other more than ever for strength and support. In moments of conflict, they feel a compelling cohesiveness to their group identity. On the other hand, they need to maintain an outward orientation as well, to stay connected to a broad and growing social base. This is a delicate balance to strike even when leaders are prepared for this tension, which is often not the case.

Take, for example, Students for a Democratic Society—the original SDS that fell apart in dramatic fashion in 1969. The *political identity paradox* was operating at the center of the epic implosion of this massive student organization. Key leaders had become encapsulated in their oppositional identity and became more and more out of touch.[21] Many core leaders lost the ability

---

21   More precisely: a few different, factionalizing identities.

and even the inclination to relate to their broader membership—a huge number of students at the time—let alone to the broader society. In the process, some of the most committed would-be leaders of that generation came to see more value in holing up with a few comrades to make bombs than in organizing the masses of students who were coming out of the woodwork to take coordinated collective action. This is the tendency toward insularity and isolation taken to the extreme. Dedicated radicals cut themselves off, like lone guerrilla fighters in enemy territory. It might have felt glorious, but it was a suicide mission.

The political identity paradox speaks to the need for political groups to develop both strong *bonding* and strong *bridging*.[22] Without strong internal bonding, group members will lack the level of commitment required for serious struggle. But without strong external bridging, the group will become too insular and isolated to forge the kind of broad alliances that are essential to winning meaningful changes in society. Good leaders must learn to perform this extraordinary balancing act.

Just because this political identity paradox seems to be written into the DNA of political groups does not mean every political group that develops a strong cohesive identity will inevitably become insular or delusional. Self-reflective and strategic organizations can build the group's identity and cohesion while simultaneously staying outwardly oriented and guarding against insular tendencies. Maintaining clear and measurable campaign goals is one of the most important safeguards. Other basic safeguards can also be codified into a group's regular practices. Testing political messages with people outside of the group—ideally with folks who are part of the group's target audience—is one basic, but always worthwhile, practice that can inform a group's strategic thinking and guard against groupthink and insularity.

More than any one particular practice, though, *good leaders* can play a critically important role in shaping a strategic and

---

22   Robert Putnam introduced the terms *bonding* and *bridging* to describe
        two essential kinds of social capital, based respectively on strong social
        ties and weak social ties. Putnam, *Bowling Alone.*

outwardly oriented culture within highly cohesive groups. One way that good leaders do this is by themselves modeling an orientation toward the periphery, rather than toward the center of the group. Whether they acknowledge it or not, leaders—both formal and informal leaders—tend to enjoy a relatively high level of status within groups. Good leaders can take responsibility for this by "flipping the script" of orientation within the group. It is tempting for those who are in the center of a group to orient their attention only towards others who they see as being in the center; i.e., other people they perceive to be especially important (or "cool"). This sets a negative pattern for the whole group, where members orient themselves to elbow their way into the center of the group, and everyone ignores the group's periphery. This "in-crowd" dynamic shuts out wisdom that resides at the periphery. It turns off new people and potential recruits, and tends to encourage imitative rather than innovative behavior. Instead, good leaders need to make the time and effort to talk with new people, shy people, people who hold less status in the group, and, especially, people who are not even "in the room"; for example, people who are part of the group's intended social base of support. This kind of exemplary outward-facing leadership establishes a positive pattern for the whole group and sets a higher bar for what it means to be a good leader. Group members can see a positive path to contributing to the group and to winning the esteem of others—not by pushing ahead of others, or trashing outsiders, or parroting the cool kids, but by attending to others and making everyone feel valued. This helps to keep the group's attention oriented toward the periphery instead of the center; toward the tasks of welcoming newcomers, plugging people in, and turning *potential* allies into *active* allies.

As a certain sailor once said, "Whoever wants to be a leader among you must be your servant."[23] And like that sailor, good leaders are both strategic and *hardcore*—and they help to define what it means to be *hardcore*. A close relative of the political identity paradox is the tendency within highly cohesive political

---

23   Jesus of Nazareth, *The Bible*, Matthew 20:26.

groups to want to *turn up the heat*. It seems written into the social DNA of oppositional political groups: when group members'
level of commitment increases, they want to go further. They
want to be more *hardcore*.

Author and social commentator Bill Bishop offers insight
into this dynamic:

> There have been hundreds of group polarization experiments,
> all finding that like-minded groups, over time, grow more ex-
> treme in the direction of the majority view ... people are con-
> stantly comparing their beliefs and actions to those of the
> group. When a person learns that others in the group share his
> or her general beliefs, he or she finds it *socially advantageous
> to adopt a position slightly more extreme than the group aver-
> age*. It's a safe way to stand out from the crowd. It brings notice
> and even approbation ... Everyone wants to be a member in
> good standing with the dominant group position. It's counter-
> intuitive, but people grow more extreme within homogeneous
> groups as a way to conform.[24]

In other words, there is a tendency within groups for members to kind of out-"group" each other; to take the essence of
the group—its distinctive culture, values, and rituals—to new
heights; to become more *hardcore*. In oppositional political
groups, this can play out as a tendency toward tactical escalation
and increased militancy. And this latter aspect can sometimes
be a good thing—but not inevitably. It all depends on the details
of *how hardcore is defined* within the culture of the group. If it
is grounded in clear political goals, an overarching strategy, and
in relation to a social base, then escalation can move a cause forward. If it is self-involved posturing, it can send the group into a
dangerous or dysfunctional downward spiral.

Compare the trajectory of Students for a Democratic Society
(SDS) with that of the Student Nonviolent Coordinating Committee (SNCC). Both were among the most important radical youth

---

24   Bishop and Cushing, *The Big Sort*, 67–69. My emphasis.

organizations of the 1960s. SDS imploded in 1969 and the Weather Underground was born because some leaders succeeded in defining hardcore to mean immediate armed guerrilla struggle against the US government—an absurd prospect for their context. In the case of SNCC, on the other hand, some very astute leaders defined hardcore to mean efforts such as going into the most segregated areas in the South and organizing some of the poorest, least educated, and most disenfranchised people in the entire country. SNCC engaged in other more visible "hardcore" tactics as well.

In both cases, hardcore really was *HARDCORE*. You can't satiate the desire for hardcore with anything less! Members of both groups demonstrated overwhelming levels of commitment to the values of the groups they belonged to. Members of both groups risked their lives, were imprisoned and brutalized, and some even lost their lives. But hardcore was defined strategically in the case of SNCC, and tragically in the case of SDS and the Weather Underground. To be clear, this comparison is one of "apples and oranges"—different organizations navigating very different terrains—and the point is not at all to argue SNCC = good and SDS = bad. Indeed, within both organizations, we can find important moments when this tendency toward escalation was navigated successfully, and other times when it was not. And of course there are countless other important factors that influence whether or not a group succeeds in its political mission—and so many of these factors are beyond the group's control.

Yet this social pattern does tend to operate as a powerful force within the life of all sorts of oppositional groups, and leaders have a great deal of power to influence the specifics of how it manifests: whether it is a strategic boon or the group's doom. Good leaders anticipate the emergent desire for escalation—for being hardcore—and they own it. They model it themselves. And they make sure that the hardcore expression is designed to strengthen bonds between the group's core members and its broader political base. This should *feel hardcore* to the participants, but it must also *look like moral leadership* to the political base and to allies and potential allies within the broader public.

THE PREFIGURATIVE AND THE POLITICAL

A dominant tendency within Occupy Wall Street espoused an anarchistic philosophy called "prefigurative politics." In this chapter I examine Occupy's prefigurative politics at length, because I see it as archetypal of a much larger social movement trend in the United States over the past half century. In contrast to power politics, "prefigurative politics" seeks to demonstrate the "better world" it envisions for the future in the actions it takes today. Rather than accept this philosophy on its own terms, I position it squarely within the internal "life of the group"—and specifically the tendency toward insularity—discussed in the previous chapter. I argue that even leftist idealists have to strategically engage power politics proper, if they hope to build anything bigger than a radical clubhouse.

"There is a danger. Don't fall in love with yourselves. We have a nice time here. But remember, carnivals come cheap. What matters is the day after, when we will have to return to normal lives. Will there be any changes then?"

—*Slavoj Žižek speaking at Zuccotti Park*[1]

---

1   Slavoj Žižek, "SLAVOJ ŽIŽEK SPEAKS at OCCUPY WALL STREET: TRANSCRIPT," *The Parallax*, October 9, 2011, http://www.imposemagazine.com/bytes/slavoj-zizek-at-occupy-wall-street-transcript.

Falling in love with ourselves

In late October 2011 my cousin Hans, who was living in Brooklyn at the time, decided to come visit me at Zuccotti Park, where for the last few weeks I'd been involved with the thriving Occupy Wall Street encampment. Hans and I are from the same little town of Bird-In-Hand, Pennsylvania. I knew that what was happening in the park would be something new for him, and I was eager to hear his impressions.

"What stood out to me," he told me at a bar around the corner, "was how you all are recreating society—or creating a microcosm of society. It's all there: a kitchen, a medical tent, a security force, a public library, even a whole alternative decision-making structure. It's fascinating!"

Much has been made about the "prefigurative" aspects of Occupy Wall Street and the occupy encampments across the country, when they existed. The camps served as more than just a protest, more than just a tactic. Participants consciously attempted to model the kind of society that they were striving to build, with an open invitation to anyone who wanted to join. In the two months of the physical occupation of Zuccotti, newcomers like my cousin could walk in off the street and join our world—could even speak up during a General Assembly meeting if they felt so moved. Everyone's participation was ostensibly welcomed. A modified consensus decision-making process was used in General Assemblies and in working group meetings so that decisions would have to take into account everyone's input and ideas, thus prefiguring a kind of "direct democracy" seen as lacking in the wider world, particularly in the realm of mainstream politics.

"It's kind of utopian," Hans suggested.

"I hope not!" I replied.

Unlike many of my Occupy comrades, I was never enamored with the "direct democracy" of the General Assembly. While I believe that democratic participation is a key ingredient of grassroots organizing, I have often found consensus-based processes of decision-making to be deeply dysfunctional, especially when attempted with large numbers of participants.[2] I take that in stride and with patience. Social movements are messy and it can take time to figure out good and functional processes for effective and accountable decision-making and organization. What was especially worrying me about the dominant culture within Zuccotti, though, was how these processes and their accompanying prefigurative rituals came to *stand in for strategy* for many Occupy participants. Particular forms of process—from "mic-checks" to "sparkle fingers" to making space where everyone who wants to can speak—were often confused with political content (i.e., goals or a platform) and with strategies for achieving the latter.[3] This is not to denigrate the importance of collective ritual in protest movements. As I have already discussed at length, collective ritual fosters strong group identity, cohesion, and solidarity; participants' willingness to give of themselves depends on this strong sense of solidarity and identity. But if our intention is to change the world—not just prefigure a utopian vision, with no idea about how to actualize it—then these collective rituals must take their place within a larger overarching strategic framework.

Discussing the utopian impulse, Antonio Gramsci wrote, "The attribute 'utopian' does not apply to political will in general, but to specific wills which are incapable of relating means to

---

2   For a critique of formal consensus decision-making process, and its religious origins, see L.A. Kauffman's article "The Theology of Consensus," *Berkeley Journal of Sociology* 59 (2015): 8–13.

3   OWS popularized the "human microphone," a means of amplifying participants' voices when amplification equipment was unavailable or prohibited. Starting with the phrase, "Mic check!" individual speakers break up their remarks into succinct segments that are loudly repeated in unison by other participants within earshot. "Sparkle fingers" is one of many hand gestures regularly employed by OWS participants during meetings and assemblies. Participants twinkle their fingers as a kind of silent applause to indicate agreement with what is being said. While mic checks and sparkle fingers often serve functional purposes during meetings and street protests, they also serve as rituals that reinforce an Occupy group culture.

end, and hence are not even wills, but idle whims, dreams, long-ings, etc.[4] Gramsci elaborated a definition of utopianism that goes further than its popular notion of rosy-eyed visions of how the world could one day be. He dismisses utopianists not for the content of their vision of the future, but for their lack of a vision or plan for how to move from Point A to Point B, from present reality to realized vision. In other words, dreaming about how the world might possibly someday be is not the same as political struggle—even when your dreams are punctuated with dramatic "prefigurative" public spectacles.

Public performance and backstage

A prevailing narrative about the global wave of uprisings, begin-ning circa 2011, has explained these movements as exhibiting a new kind of politics. Ostensibly "prefigurative" and "leaderless," such movements seem on the surface to be playing an entirely dif-ferent game than traditional social movements or political chal-lengers. But should we take these movements' self-descriptions at face value? Can they succeed politically while ignoring or eschew-ing the realm of power? And is "prefigurative politics" really the only story to be found within these novel mobilizations?[5]

In answering these questions, we have to distinguish be-tween social movements' mythologies and their operations. Con-sider Rosa Parks and the Montgomery Bus Boycott. We know that Parks was not merely tired when she refused to give up her bus seat. She was acting with agency, and the appearance of spontaneity was part of an intentional performance designed for strategic effect.[6] It was fine—intended even—for most people to see and sympathize with her as a tired woman who had simply

---

4   Antonio Gramsci, *Selections from the Prison Notebooks*, ed. and trans. Quentin Hoare and Geoffrey Nowell Smith (New York: International Publishers, 1971), 175.

5   This paragraph borrows language (my own) that frames a forum in the *Berkeley Journal of Sociology's* 2014 call for papers.

6   Polletta, *It Was Like a Fever*, 33.

had enough. It would be a mistake, however, for social movement strategists to take her performance at face value. We must also look behind the scenes.

With the sudden and dramatic launching of Occupy Wall Street, there was a widespread tendency to take the new movement's bountiful public performances at face value. However, as in the case of Rosa Parks and the civil rights movement, it behooves us to explore Occupy Wall Street's *backstage* when assessing the movement.[7] What complicates such an endeavor is that what we might usually think of as a movement's backstage—for example, decision-making processes, general meetings, working groups, planning, and so on—was not really behind the scenes with Occupy. It was all part of the public performance. To many participants, Occupy's internal democratic processes were indistinguishable from external messages. To me, Occupy's hyper-democratic process was an important *part* of the public message. General Assemblies at Zuccotti Park operated as brilliant theater, dramatically juxtaposing a visibly participatory people's movement against a rotted political system that has effectively disenfranchised most Americans. The downside was that General Assemblies were not functional forums for actual decision-making. Because they were so cumbersome and easily derailed, many of the most active Occupy Wall Street organizers, myself included, eventually stopped attending with much frequency. We were too busy attending to tasks to be able to sit through hours upon hours of exasperating do-nothing meetings. Thus, much of the real decision-making was pushed *back*-backstage into underground centers of informal power.

Because of the quasi-official storyline about having "no leaders," few were willing to openly admit exercising leadership, even when it was clear to them—and should have been clear to many—that this was in fact what they were doing. For example, one active participant in Occupy Providence, Mike McCarthy, candidly discussed in an interview his own informal leadership

---

7   Erving Goffman, *The Presentation of Self in Everyday Life* (Garden City, NY: Doubleday and Anchor Books, 1954).

and even admitted to manipulating the official process.[8] Mc-
Carthy's informal leadership is a common Occupy story. What
is less common is his candor in recounting his own actions and
role. For my part, I was self-consciously part of one of these
centers of informal power in New York City, for close to a year,
beginning in October 2011.[9] Like McCarthy, I, too, "was never
for the no leadership thing."[10] And I concur with OWS participant journalist Sarah Jaffe that "the 'leaderless" structure of
Occupy masked the fact that a small core group of people did a
large amount of the work."[11] Such sentiments are a more accurate reflection of reality than many of Occupy's self-proclaimed
or on-paper processes.

My work with Occupy Wall Street was primarily with the
public relations working group, the movement-building working
group, Occupy Homes, and coordinating with allied organizations (e.g., labor unions, nonprofit advocacy organizations, faith
communities, and more). My goals and many other core participants' goals were absolutely political, in the sense that we saw
the nascent movement and the moment through a lens of a long-
term political struggle. Indeed, Occupy Wall Street constituted
one of the biggest political openings for the US left that many of
us had ever seen in our lives. This is why I take issue with people—critics and supporters alike—who have cropped politics out
of the picture of OWS, as if it were little more than a metropolitan
version of Burning Man. Media theorist Douglas Rushkoff, for
example, suggested that OWS "is more like a university than a
political movement" and that it is "not a game that someone wins,
but rather a form of play." He and others can hardly be faulted for

8   Robert J. Wengronowitz, "Lessons from Occupy Providence," *The Socio-
      logical Quarterly* 54, no. 2 (2013): 215.
9   While the encampment at Zuccotti Park was evicted on November 17,
      2011, Occupy-related actions and campaigns (e.g., Occupy Homes,
      Strike Debt, and Occupy Sandy) continued well into 2012 and beyond.
10   Wengronowitz, "Lessons from Occupy Providence," 215.
11   Sarah Jaffe, "Occupy as a Humbling Experience," *The Sociological
      Quarterly* 54, no. 2 (2013): 201.

these characterizations though, as many core participants were also describing Occupy as "post-political," as if this would be a positive development.

So, while Occupy did often approach the edge of degeneration into a utopian sideshow, such tendencies were always only part of the story. The movement was also brimming with grassroots political actors intent on a main-stage intervention. As Frances Fox Piven explains, OWS "succeeded in putting the issue of extreme inequality in the political spotlight, ... made Wall Street its target, and ... reached out to find allies."[12] Piven describes how many core participants engaged continuously in classic political organizing tasks like "reach[ing] out to potential allies among workers, students and community groups." These efforts bore fruit, as "unionists rallied to defend Zuccotti Park when the Mayor first threatened to evict the Occupiers, and joined them in their marches."[13] Some of us worked relationships with sympathetic city council members; some negotiated with the local community board; and some strategized with unions, community groups, and national advocacy organizations. While the news cameras and our own social media zoomed in on the public performance in the park, these behind-the scenes tasks were part of a scaffolding that propped up the temporary platform.

What is politics?

What would it even mean for something like Occupy to be *post-political?*" Part of the problem here is how the words *politics* and *political* are routinely thrown around casually and without precision. What does it mean for something to be *political* or, for that matter, *apolitical?* For Gramsci, whether a certain tendency is political or not ultimately comes down to its engagement with extant power relations and structures. When Gramsci calls certain tendencies

---

12   Frances Fox Piven, "On the Organizational Question," *The Sociological Quarterly* 54, no. 2 (2013): 192.

13   Ibid. Unions were in fact responsible for a huge part of the turnout on the biggest days of action (e.g., October 15 and November 17, 2011).

apoliticism, his argument is not that these tendencies are not informed by or in reaction to political events or structural relationships, or that their adherents have no political opinions.[14] He is asserting, rather, that the actions of some ostensibly political groups are not genuinely intended as political *interventions*, i.e., strategic attempts to shift relationships of power and the outcomes of those relationships. Here we see an important distinction: between actions (or opinions) that are informed by or in reaction to a political situation, on the one hand, and actions that are designed to be political *interventions* to reshape the world, on the other. The expression of one's values or opinions, while informed by political realities, will not automatically amount to a political intervention—even if expressed loudly and dramatically.

To be *political*, then, is not merely to hold or to express political opinions about issues, but to be engaged with the terrain of power, with an orientation towards changing the broader society and its structures. With such a political understanding, Gramsci saw the essential task of aspiring political challengers was "the formation of a national-popular collective will, of which the modern Prince is at one and the same time the organiser and the active, operative expression."[15] With the term "modern Prince" Gramsci was referencing Machiavelli's *The Prince*, but what he meant by this was a revolutionary party that must operate as both the unifying *symbol* and the *agent* of an articulated collective will, i.e., an emerging alternative hegemony that brings disparate groups into alignment.

How does Occupy Wall Street measure up to Gramsci's political vision? OWS did not have a revolutionary party, in the sense that Gramsci elaborated. Indeed, Occupy shared many features with the anarchist movement that Gramsci criticized.[16] Yet, despite this anarchism—with all of its ambivalence and hostility towards the notion of building and wielding power, leadership, and organization—OWS did, in its first few months of existence, step partially into this dual role of "operative expression" and

---

14   Gramsci, *Prison Notebooks*, 147.

15   Ibid., 133.

16   Ibid., 149.

"organiser" of a newly articulated "national-popular collective will." Indeed, OWS's initial success in the realm of contesting popular meanings was remarkable. Emerging practically overnight, the nascent movement broke into the national news cycle and articulated a popular critique of economic inequality and a political system rigged to serve "the one percent."

Moreover, OWS managed to momentarily align remnants and residue of a long-fragmented political left in the United States, while simultaneously striking a resonant chord with far broader audiences. Its next logical political step, had it followed a Gramscian political "roadmap," would have been to build and consolidate its organizational capacity by (1) constructing a capable and disciplined organizational apparatus, and (2) activating the above-mentioned organizations and social bases into an alternative hegemonic alignment capable of shifting political outcomes (i.e., winning).

Unfortunately, Occupy was deeply ambivalent about even attempting such operations. Nonetheless, it is important to draw attention to the tendency within OWS that *did* make such attempts, and that even enjoyed notable successes, however localized or limited these may have been.[17] As I've described above, there were two main tendencies within the core of OWS: one oriented toward *strategic politics* and the other toward *prefigurative politics*.[18] To follow a Gramscian roadmap, the former tendency would have had to build a mandate within the movement for strategic political intervention, to a greater extent than it did.

---

17   Many commentators, including grassroots organizers who should know better, now speak about Occupy as if this tendency did not exist. Whether we are discussing elections, social movements, legislative campaigns, or revolutions, the question of whether a political contender wins or loses tends to have a totalizing effect upon the post-game analysis of "Monday morning quarterbacks." Analysts often make the mistake of inferring that the loser did *none* of a thing that they actually did *insufficiently*.

18   Wini Breines introduces this juxtaposition of *strategic politics* and *prefigurative politics* in her scholarship on the New Left. Wini Breines, *Community and Organization in the New Left, 1962–1968: The Great Refusal* (New York: Praeger, 1982).

As for the prefigurative politics tendency, Gramsci would likely not have considered much of its "politics" to be politics *at all*. This latter tendency viewed decision-making processes and the physical occupation of public space as manifestations of a better future *now* (i.e., prefiguration), rather than as tactics within a larger strategy of political contestation. The prefigurative politics tendency confused process, tactics, and self-expression with political content and was often ambivalent about strategic questions, like whether Wall Street was the named target or most anything else in its place.[19] It celebrated "'the act for the act's sake', struggle for the sake of struggle, etc."[20] Such an inability or disinterest in engaging questions of political strategy—i.e., "how to get from Point A to Point B"—resemble Gramsci's critique of utopianism ("specific wills which are incapable of relating means to end, and hence are not even wills, but idle whims, dreams, longings, etc."). He may well have called it "apoliticism."

Lifeworld

I want to suggest that in the "prefigurative politics" on display at Zuccotti Park, Gramsci's negative concept of utopianism interacted with, and was fueled by, the tendency toward insularity that I have been discussing in the first three chapters of this book. To recap, I have explained this as the tendency to elevate the internal *life of the group* over the group's external political accomplishments. In order to excavate deeper layers of this tendency, I now turn to Jürgen Habermas's concept of the *lifeworld*—specifically his discussion of subcultural tendencies oriented towards the revitalization of the lifeworld.

Prefigurative politics purports to be about modeling or prefiguring visions of utopian futures here and now. Indeed, such prefigurative spectacles did seem to create a palpable *feeling* of

---

19   Indeed, consider the bizarre attempt to occupy land owned by Trinity Church on December 17, 2011, in what may have been the most epic single moment of Occupy's unraveling.

20   Gramsci, *Prison Notebooks*, 147.

utopianism at Zuccotti Park for many participants. *Utopianism as a feeling* is hardly about the future; rather, it is felt, deeply, here and now. During my time as an active participant at Zuccotti Park, I began to wonder if the heightened sense of an integrated identity was the "utopia" that many of my fellow participants were seeking. What if the thing we were missing, the thing we were lacking—the thing we longed for most—was a sense of an integrated existence in a cohesive community, i.e., an *intact lifeworld*? What if this longing was so potent that it could eclipse the drive to affect larger political outcomes?

Habermas argues that under a system of advanced capitalism and bureaucracy, both bureaucratic and capitalist logics have penetrated and colonized the *lifeworld*, encroaching upon, and even annihilating, the realm of traditional and organic social practice and organization. The fabric of community is profoundly disrupted, and we feel this loss deeply. In such contexts, social movements have dramatically shifted in their political contents, forms, demographics, and the motivations of their participants. Perhaps especially consequential is how social movement participants in advanced capitalist nations may be more likely to emphasize fine distinctions between their own groups and the broader society than they are to look for commonalities. That is, they are more likely to *marginally differentiate* themselves and their groups as a means of finding and deepening a sense of solidarity and belonging that they feel themselves lacking. Habermas writes: "For this reason, ascriptive characteristics such as gender, age, skin color, neighborhood or locality, and religious affiliation serve to build up and separate off communities, *to establish subculturally protected communities supportive of the search for personal and collective identity*. The revaluation of the particular, the natural, the provincial, of *social spaces that are small enough to be familiar*, of decentralized forms...all this is meant to foster the revitalization of possibilities for expression and communication that have been buried alive."[21]

---

21   Jürgen Habermas, *The Theory of Communicative Action, Volume II* (Boston: Beacon Press, 1984), 395. My emphasis.

My point here is not to diminish the importance of a group's internal life and the sense of community, meaning, and belonging experienced by participants. I would even posit that such spaces are indispensable to social movements' ability to deepen political analysis and foster the level of solidarity and commitment that oppositional struggle requires. The problem here is a matter of imbalance: when a group's internal life becomes a more important motivator than *what the group accomplishes* as a political vehicle for change. To the extent that a group becomes self-content—encapsulated in the project of constructing its particularized lifeworld—what motivation will participants have to strategically engage broader society and political structures? Why would group members want to claim and contest popular meanings and symbols if the group's individuated lifeworld can be further cultivated by an explicit rejection of such contests and by eschewing the popular? If participants are motivated by hope of psychic completion—by community and a strong sense of belonging—and such motivation is insufficiently grounded in instrumental political goals, their energies will likely go into deepening group identity over bolstering the group's external political achievements. The problem is that the group's particularized lifeworld can be strengthened without it ever having to actually *win* anything in the real world. Indeed, this may help to explain why some ostensibly political groups have been able to maintain a committed core of participants for decades without ever achieving a single measurable political goal.

In short, the utopianism described by Gramsci is encouraged by the extraordinary motivational shift described by Habermas. The latter theorist discusses two factors that combine to encourage this motivational shift: (1) the drive to construct a refuge from the pervasive logics of capitalism and bureaucracy, i.e., an intact *lifeworld*, and (2) the backdrop of an expanded middle class whose members can take for granted a certain level of material sustenance and comfort, so that individuals are freed up to expand their political concerns beyond basic material needs, thereby diminishing the imperative to articulate *common* class interests or build effective vehicles for their advancement. In

Habermas's words, "The lifeworld, more or less relieved of tasks of material reproduction, can in turn become more differentiated in its symbolic structures and can set free the inner logic of development of cultural modernity."[22]

Political scientist Ronald Inglehart made a similar argument, based partly on Abraham Maslow's hierarchy of needs. Once our basic survival and material needs are provided for, we can then focus our attention on social networks and individual self-expression. Projecting this schema onto generational shifts, Inglehart posited an explanation for why dramatic outbursts of a remarkably self-expressive style of collective action hit every highly industrialized society in the world simultaneously in the late 1960s.[23] The "kids of the baby boom" grew up with relative abundance, unlike their parents who had been shaped by both the Great Depression and the Second World War. We must, of course, be careful not to throw the entire generation into a single bucket—stratification by economic class, race, gender, sexual orientation, and locality, among other categories, obviously produced highly divergent experiences. Yet the overall expansion of a comfortable middle class—with its individualist logics of self-fulfillment, self-development, self-expression, consumption, and upward mobility—clearly shaped a significant portion of this generation. Inglehart's argument dovetails with a prescient framework put forward by David Riesman in *The Lonely Crowd*, over a decade before the social upheaval and social movements of the 1960s. Riesman argued that a new *other-directed* character structure, arising from a backdrop of material abundance, was becoming predominant in the United States. Young people who were socially molded into this character structure—in contrast to their *inner-directed* parents—were more concerned with *the morale of the group* than with *what the group produces*.[24] It is not hard to see how such shifts could encourage movement participants who are self-expressive to the

---

22   Ibid., 385.

23   Inglehart, *The Silent Revolution*.

24   Riesman, *The Lonely Crowd*.

point of being effectively disinterested in political instrumentality, strategic calculus, and broader outcomes.

Habermas is making a kind of psychological wholeness argument. And it is important to not underestimate the power of such a drive, which is produced by the alienating effects of advanced capitalism. Moreover, we must be careful to not view this psychological level only as a negative constraint on effective collective action. The benefits of the profound sense of integration experienced by some social movement participants are not only personal or psychological on the individual level. Again, a *cohesive sense of group* dramatically increases participants' willingness to give of ourselves, our time and energy, and even to risk our safety for the sake of a greater good. Developing a strong movement core so thoroughly oriented toward the group—i.e., the campaign, the struggle, etc.—is essential for effective political challengers.

But such cohesion is a double-edged sword. Insofar as participants are motivated by the hope of psychic completion, as opposed to concretely changing X in the world, they are likely to fixate on the group's internal *lifeworld* more than the group's external political *accomplishments*. This helps explain how a group's internal processes can come to stand in for a strategy; how "tactics" can become valued more for their self-expressive and group-affirming capacities than for their instrumentality; how a would-be political group can gravitate toward self-referential rituals and rhetoric; and how the core of an initially popular movement like Occupy Wall Street can quickly degenerate into insularity, impotency, and narcissism.

"There is a danger," Slavoj Žižek warned us at Zuccotti Park. "Don't fall in love with yourselves. We have a nice time here. But remember, carnivals come cheap. What matters is the day after, when we will have to return to normal lives. Will there be any changes then?"[25] Žižek warned us to not fixate on our own image in the mirror; to not let love of our own liberation devolve into narcissism. Our challenge is to build and celebrate our

---

25   Žižek, "SLAVOJ ŽIŽEK SPEAKS."

community-in-struggle—including the deeply motivating feel-ings of belonging and solidarity we experience—while also keep-ing our eyes on the prize of real-world political change. Valuing the internal life of the social movements we are part of—our spac-es, our culture, our rituals, our processes, etc.—and the accom-panying sense of wholeness is important, but we have to balance this with the value we place on what our movements achieve in the world beyond ourselves.

Again, the utopianism described here is not just about an idealistic vision for the future. There is an aspect of utopianism within intense challenger movements like Occupy Wall Street, and the utopian drive in these situations may be as much about immediate participant experience as it is about an envisioned ideal future. The incarnated utopian space (e.g., Zuccotti Park) provides an integrated group identity that fills a lack for many core participants. The lack is caused at least partly by the frag-mentation of modern life—the dispersal of our identities across many spheres (e.g., workplace, family, religion, interest, hobby, or neighborhood) and the accompanying anxiety caused by the con-stant juggling of our selves.

Who are we? Each of us contains many selves, many perfor-mances, each of which emerges in relation to different groups and circumstances. But those who can step fully into one single radically totalizing identity are able to fill this lack and longing, even if temporarily, with an integrated sense of self and of be-longing in a beloved community. Out of many identity fragments emerges a singularity: the revolutionary, the occupier. Even those who are unable to step in quite so fully can still experience this utopian space vicariously as representing the *potential*, the *idea*, or the *symbol* of completion; of filling the lack.

The danger with this arrangement is political. Because this utopian space is what fills our lack, the *achievement of the space* can be exalted over *what the space achieves*; the life of the group over the group's capacity to act as a vehicle for change.

Two tendencies

However, as I have already suggested, this was not the only tendency within Occupy Wall Street. As the movement launched, its
prefigurative politics tendency was the most visible, as it celebrated the utopian microcosm it created in Zuccotti Park, and fixated
on its own decision-making process and the physical occupation of
public space. There was, however, another strong tendency, though
often less visible, that bore a greater resemblance to a Gramscian
approach to political struggle. This *strategic politics* tendency was
simultaneously succeeding in injecting strategic political messages
(most notably, "We are the 99%!") and aligning hitherto fragmented political actors—such as labor unions, community groups, and
national organizations—behind the scenes.[26] In the beginning of
OWS, prefigurative politics and strategic politics co-existed uneas-
ily; many core Occupy participants engaged in both kinds of tasks
or oscillated between the two tendencies. Within three months,
however, core members factionalized, and the tendencies became
much clearer—and recognizable as *ideal types*.[27] Admittedly, Occupy was made up of an impressive number of moving parts, so it
is a simplification to try to categorize such variegated components
into two overarching tendencies. Nonetheless, it is my assessment
that these two tendencies each had enough coherence and adherents to be reasonably treated as *things*, however amorphous,
and that additional political tendencies can either be treated as
sub-tendencies under these two, or discarded—for purposes of the
strategic analysis here—as relatively small, eccentric, or inconsequential to this analysis.

---

26   To be clear, informal leaders from *both* tendencies operated both back-
      stage and out in the open (i.e., engaging with Occupy's official appara-
      tuses, like working groups and General Assemblies). Informal leaders
      of the *prefigurative politics* tendency were, however, understandably
      less likely to admit to this reality.

27   Sociologist Max Weber is most associated with the concept of an *ideal
      type*, which is an analytical tool used to apprehend social categories by
      identifying and emphasizing their essential distinguishing features.

Dualisms

hegemonic contest	lifeworld
unification	marginal differentiation
instrumental	expressive
what the group accomplishes	life of the group
strategic politics	prefigurative politics
ethic of responsibility	ethic of ultimate ends
politics	values

Figure 1: dualisms

I introduce the dualisms in Figure 1 in order to shed light on underlying logics of these two tendencies in OWS. The dualisms overlay each other, but are not identical. Starting at the top, I juxtapose Gramsci's conception of a *hegemonic contest*—a strategic intervention into the realm of politics (with the aim of prevailing)—with Habermas's elaboration of the *lifeworld*, which, in advanced capitalist nations, can function as a kind of sacred refuge from political-instrumental logics. The second dualism relates to the first: *unification*, a necessary operation and orientation within a hegemonic contest to find common ground and articulate a common sense, is juxtaposed with the tendency toward *marginal differentiation*—i.e., emphasis on distinguishing particulars, which Habermas (among others, e.g., Riesman, Inglehart, Bourdieu) argues becomes more prevalent as the middle class expands in post-scarcity societies. Following this is *instrumental / expressive*, a dualism often discussed by social movement scholars.[28] The term *expressive* misses something important, however, insofar as it can imply *self*-expression and individualistic motivation. Seeing this motivation as profoundly group-oriented, I prefer the next dualism, *what the group accomplishes / life of the group*. Moving

---

28   For example: Francesca Polletta and James M. Jasper, "Collective Identity and Social Movements," *Annual Review of Sociology* 27 (2001): 283–305.

down, I situate so-called *prefigurative politics* on the right side of
the dualisms, to suggest that the concept is highly related to the
dualism halves above it—*lifeworld, marginal differentiation, expressive* motivations, and the *life of the group*—and is ambivalent
or even hostile towards the opposite halves. This dualism corresponds with the next one down: Max Weber's juxtaposition of an
ethic of responsibility versus *an ethic of ultimate ends* (which I will
discuss in the following chapter); *strategic politics* stems from the
former, and *prefigurative politics* from the latter.[29] The final dualism, *politics / values*, names the two overarching realms and thus
contains the two distinct levels of analysis that I argue are indispensable in apprehending collective political action; this dualism
roughly encapsulates all of the above dualisms.

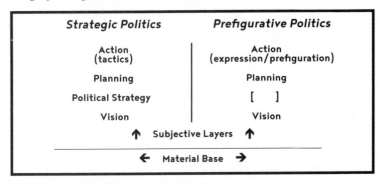

Figure 2: subjective layers of action

Figure 2 depicts subjective layers that precede collective action, under two models, as ideal types: *strategic politics* and *prefigurative politics*. Both models of political subjectivity are constructed upon, and shaped by the details of, a material base. The
strategic politics model then starts with a *vision* of the world that
the collective actor desires; the ultimate goals it hopes to attain.
On top of this ground is the layer of *political strategy*, where the

29   Max Weber, "Politics as Vocation," in *From Max Weber: Essays in Sociology*, ed. H. H. Gerth and C. Wright Mills (New York: Oxford University Press, 1946), 120.

actor assesses what parts of its vision might be achievable when—
and how. This is where the actor assesses the terrain in which it
must operate: its opponents, allies, potential allies, targets, resources, constraints, opportunities, etc. Informed by this layer, the
actor engages in *planning* for its actions. Its *actions* (the top layer)
then can be seen as *tactics* designed to move forward an underlying political strategy, which is designed to move the actor closer
to realizing its vision (or to achieve measurable pieces thereof).[30]
The *prefigurative politics* model likewise starts with the layer of
vision (also atop a material base), but it skips over—and glosses
over—the layer of *political strategy*. Instead it plans actions to directly manifest the essence of its vision. As such, its *actions* are not
tactics—insofar as tactics are steps to move forward a strategy—
but are rather direct *expressions* or *prefigurations* of the actor's
vision. *Means* and *ends* are one and the same in this model.

In Figure 2, the two models can easily be confused, at first
glance. On the one hand, the *strategic politics* model incorporates
prefigurative elements into its design; its tactics also reference
and "prefigure" the actor's vision, as part of a strategic communication operation aimed at mobilization. But these operations are
subordinate to political considerations. The famous lunch counter
sit-ins in the US South during the civil rights movement provide
an excellent example of this kind of prefiguration of the actor's vision for the world—as a key communications component within a
larger political strategy. On the other hand, the prefigurative politics model often uses buzzwords like "strategy" and "organizing"
without ever defining them; misappropriating a political vocabulary, while mistakenly assuming that any plan of action automatically implies the existence of a strategy. In this case, the implicit
"strategy" was to inspire more and more people to spontaneously
join the prefigurative action, led by the hope that the revolution

---

30   In real life *strategic politics* is not as monolithic as an ideal type might
     suggest. Among those who embrace strategic politics, there remain
     abundant disagreements on what counts as strategic (or unstrategic).
     Moreover, strategic and tactical disagreements often also correspond to
     divergences between different groups' interests and goals.

would come and the system would eventually collapse, by way of spontaneous mass defection.[31] As more and more people occupied more places, the Occupy movement would keep expanding. Such notions amounted to little more than wishful thinking.

That *prefigurative elements* can (and often should) be included within a *strategic politics model* is an important point. With Occupy, my aim is not to dismiss the value of the movement's prefigurative elements, such as the "people's kitchen," the free library, "mic checks," and so on. Indeed, I found many of these elements both inspiring and practically useful; I took part in them and I celebrate them. My argument is against a theory of change that is made up of *only* these elements, without attention to whether they fit into a larger political strategy. I am neither against manifesting our visions and values in our internal organizing processes, nor against staging actions that put these visions and values on public display; my critique, rather, is of the notion that such practices can somehow substitute for strategic engagement at the level of political power. Insofar as prefigurative elements *supplement* a strategic politics, I am all for it; however, in its contemporary usage, I interpret the phrase "prefigurative politics" as a claim to *replace* strategic politics, as defined here, altogether. I will return shortly to the question of whether such an interpretation is warranted or fair.

Thus, both sides of the dualisms shown in Figure 1 can be contained as balanced complements within the *strategic politics* ideal type shown in Figure 2, but the same is not true of the *prefigurative politics* ideal type. The former *qua ideal type* has to achieve an optimal balance between *instrumentality* and *expressiveness*—when manifested as a working *model*, it *strives* for this balance—while the latter ideal type does not have to even recognize the legitimacy of the need for such balance. Following

---

31   Richard J. F. Day sees such defection unfolding over a longer period of
      time; a process that he sympathetically describes as "the exodus from
      the neoliberal order." Richard Day, *Gramsci Is Dead: Anarchist Cur-
      rents in the Newest Social Movements* (Ann Arbor, MI: Pluto Press,
      2005), 215.

the logic of the dimension of *values expression* in which it has emerged, *prefigurative politics* is equipped to only see the dimension of politics negatively; the *whole dimension* is labeled and shrunk down to a single negative point of reference within a particularly narrated values dimension (i.e., the *lifeworld*). From the vantage point of this sacred lifeworld, anything that is associated with power, authority, or politics proper, is considered to be a part of or imitative of a monolithic system, and must be opposed on principle.

It should be clear by now that I am not convinced by the prevailing narrative about Occupy Wall Street having "no leaders" and amounting to a new kind of "prefigurative politics." I am not only arguing that such an approach is politically unviable; I am suggesting that it never happened, except as mythology and public performance. It is clearly *part* of the story, but it could not have existed without the existence of a more politically instrumental tendency. What I have been building up to is a conceptual structure in which to properly situate "prefigurative politics." I situate "prefigurative politics" squarely within the *life of the group*, and I contrast it with the *strategic politics* that groups engage in to achieve ends beyond their own existence. I do not accept prefigurative politics' account of itself. In many instances, I do not even accept that it is politics *at all*.

If prefigurative politics has its basis in attempts to construct a particular *lifeworld*—i.e., in expressing values and affirming the *life of the group*—and it eschews engagement and contestation in the larger common realm of power and politics, then we might ultimately view it as a project of *private* liberation. A private endeavor need not view itself as such in order for it to be functionally so; if the benefits of its efforts are limited to its own participants, it is functionally private. It should be clear enough by now that the point here is not to diminish the value or meaningfulness of these internal benefits to group participants, but to advocate for balancing this with a broader political orientation. All of this points to the need—perhaps greater than ever before in history—to intentionally ground our projects of liberation in concrete political goals and accompanying political strategies. We have to acknowledge and be strategic about "what's in it for us," in terms of our sense of identity, community, and wholeness (i.e., the life of the group). We have to navigate and find a balance between the *expressive* and the *instrumental* aspects of collective action; between within-group *bonding* and beyond-group *bridging*;[32] between the *life of the group* and *what the group accomplishes* aside from its own existence. Because, frankly, we (i.e., many social movement participants in advanced capitalist nations) have material circumstances and a predominant disposition that incline us towards self-involvement to the point of insularity.

Another question presents itself concerning material circumstances and dispositions: If, as I have argued here, the *prefigurative politics* model is partly the product of a *disposition* that is itself produced by *material conditions*, we might then wonder whether both model and disposition will grow stronger or weaker in response to changes in material conditions that are well underway. Now that the welfare state is being actively challenged and eroded, and the middle class can no longer take its status and material comforts for granted, will we see a decline in prevalence of the characterological disposition and corresponding tendencies in contemporary social movements discussed above? Because these tendencies were so visible and pronounced in Occupy, maybe even to an unprecedented extent, it would be easy to assume that this disposition is presently more widespread than ever before. There is, however, a perhaps more optimistic alternative hypothesis: that (1) this disposition has already peaked in the United States—perhaps several years ago—and is currently in decline; that (2) the popular framing of "We are the 99%!"—as well as many of Occupy's savvy "backstage" features—could itself be submitted as evidence that the disposition toward marginal differentiation is shifting to a disposition toward claiming and contesting the popular; but (3) Occupy came onto the scene at the tail end of a 40-year devastating decline and fragmentation of the US left (partially attributable to this disposition!); and (4) the strategically inclined young leaders who came out of the

---

32   Putnam, *Bowling Alone*.

woodwork during Occupy's inauguration found very few resources in terms of mentorship, apprenticeship, development, and support; and (5) finding a seriously gutted left infrastructure, they had to flail about as political orphans, make a lot of otherwise avoidable clumsy mistakes, and ultimately lose the reins of a potentially powerful vehicle.

If the alternative explanation is true—if the disposition has already peaked—that could mean a greater influx of strategically oriented young leaders come the next round. Demographic research of the movement provides evidence that Occupy's participants came disproportionately from the middle class, but that their economic existence and prospects were growing increasingly precarious.[33] It is my experience that alongside the loud and visible *prefigurative politics* of Occupy Wall Street, there was also a strong *strategic politics* practiced by many core participants; indeed, that such participants constituted a major tendency within OWS; a tendency that often prevailed, and when it did not, it was not for lack of trying.

Origins and proponents

How can the reader be sure that the author is not arguing against a caricature of prefigurative politics? Have I set up a straw man? Surely not everyone who uses the phrase "prefigurative politics" is unconcerned with political strategy in the ways I have elaborated in this chapter. Indeed, the ambiguity of the term makes it difficult to argue a clear case against it. To construct a counter-argument, I have had to first make clear my own theoretical interpretation of the phrase "prefigurative politics"—to construct an *ideal type* of the concept. Have I been fair in doing so?

---

33 Ruth Milkman, Stephanie Luce, and Penny Lewis, *Changing the Subject: A Bottom-up Account of Occupy Wall Street in New York City* (New York: The Murphy Institute; The City University of New York, 2013); Hector Cordero-Guzman, "Main Stream Support for a Mainstream Movement," *Unpublished draft*, October 19, 2011, https://occupywallst.org/media/pdf/OWS-profile1-10-18-11-sent-v2-HRCG.pdf.

First, a brief word must be said about *ideal types*. What is the difference between a *straw man* and an *ideal type*? Part of the idea of an ideal type is that it rarely, if ever, actually exists in pure form in the real world, yet constructing ideal types can be useful for apprehending the essence of a concept or thing. That may sound a lot like a straw man. The difference—and this is no small detail—is that a person who is setting up a straw man does not usually admit that they are doing so, i.e., that they are intentionally oversimplifying complex phenomenon for the sake of strengthening their argument or position. In constructing ideal types and posing dualisms, the point here is not to box the world into inflexible dichotomies, but, rather, to clarify thinking about different kinds of logics and motivations that are often difficult to understand without such thought exercises—precisely because the concepts do, indeed, get so thoroughly mixed up with each other in the messy details of the real world.

However, the fact that I have constructed an ideal type and stuck the label "prefigurative politics" on it does not answer the question of whether my construction and the label really belong together. There is no way around the ambiguity of the phrase "prefigurative politics" and the fact that, as its usage has increased—and as it has become a buzzword within some contemporary social movements—the people who have come to use or identify with it now often intend divergent meanings. Is it accurate or useful, then, to interpret the phrase "prefigurative politics" as I have: as a claim to *replace* strategic politics altogether? I have debated this question for some time, in my own head and with comrades. Essentially, my choice was between interpreting "prefigurative politics" as either (1) an assertion by its proponents that political contestation is unnecessary or obsolete, or (2) allowing a more ambiguous interpretation that could basically mean "values expression," "foreshadowing" the world that we want, changing internal group norms in socially positive ways, or any combination of the above. I chose the first interpretation. However, I am in favor of engaging with all of the *elements* of the second, more open, interpretation. One important reason that I ultimately went with the first, more limiting interpretation in constructing an ideal type of prefigurative politics is because this is the essence of what I have encountered the most, in practice, by people who use the phrase most emphatically—who explicitly espouse "prefigurative politics" as such. Not everyone, to be sure, and that is why I remain ambivalent about this choice. However, my choice is not based only on what I view to be the predominant usage of the phrase. The two words, put together, can themselves suggest such an interpretation: the "politics" part of the term infers an *alternative* or *replacement* for regular politics, i.e., for logics of power and contestation generally. Such an assertion is corroborated by another aforementioned phrase that was frequently heard—intended positively—at Occupy: *post-political*. If some advocates of prefigurative politics conceptualize it in a less totalizing way than I have presented it here, then my critique may not apply to their conceptions. Fine. Yet, this is not my own novel interpretation of the phrase; I am hardly going out on a limb. Among prefigurative politics' most vocal and theoretically developed contemporary proponents, Manuel Castells, Richard J. F. Day, and David Graeber seem to concur with my claim that it aims to *replace*—in Day's words, to "render redundant"—*strategic* politics, especially if the latter is defined in terms of *hegemonic contestation*.[34] These theorists might even agree with me on the essentials of the term's definition; where we would disagree is on the question of whether such a concept could ever enable a movement to ascend any higher than a low plateau.

Before concluding this chapter, I want to point readers to the remarkable scholarship of Wini Breines and her excellent book *Community and Organization in the New Left, 1962-1968.* Breines's work on the subject of prefigurative politics—and how it emerged and played out in the New Left—is unparalleled; a treasure trove for readers who are interested in the subject of prefigurative politics (including those who would like to further evaluate my interpretations of the concept). While I am indebted to Breines for her impressive scholarship, she is in no way responsible for where I go with her ideas. Breines is very sympathetic

---

34   Day, *Gramsci Is Dead*, 18.

towards the New Left's experiments with participatory democracy, as well as its wariness towards hierarchy and bureaucracy. Her book illuminates the prefigurative politics of groups like
SNCC and SDS, partly by elucidating the self-understood rationales of its advocates. Most movement participants wanted the
best of both worlds, Breines argues. They sought to model greater equality and participation in their organizational forms and
practices, and, at the same time, they wanted their groups to be
politically effective. These two desires were not seen as mutually
exclusive, for the most part—at least not initially.

My discussion of prefigurative politics in this chapter, then,
may come off as less generous than hers. This may, however, be
due to the different eras and purposes for which she and I write,
more than any irreconcilable differences in our analyses. Breines was writing largely to provide a fuller picture than the one
painted by left critics who were harshly dismissive of the New
Left's prefigurative experiments. The critics—among whom we
find many active movement participants and leaders—often saw
the New Left's experiments as self-expressive to the point of being self-indulgent and narcissistic. Breines does not disagree entirely with these assessments—indeed, she thoroughly explores
them and acknowledges the elements of truth they hold—but she
balances these critiques by also drawing attention to the positive values of democracy, participation, social equality, and,
perhaps most importantly, *community*, that movement participants were passionately pursuing. My own emphasis on the drive
for community—and invoking Riesman's *morale of the group*
and Habermas's *lifeworld*—mirrors much of Breines's analysis.
Moreover, my elaboration of the ideal types of *strategic politics*
and *prefigurative politics* is based on her original juxtaposition
of these very terms.

The backdrop for my writing and purposes, however, is a
dominant narrative about the recent wave of global uprisings that
takes for granted their purported leaderlessness and prefigurative politics. The culture in the academy has changed considerably since the publication of Breines's book as well. Where many
established academics in the 1960s and 1970s may have failed

to recognize the merits of the New Left's prefigurative politics on its own terms—through its own subjective standpoint—today many scholars are *too deferential* to contemporary movements' own self-presentations. Movements always have a propagandistic face—or at least they *had better* if they hope to mobilize people—so it is just silly for scholars or strategists to take movements' self-presentations at face value. The tendency to do so is likely related to a contemporary approach to studying social movements that, somewhere along the way, started to feel like a trip to the zoo: the focus became more on movements' unique and eccentric features than their *indication* of broader social, economic, and political crises or their potential for catalyzing large-scale change.

This shift in backdrop becomes clearest in Breines's concluding remarks, when she humbly suggests that her "attempt to reconstruct sympathetically the prefigurative and utopian features of the New Left may be faulted in various ways, but *not for being fashionable*."[35] Today a sympathetic, even deferential, view of the "prefigurative and utopian features" that manifested in the recent global wave of uprisings can be faulted *precisely* for being *fashionable*. Fashion has flipped, as fashion is sometimes known to do. Indeed, the exercise of leadership and the widespread usage of classic political organizing methods, tools, and infrastructure in today's movements are what has been consistently downplayed, denied, and cropped out of the picture. Thus, my purpose, like Breines's, is to tell an under-told story—it's just that the part that is under-told has flipped.[36]

---

35 Breines, *Community and Organization in the New Left*, 151. My emphasis.

36 To be clear, Breines does a thorough job of telling *both* "stories." She provides a rich presentation of both tendencies—strategic politics and prefigurative politics.

ASPIRING HEGEMONIC

*Having already explored the radical left's tendency toward
self-righteous insularity and impotence, I now make the moral
and strategic case for political power. And embracing the need
to build collective power is only a humble start. If we are to bring
about the world that we imagine, we have to learn to wield power
as well. Our task is not to critique hegemony impotently from the
sidelines. Our task is to become hegemonic.*

"The genius or demon of politics lives in inner tension
with the god of love..."

–Max Weber[1]

"Power properly understood is nothing but the ability
to achieve purpose. It is the strength required to bring
about social, political and economic change... And one
of the great problems of history is that the concepts of
love and power have usually been contrasted as opposites–polar opposites–so that love is identified with a
resignation of power, and power with a denial of love...
Now, we've got to get this thing right. What is needed
is a realization that power without love is reckless and
abusive, and love without power is sentimental and

---

1   Weber, "Politics as Vocation," 126.

anemic… It is precisely this collision of immoral power with powerless morality which constitutes the major
crisis of our times."

–*Martin Luther King Jr.*[2]

Resigned sideline critique

For Martin Luther King Jr. "the major crisis of our times" is that
"the concepts of love and power" have been framed as opposites
in the public imagination. Accompanying this false dichotomy
we can see a very real social bifurcation in the realm of politics:
in their vocations and avocations, those who are driven by the
ideals of love and compassion and those who are driven by, in
Max Weber's words, "power for power's sake" have self-segre-
gated; the latter operate at the center of the realm of politics,
the former on the sidelines.[3] They have constructed separate do-
mains, each with its own logic that is incompatible with the other's; almost untranslatable, separated by a great chasm. They
have specialized, and their respective specialties hold vastly
unequal shares of influence on the direction of society. A consequence of this bifurcation is that those who strive for *power
for its own sake* tend to get what they strive for: power.[4] And
what about those who self-select to devote themselves to higher
ideals? They get to surround themselves with others who share
their ideals. They get to express their ideals together, perhaps
punctuated with creative collective rituals, but without much
realistic hope—perhaps not even the intention—of ever arming
their ideals with power.

One category gets to play the field, while the other gets to
critique the game from the sidelines. Not a winning scenario

---

2   Martin Luther King, Jr., "Where Do We Go From Here?" *Annual Re-
     port Delivered at the 11th Convention of the Southern Christian Leader-
     ship Conference* (Atlanta, GA, 1967).

3   Weber, "Politics as Vocation," 78.

4   As a category of self-selectors; obviously to varying degrees amongst
     themselves, and not in every individual case.

for Team Change. This is of course an over-simplification. *Power-seekers* and *idealists* presented as such are what Weber would call *ideal types*: categories whose essential features are emphasized or exaggerated in order to be recognized as such. In the real world, many shades exist between these two poles. A central argument of this book is that we need more of those shades between; specifically, we need more people who are driven by love and social justice to *refuse to cede power to the powerful*. We need more "idealists" to step up to study and navigate the terrain of power and politics. Of course, political terrain is messy and can be morally perilous. But is that a legitimate excuse for allowing the power-hungry to have all the power, uncontested, while we content ourselves with a righteous but resigned sideline critique?

Consider an example that epitomizes resigned sideline critique: the bumper sticker slogan "I'M ALREADY AGAINST THE *NEXT* WAR." On my daily commute home, I pass a parked truck displaying this bumper sticker—and I cringe. This sad message proudly proclaims resignation to a future in which there are inevitably more wars, while the individual dissenter can celebrate their moral commitment to stand among the righteous few protesting tomorrow's wars as fervently and impotently as they protest today's. This message epitomizes the problem of settling for—even celebrating—a resigned self-expressive dissent. Such sideline critique can take many forms. Even militant action in the streets has the potential to become little more than an edgy expression of the participants' identity as dissenters, rather than a meaningful political intervention.

If *critiquing* power is the forte of the modern American left, *contesting* power—let alone *exercising* it—surely is not. One can develop a robust political critique without bothering with questions of power and strategy, but not a robust political operation. We will never attract large numbers of people to join us in our collective efforts—not for more than a hot second—if we fail to rigorously and practically engage such questions. Our historic task, if we are serious, has to extend well beyond sideline critique. We have to arm our critiques with power.

Reasons for ambivalence

There are many reasons to be deeply ambivalent about power. A cursory glance at the past century alone should provoke in any sensitive person a serious wariness about power and the horrors of which it is capable; including tragic examples of once-well-intentioned revolutionary leaders becoming tyrants amidst the messy process of struggling for and executing political power. Surely the dismal historical backdrop of the 20th century (and early 21st century) has spurred the development of a robust critique of power within the left. A comprehensive examination of these critiques is well beyond the purpose of this book, but the basics are fairly straightforward. Power corrupts. History's worst horrors have been ordered by very powerful people—people who spouted both right- and left-wing ideologies. For good reason, this predisposes social justice advocates to be generally wary of power and authority. In the words of Kenneth Keniston, "Fear of the abuse of power, of irrational authority, and of dominating leadership is in many respects a legitimate reaction to a world in which power, authority, and leadership are used cruelly rather than benignly."[5]

We are also ambivalent about power because of our aspirational vision for humanity. What is it that we ultimately want to see in the world? Social justice. Economic equality. Ecological sanity. Social organization based on compassion, solidarity, and mutual aid. A world free from oppression, where systems of racism, patriarchy, bigotry, militarism, and economic exploitation can only be found in history books. Even a world free from *coercion*, where people are truly free to make their own choices. Our ambivalence about power thus stems from the fact that we ultimately want to equalize power and strip it of its coercive capacity. It is little wonder then that *coercive means* for such righteous ultimate ends would intuitively seem self-contradictory and even hypocritical.

---

5   Kenneth Keniston, "Young Radicals and the Fear of Power," in *The Politics and Anti-Politics of the Young*, ed. Michael Brown (Beverly Hills, CA: Glencoe Press, 1969), 56.

But can we eliminate coercion altogether? Even if we were to believe this to be possible in the (very) long-term, does that mean that the best way to do so is to refrain from engaging in any kind of coercion starting right now? Is it really on us to "unilaterally disarm" in the realm of politics? If so, what is our *theory of change*? Do we believe that people will be inspired by our brave acts of eschewing power; that more and more people will join us until "the system" eventually collapses because no one believes in it anymore? When in the history of the world has any such thing ever occurred? And what happens in the meantime when a family is struggling to survive on poverty wages? Or when our government attempts to start another war of aggression? Are our moral appeals our only leverage to intervene in such matters? Does anyone really believe that moral appeals, unaccompanied by a political force, will convince anyone in power to act against their own narrow interests?

Very few people would admit to such naïveté. Most of us know full well that "power concedes nothing without a demand."[6] Yet social movements do sometimes get confused—or are in denial—about the fact that raising such a demand effectively amounts to an act of *coercion*. We aim to coerce someone to do something that they do not want to do—or to *not* do something they are intent on doing—and occasionally we succeed. We may fancy that we are not coercive, because in our acts of protest or obstruction we are trying to *stop coercion*. We are attempting to stop elites from exploiting workers or waging wars or destroying habitats or foreclosing on homes. We are pushing back. They are the aggressors and we are righteously raising our voices or standing in the way to stop them. Indeed, the more powerful our opponents are and the more lopsided the conflict, the more righteous our own opposition to power seems. Consider a scenario, though, in which our opponents have a little less power and we have a little more. What if we had enough power to not just be protesting reality, but also shaping it? And what if, in such a scenario, we had yet to convert—through moral suasion—every last racist, misogynist, warmonger, and capitalist? Would we then just live and let live?

---

6   Douglass, *Frederick Douglass on Slavery*, 42.

Or would we restrain destructive people in order to prevent them from doing destructive things?

Most of us accept that some level of coercion is necessary in the realm of collective action and politics, and we also make distinctions between levels and kinds of coercion. Maybe we are even able, in James Forman's words, to "distinguish between a revolutionary organization seeking power, and power as it had been corruptly wielded by the managers of capitalist America."[7] Yet lack of clarity and nuance on such questions often results in an ambiguous kind of gravitational force that pulls our energy and emphasis towards certain forms of collective action, and away from others. This "gravity" operates in the service of a moralizing narrative. It might help to explain why, for example, so many young radicals in the United States love to talk about the Zapatistas in Mexico or the horizontally organized recuperated factory movement in Argentina, but are silent about the Chavistas in Venezuela.[8] Is it not because the latter have succeeded in winning some level—however limited a degree—of state power, while the former have appeared to stay neatly outside of "the corrupt system"?[9] As I discussed in *the story of the righteous few*, we can grow so accustomed to estrangement from power that our political marginalization becomes a central feature of our identity. We are only comfortable with getting near power in dramatized opposition to it—on our side of a clearly marked line of scrimmage. In the process, we doom ourselves and our political imagination to eternal outsiderness.

7   James Forman, *The Making of Black Revolutionaries* (New York: Macmillan, 1972), 425.

8   Some are even infatuated by the dramatic protests against the Venezuela government, with zero attention to the political interests and ideology of the opposition.

9   On the other hand, the recent rise of Podemos in Spain and of Syriza in Greece—and the interest of many young leftists in the United States in these vehicles, let alone the Bernie Sanders 2016 campaign—may be a good indicator that this "force of gravity" is flipping; that a new political "zeitgeist" may be at hand.

For reasons that should be clear by now, being eternal outsiders might not bother us in the least. If constructing a cohesive *lifeworld* becomes the central preoccupation of an ostensibly political group, then its outsiderness—even its *fringeness* or *marginality*—can further emphasize its distinctiveness and cohesion. Here strategic political logics may fall on deaf ears; upon ears that have heard enough of such logics. To extend Habermas's argument outlined in the previous chapter, we are barraged daily with endless manifestations of manipulative logics whose central goals are private profit and coercive control, and we are repulsed by these logics that penetrate and colonize most everything they touch, leaving injustice and alienation everywhere in their wake. Against these oppressive logics we attempt to scrape together beauty, art, and poetry—and, most fundamentally, community. We build a scrappy little alternative clubhouse near the perimeter of the ever-advancing logics of capitalism and bureaucracy. Our little clubhouse sometimes serves as a makeshift base of operations for scrimmages with the authorities. Occasionally when these scrimmages heat up, the authorities will raid or burn down our meager fortifications. But we always rebuild. For the most part we are permitted to keep our little clubhouse. Defending it—its culture and meanings and rhetoric and symbols—becomes our prize.

And somewhere along the way we seem to have lost faith in the possibility of really winning against these logics and systems in the world beyond our little clubhouse; the possibility of gaining ground again in the terrain of society. The clubhouse becomes our starting place—the source of all of our reference points—and society is written off as a lost cause. And the logic of political strategy? We don't want to hear the logic of political strategy in our clubhouse. This is a liberated, "prefigurative" and "post-political" space. We don't need strategy or organization or leadership or money in our clubhouse. All those things remind us of the insidious logics against which we define ourselves and our projects. Such a disposition was strong, if not predominant, amongst core participants of Occupy Wall Street. And it is my view that this paralyzing allergic reaction to power was as responsible for stunting the movement's growth as any external repression that we faced.

A caveat must be added concerning the relationship between guarding the *lifeworld* and negative attitudes about power: We have to be careful about conflating tendencies towards self-involvement, insularity, and purism, on the one hand, with valid and important progressive critiques of power, on the other hand. These are obviously different concepts. Yet it can be difficult to neatly separate them in practice, because the former concept often dresses itself up in the rhetoric of the latter. In other words the drive to guard the *lifeworld* can lead to a kind of purist negative reaction to power of all kinds, but this purism is narrated in the language of a legitimate critique of power. In so doing, complex and nuanced critiques morph into simplistic, self-righteous axioms that effectively add up to a politically paralyzing allergic reaction to whatever is labeled "power." We might, for instance, invoke the "iron law of oligarchy" as a catchphrase that excuses us from having to take responsibility for the task of building political organization.[10]

Let us not, however, develop an allergic reaction to the allergic reaction; it remains important to critique power and to keep vigilant about its dangers. Let's just not do it from the sidelines! Instead, we have to engage an advanced progressive critique of power, even as we lean into the hard work of building and wielding it together.

Ethic of responsibility

We all make everyday compromises in our values in order to navigate the real world as it is. For example, I may believe that humanity is ultimately capable of achieving the ideals of full communism, but right now—seeing as how capitalism is "the only game in town"—I work for a paycheck because I need to eat and pay rent. Most of us accept that we have to make such compromises in the full expression of our ideals—in an everyday kind

---

10   Robert Michels, *Political Parties: A Sociological Study of the Oligarchical Tendencies of Modern Democracy*, trans. Eden and Cedar Paul (New York: The Free Press, 1962), 342.

of way—for our own economic survival "in the meantime." Yet sometimes radicals are unwilling to extend such practicality to the realm of politics for the greater collective good. Instead, they approach political action as a space for the full, uncompromised expression of their political ideals and vision. Conceptualized as such, collective action becomes our sacred space. This is important: *the terrain of politics is not that space.* It's about doing what we can to improve real people's lives—to mitigate real suffering and oppression—in the here and now. We work hard and come away with clearly limited gains. We don't "settle" for these, but, rather, we accept them *for now*—maybe we even *celebrate* limited and compromised victories, because they are consequential and they are signs of our momentum—as we plan for how we will win bigger gains tomorrow. The tactics and strategies we use are about getting the job done, not about perfectly reflecting a utopian vision.

Does this mean that our engagement in this terrain should not be informed or constrained in any way by our values? Of course not. In fact, I'm arguing that we should intervene in politics by actually *taking responsibility* for constructing the world that we want to see: a world where there is more compassion and social justice. In our public demands, we may rightly—and also strategically—place responsibility for problems and crises squarely on those who currently hold the most political power in society. However, we also know full well that to have a *demand that actually demands* something from the powerful—i.e., that makes them *do something*—requires a political force behind it. We have to take responsibility to construct such a force. Otherwise we are just shouting at the wind. We have to take direct aim at the problem of political will; at our current lack of capacity to take sufficiently powerful collective remedial action to confront the social, economic, political, and ecological crises before us. We have to ground our efforts upon the assumption that truth is not its own arbiter; that right does not equal might; that even the most refined analysis is all for naught if we are unable to comprehend that our constraints are primarily *political*; that our problem is one of power, leverage, and will.

This leads us directly to the aforementioned ethical questions about political power itself. In examining questions of ethics in politics, Max Weber provides an important distinction between "two fundamentally differing and irreconcilably opposed maxims: conduct can be oriented to an 'ethic of ultimate ends' or to an 'ethic of responsibility.'"[11] The adherent to an *ethic of ultimate ends* strives to "do the right thing," no matter how it all turns out—even if a righteous stand seems destined to fail. (This ethic shares much in common with the *story of the righteous few* discussed in chapter three.) The adherent to the *ethic of responsibility*, on the other hand, thinks about the likely reactions to her action, and adds these likelihoods into her strategic calculus. Neither person has a crystal ball through which they can see the future, but the latter person takes responsibility for making her best educated guess about how her actions are likely to interact with a complex unfolding reality. The former person, on the other hand, embraces stand-alone righteous action for its own sake—let the chips fall where they may. "This is not to say that an ethic of ultimate ends is identical with irresponsibility, or that an ethic of responsibility is identical with unprincipled opportunism. Naturally nobody says that. However, there is an abysmal contrast between conduct that follows the maxim of an ethic of ultimate ends—that is, in religious terms, 'The Christian does rightly and leaves the results with the Lord'—and conduct that follows the maxim of an ethic of responsibility, in which case one has to give an account of the foreseeable results of one's action."[12]

Consider the question of whether the United States government should listen to me when I make a moral argument about why not to invade Iraq. Of course I think that it *should* listen to me! But *will* it? Clearly we know that the answer is *no*. Not unless I am speaking from a base of political power that has the capacity to meaningfully interfere with other things that matter to the government (or to specific agencies or individuals therein). Here, then, with an ethic of responsibility, I account for the fact

---

11   Weber, "Politics as Vocation," 120.

12   Ibid.

that governments will probably not do "the right thing" unless they have sufficient incentive. I therefore set out to help build and wield a sufficiently powerful political force to create the needed incentive (i.e., coercion). Taking another step forward with an ethic of responsibility, I have to account for the fact that most of my fellow Americans will not necessarily be eager to drop other commitments in their lives in order to help assemble such a political force—even those who agree with me on the issue. With an *ethic of ultimate ends*, I might dismiss such people as brainwashed apathetic "sheeple." But instead—with an *ethic of responsibility*—I look to *incentivize* their participation in a popular antiwar effort. I study the roadblocks to participation, and I attempt to make it easier for people to get involved.

Such an ethic of responsibility is fundamental to political organizing.[13] Organizing involves incentivizing, facilitating, and structuring the participation of many people—forming many fragments into a coherent political force that is powerful enough to then incentivize certain actions by the state and other powerful actors. An ethic of responsibility attempts to understand people as they really are, and to engage them in a way that adjusts for the ways they are constrained, their limitations, and their idiosyncrasies. An *ethic of ultimate ends*, on the other hand, requires no organizing of the social sphere whatsoever—it only requires righteous stands, by whoever steps forward to take them.

In what contexts, then, does an *ethic of ultimate ends* seem compelling, even within a realm that is ostensibly explicitly about *political* engagement? Such an ethic might seem especially compelling in a context in which people have no direct experience of real political agency—i.e., no experience of engaging in collective action that has made a clear and measurable difference. If a person has no taste of what it is to affect political outcomes or to alter the terrain—e.g., if they have never won a campaign—then they might well cede the terrain itself and assume the most righteous location there within, which

---

13   The same is not necessarily true for "activism"—for reasons that have already been elucidated in chapter one.

may be Golgotha.[14] Along these lines, if a political goal is too big to believably accomplish anytime soon—e.g., ending capitalism—then winnable interim victories have to be articulated, if we don't want our core dedicated folks to gravitate toward the self-righteous over the political. Long-time grassroots organizer Bob Wing once put it this way to me: "If winning feels impossible, then righteousness can seem like the next best thing." Righteous action at least keeps alive the idea of courageously standing up for justice in the face of overwhelming odds, and surely, there are times when such hopeless stands are the only option available to conscientious people. But let us not fetishize such moments of despair. Better options are nearly always available.

Aspiring hegemonic

It is with such an ethic of responsibility that political challengers must approach political—and I would say *hegemonic*—struggle. If we hope to find fissures and footholds within "the system"— and not just make a brave but doomed righteous stand against it—then we have to engage with the terrain of power and politics, not just wash our individual hands of the whole corrupt business.

Let us then examine more closely the concept of hegemony. Hegemony, as I use the term throughout this book, is *leadership or predominant influence exercised by one particular group within national, regional, or local political spheres.*[15]

Within social justice–oriented challenger movements, we can immediately imagine a protest to the title of this book: *Isn't hegemony precisely what we are fighting against?* Some on the left, especially within anarchist tendencies, have argued affirmatively that, yes, hegemony itself is something that the conscientious person should oppose. Many more, while not arguing this explicitly, have inferred an inherently negative meaning by only using the

---

14   Golgotha is the hill where Jesus Christ is said to have died on the cross, according to the Bible.

15   While the international sphere is extremely important, it is also beyond the scope of this book.

term to refer to oppressive systems and regimes of elites. I am well aware that the title of this book may be read by some of my comrades as a provocation, insofar as it suggests that hegemony is not in and of itself something to stand against, but rather something to *attain*. To be clear, it is *intended* as a provocation.

It is tempting to approach hegemony by starting with those examples of hegemonic orders that we find most abhorrent, and to then define the concept by its association with one-dimensional villains. This approach fails to provide much clarity about the concept of hegemony and how it operates. Let us instead approach hegemony by a less direct route, from another angle, through one of its essential components: the concept of *common sense*. What is common sense? Common sense is what everyone knows so intuitively that it does not even need to be spoken aloud. Common sense is as invisible as the air, as unnoticed as water is to a fish. However, common sense can never be *fully common*. It never attains a complete universality, wherein *everyone*—every particular that comprises the "universal"—agrees fully to the assertions of "common sense." Yet the idea of common sense—the literal interpretation of its two parts—infers this universality, or at least commonality to a given group of people. Furthermore, common sense exists not only as an idea, but also as a *form* that contains particular political *contents*. In other words, a particular notion could be the common sense, or an opposing notion could be the common sense—and which one has ended up as such is a contingent outcome. In the words of Chantal Mouffe: "Things could always be otherwise and every order is predicated on the exclusion of other possibilities. Any order is always the expression of a particular configuration of power relations. What is at a given moment accepted as the 'natural' order, jointly with the common sense that accompanies it, is the result of sedimented hegemonic practices."[16]

Whatever content ends up occupying the form of common sense will considerably appreciate in value by virtue of the normative power—the seeming "naturalness"—of common sense.

---

16 Chantal Mouffe, *Agonistics*, 2.

Thus, whomever has defined the *prevailing common sense* has equally defined the *hegemonic narrative*—i.e., has won a hegemonic contest over meanings in the culture.

We have to ask ourselves: are we, on principle, against our own achievement of such a feat? Before answering, let us consider the *contents*—i.e., the values and agendas—to which we are partial. Do we want the values of compassion, social justice, and equality to be universally embraced? Do we want tangible expressions of these values to be *popular*? Do we want trespasses against these values to be widely regarded as *deviance* from a *norm*? Or would we rather throw these *particular* values (e.g., compassion, social justice, and equality) into a sea of equally valid *particulars*—after all, who are we to judge particulars?—a sea that includes values of, say, bigotry and xenophobia? Are we indifferent to whether a prevailing value in society is "From each according to ability to each according to need" or whether it is "Greed is good!"? In other words, is there a contest between different values and interpretations of reality? If so, are we concerned about who or what wins that contest? That is, do we want the values that we regard as socially beneficial to an inclusively defined public to win out against the ones that we regard as exclusionary, destructive, and oppressive?

I hope the answer is an emphatic *"yes!"* Of course the interpretations of what counts as social justice and equality will be messy and contingent, depending on interests and situations, but if we can at least agree that we want a society based firmly on these values, then it follows that we are not inevitably or invariably against hegemony itself—at least on this level of meaning, culture, and common sense—but against *particular* hegemonies. Again, this is to define hegemony as more of a *form* than an inherent *content*. Something will be the prevailing common sense—the question is: "what?" The form could be filled with capitalist or socialist content, racist or antiracist, patriarchal or feminist, and so on.

This is not at all to suggest that the form itself will have no bearing on the content, including potentially corrosive effects. Indeed, an essential question with which a social justice left must wrestle is to what extent and with what consequences do hegemonic forms bleed into hegemonic contents. Mindful of the many pitfalls and dangers that engagement in such a contest entails, we must nonetheless engage it. We are not neutral about the issues or unconcerned about the outcomes. That is precisely why we have entered the realm of politics in the first place.

An important aspect of a hegemonic contest then is the *contest over the contents of common sense*. In such an elaboration of hegemony, common sense is itself one of the central underlying structures of hegemonic orders and hegemonic contests between political contenders. Common sense organizes the "ground" of popular meanings. A political order's ability to resonate with and shape popular meanings is the basis of its legitimacy. Thus, shifting the ground of common sense creates the potential to shift the structures and power relations of society—though not without a considerable level of accompanying organization (i.e., not without also winning an *institutional contest*). It is impossible for this ground of meaning to be politically neutral. Here we can think of common sense as part of the structure or *form* of hegemony itself, and we can think of particular prevailing ideas as the ideological *contents* that prop up a particular *hegemonic order*. Similarly, we can think of ideas that challenge status quo power relations as the ideological contents of a particular political challenger force (i.e., an *aspiring* or *insurgent hegemony*).[17] If, however, we see he-

---

17   I prefer these terms in place of *counter-hegemony*, a term that I think causes needless confusion. Specifically, *counter-hegemony* can imply either (1) an opposition to the idea of hegemony itself, i.e., to be against *all* manifestations of hegemony regardless of their contents, or (2) an opposition to a *particular* hegemonic order. When I do use the term *counter-hegemonic*, I mean the latter definition. In my view of political terrain, particular actors and alignments construct and maintain particular hegemonies. A hegemonic order's political challengers are not *counter-hegemonic*—insofar as the first definition would suggest (i.e., opposing hegemony itself)—but are themselves *aspiring hegemonies*. I usually use variations of this latter term—as well as the more plainspoken term *political challenger*—in place of *counter-hegemony*. These challengers want their ideas and agendas to prevail. My concern with

gemony as invariably bad—something to always *stand against*—but we are unclear about when we are referring to a particular *content* and when we are referring to a *form* (i.e., a socio-political pattern or structure, e.g., "common sense"), then we are here again dooming our social justice agenda to eternal impotency. We cede the terrain that we need to learn to navigate if we are to ever replace the content of elites with a content aimed at serving everyone. We cast ourselves as permanent armchair critic. And let us not deceive ourselves—something will always fill the space that we refer to as *common sense*. It abhors a vacuum. We engage in a hegemonic contest to fill the container of common sense with contents that are intended for the benefit of an expansive and inclusive public—even for the benefit of humanity in the broadest sense—instead of private profit and power.

One might argue that common sense is such a powerful and manipulative force that the only conscionable thing to do is to attempt to shatter common sense itself. Indeed, the attempt to do so (at least through textual critique) is arguably the central theme of the movement of postmodernism, which insists, in the words of David Harvey, that "we cannot aspire to any unified representation of the world."[18] Postmodernism "emphasizes the fragmentary, the ephemeral, and the chaotic ... While expressing a deep scepticism as to any particular prescriptions as to how the eternal and immutable should be conceived of, represented, or expressed."[19] Postmodernist thinkers astutely grasp how a universalizing meta-narrative—precisely the operation of "common

---

the confusing term *counter-hegemonic* is an extension of my concern about left ambivalence about power more generally. The *counter* part reinforces our eternal outsider status and casts doubt on whether we even want power. It is similar to how the term *counter-culture* suggests the creation of sideshow alternative subcultures, rather than contention on the main cultural stage, i.e., to claim and contest popular meanings, symbols, narratives, and institutions.

18   David Harvey, *The Condition of Postmodernity* (Cambridge, MA & Oxford UK: Blackwell, 1990), 52.

19   Ibid., 116.

sense"—is the power move *par excellence*. By deconstructing meta-narratives they attempt to dismantle "common sense" altogether. Let us briefly examine the impossibility and self-defeating nature of such an undertaking. My argument is that the existence (of the powerful operation) of common sense is inevitable—though always shifting and contestable—because "common sense" is *inextricable from human communication itself.* There is no clear line between *dominant* ideas and *common* understandings. Verbal and symbolic communication itself is a process of establishing and utilizing common words and symbols to reference commonly held meanings (for multiple social and material purposes).[20] As soon as two people encounter a four-legged creature that barks and wags its tail and they agree to call it a "dog," there exists a degree of common sense. However, human systems of *signs* and *signified* go well beyond a direct relationship between words and simple objects. We invent words for complex phenomena, for persons and reputations, for abstract ideas, and for succinctly referencing whole stories about origins, causes, blame, trajectories, power relations, and so on. We invent and reinvent language, but not from scratch; we are born into a world of pre-defined words and symbols that we regurgitate and whose meanings we have to learn. These common meanings structure the thoughts in our heads. Thus, the specifics of the references, inferences, and emotional associations conjured by a word or symbol are hugely consequential, including at the level of social and political power. The process of constructing *common understandings*, then, is inseparable from that of constructing *dominant ideas*. Many such ideas are benign or even commonly beneficial. But many are not. For good or for ill, though, we cannot wish the phenomena of common sense away. More precisely, we cannot dispose of the structure of common sense without giving up symbolic communication itself. Yet, this structure presents myriad problems of power; we know that the *contents* of common sense can never be neutral. Desires, wills, and power relationships are all organically

---

20   By *commonly*, I do not mean *universal*, but common to a *particular* social group.

woven into the fabric of common sense. Yet, this "weaving in" is a dynamic and contestable process—a terrain. Astute political actors engage this terrain strategically. The structure of common sense will not cease to operate by virtue of our abdication. "There will," in Chantal Mouffe's words, "always be a struggle between conflicting hegemonic projects aiming at presenting their views of the common good as the 'true' incarnation of the universal. No rational resolution of that conflict will ever be available."[21]

If progressive forces do not muster a challenge within this terrain, our opponents will be happy to win the contest by acclamation. Indeed, this is an important part of the story of the advance of neoliberalism over the past half century, and this is why David Harvey is so critical of postmodernism. Here it is worth quoting him at length:

> Postmodernism has us accepting the reifications and partitioning, actually celebrating the activity of masking and cover-up, all the fetishisms of locality, place, or social grouping, while denying that kind of meta-theory which can grasp the political—economic processes (money flows, international divisions of labour, financial markets, and the like) that are becoming ever more universalizing in their depth, intensity, reach and power over daily life.
>
> Worst of all, while it opens up a radical prospect by acknowledging the authenticity of other voices, postmodernist thinking immediately shuts off those other voices from access to more universal sources of power by ghettoizing them within an opaque otherness, the specificity of this or that language game. It thereby disempowers those voices (of women, ethnic and racial minorities, colonized peoples, the unemployed, youth, etc.) in a world of lop-sided power relations. The language game of a cabal of international bankers may be impenetrable to us, but that does not put it on par with the equally impenetrable language of inner-city blacks from the standpoint of power relations.

---

21   Mouffe, *Agonistics*, 79.

The rhetoric of postmodernism is dangerous for it avoids confronting the realities of political economy and the circumstances of global power.[22]

To be clear, even when we are oriented toward the task, it is typically quite difficult to successfully challenge prevailing common sense. To *truly challenge* the prevailing common sense is not merely to move from deconstructive critique to active dissent or defiance. Common sense tends to inoculate the broader populace against its dissenters. To actually challenge the prevailing common sense is to undermine its very premises in the popular vernacular, which requires an effective claiming and contestation of popular meanings, symbols, and narratives. In chapters seven and eight, I explore in greater depth key patterns within such contests of meaning, as well as conceptual tools for engaging these contests. For now, it is sufficient to acknowledge that underdogs do sometimes win such contests, even if rarely. And when an underdog wins, this only constitutes one level of the hegemonic struggle. If we, political challengers, win an uphill struggle over meanings and narratives—if our values gain cultural hegemony and become the prevailing common sense—we have to extend the hegemonic contest beyond symbols, narratives, and meanings, and to move into the terrain of institutions, policies, and consolidation; to give political "legs" to our moral and cultural victories, in order to change social relations and material conditions.

Now, let us make an important conceptual distinction between the idea of *contesting meanings* and the idea of *contesting state power*. A corresponding distinction, respectively, is between the level of *meanings and culture* and the level of *organizational and political capacity*. In a hegemonic contest, a political actor must favorably define the prevailing common sense—at least those parts of common sense that relate to the core components of the challenger's agenda. When a challenger movement succeeds in doing so, it may provoke a *crisis of legitimacy* for elites, whose hegemony had been, until then, maintained largely through a

---

22   Harvey, *The Condition of Postmodernity*, 116.

common sense that legitimated and obfuscated their privilege and power.[23] Such legitimacy is what makes it easier—and ultimately *possible*—to rule. When an underdog challenger wins such a contest over meanings, however, the challenged hegemon does not throw his arms up and walk away from the field, defeated. Of course not. He throws down. He musters whatever infrastructure he can to squash the threat to his power. If he is at the helm of state power, this infrastructure is substantial. Indeed, challengers would have no hope at all, except that, by winning a contest over common sense, they set the stage for fissures amongst elites and widespread defection within the infrastructure of the state, political society, and civil society. Depending on many contingencies, this defection could potentially reach a powerful crescendo, threatening a scenario wherein everything the hegemon does will backfire—a spiral that might just end in his tribunal.[24]

There are some in the social justice left who have no qualms about engaging in the one level of a hegemonic contest—the level of meanings, culture, and common sense—but who, on principle, oppose engagement in another level—the level of an institutional ground game whose victory is tied to its capacity to consolidate victories in the state, whether that be winning concessions or wresting the helm.[25] I call the former contest over popular mean-

---

23   We have to be careful about attributing causation here. Events like the stalling of the economy or failure in war can create conditions that set the stage for a political challenger to re-articulate the common sense, and while the challenger's intervention may be crucial in expanding a crisis of legitimacy for elites, in such a situation the crisis has probably already begun.

24   The image of overthrowing an individual hegemon is invoked here to paint a picture of the basic structure of a successful hegemonic challenge. Many successful challenges will culminate in less dramatic outcomes than revolutionary "overthrows" of regimes or individual power holders. They may, for example, win important concessions or policy changes without unseating anyone.

25   While some in the social justice left do *oppose* such engagement on principle (e.g., many anarchists), many more are at least *ambivalent*

ings the *symbolic contest*, and the latter contest over institutional power—which includes but also extends beyond state power—the *institutional contest*. While it can be conceptually useful to distinguish between the two (e.g., in order to develop appropriate strategies and tactics), in messy reality the two contests are inextricable—mixing together to constitute the *hegemonic contest*—and any kind of *moral* distinction between them is illusory. If it is morally acceptable to contest cultural meanings, then this acceptability should extend to contesting policy outcomes and state power. Both levels are interventions into the ground upon which all social interactions operate. To reshape this ground is to re-pattern everything that happens upon it. Both levels, to be clear, are profoundly manipulative, insofar as they are re-sculpting social terrain itself. I will return shortly to this idea of manipulation, and what we are to do with it.

Again, we can conceptualize the *symbolic contest* as the layer of a hegemonic contest that is concerned with culture, meaning, framing, and common sense. Winning this contest is indispensable, but it is certainly not enough. We also have to win an *institutional contest*, which is concerned with the leadership, organizational capacity, and ground game of a subjective political actor (e.g., a social movement or political party). To struggle against a power is to build and wield a power of one's own, which requires organization and more. This is all to say that a bottom-up power must, through contests within the layer of culture and meanings, win some degree of popular support while delegitimizing and ultimately isolating its political opponents. And to win more than just popular support—i.e., to acquire the power that can be wielded to change policies, structures, and distributions of wealth and power—we need a strong and sophisticated ground game, one that is only made possible through organization and alignment of broad social forces. Here now is how victory ultimately plays out: our once-hegemonic opposition's ambition for perpetual domination (with a different agenda than ours) has to be constrained. We win as broad a consensus as possible for a

---

about such engagement to the point of paralysis or inaction; they do not step up to engage intentionally on this level.

social justice agenda, but then we *make it so*—aspects of it, at least—well before we have won over the hearts and minds of every last opponent. If a bottom-up movement—an emergent *power*—succeeds in defining its values as the popular common sense and also succeeds in translating this broad values-shift into concrete revolutionary transformations of power and wealth relationships in society, then that challenger has now itself become *hegemonic*, or at least *powerful* enough to contend within the polity and win important gains. The state is no longer an *other* that we stand in opposition to as total outsiders; instead we become responsible for it—parts of it, at least—as it is becomes a capacity of our operation. That is the political roadmap, in a nutshell. That terrifying thing, with all its challenges, messiness, and moral quandaries, is what victory looks like.[26]

If victory as such is our destination, how will we ever reach it if we are too ambivalent about power to even bother to look at a map? The reward for eschewing the terrain of politics is the comforting illusion that, while the world is full of manipulation, the righteous individual can wash his hands of it; he can live and let live; he can even stand defiantly, but as someone who wants to be recorded by history as having stood against the inevitable. Such an individual subscribes to what Max Weber called the "ethic of ultimate ends" and what I call the *story of the righteous few*. But can a person really save his individual soul by esteeming his own righteousness above the real-life outcomes of others? Such a salvation is self-defeating and in many ways equivalent to any other less righteous-seeming coping mechanism or private retreat.

Moreover, it is illusory to imagine that an individual or group can avoid manipulation. Let us briefly examine the concept of *manipulation*—let us break it down so that it ceases to be so paralyzing in our conscientious psyches. Can you take even one breath without manipulating the common fabric of material existence? Existence implies manipulation, inasmuch as everything, unavoidably, manipulates everything else. Manipulation is inherent to the interaction of matter and energy moving in time, of

---

26   Degree is important here. Such victories are rarely "all or nothing."

cause and effect, with the latter perpetually becoming the former. Every action shifts the ground upon which everything else operates. No person is an island. There is no such thing as a fully autonomous project or space. The question is not whether but *how* to manipulate. How will you step into an "ethic of responsibility" to consciously intervene for the common good? You did not make the world that you were born into, but now you are among its living makers. You are part of the social fabric. And, in a remarkable feature of human vitality, you have agency to self-consciously contribute to the alteration of its shape and trajectory. It is folly to feign or seek purity or neutrality or to pretend that you can somehow become separate from—uncontaminated by—the sins of society, structures, or the state. Do not run for the hills. Instead, study the apocalypse, map its terrain, and plan your intervention. It is selfish to jump ship when there are not enough lifeboats for everyone. We must conspire to take the helm.

6

BEYOND THE LOW PLATEAU

Understanding the imperative to build and to wield political power does not in itself magically award us with any. The basis of an underdog challenger's political strength is "people power." Fundamentally, we need more people engaging in aligned political action. After decades of deteriorating progressive infrastructure in the United States, a central task is to rebuild our forces. Growth and expansion have to be chief preoccupations. This chapter gives attention to the level of organization and mobilization—mostly at the local level—introducing conceptual frameworks, micro-dynamics, and specific techniques that may be useful to inform grassroots organizers as they design and carry out their political operations, whether these be at a local, state, or national scale.

> "An organization which claims to be working for the needs of a community...must work to provide that community with a position of strength from which to make its voice heard."
>
> –Kwame Ture (formerly known as Stokely Carmichael)[1]

---

1   Stokely Carmichael, "What We Want," *The New York Review of Books* (1966).

Growth trajectory

Brazilian educator Paulo Freire asked, "What can we do now in order to be able to do tomorrow what we are unable to do today?"[2] Here Freire is implicitly acknowledging that every political challenger is to some degree presently lacking the capacity needed to accomplish its long-term goals; if it were not lacking this capacity, it would hardly be a political *challenger*. Rather than treat such a disadvantageous present situation as if it were static or eternal, however, Freire implores us to think in terms of a *trajectory*. If we are presently too feeble a force to win the fight today, *what can we do today* so that tomorrow we will be a little stronger, and the day after that, a little stronger still?

Before we can wield power for change, we need to build and align that power. The addition of the word *align* is necessary here because it is not only a matter of *building* our own power from scratch. Certainly we do need to build some of our own explicitly progressive political organizations, but constructing a political force is just as much about aligning with existing groups and institutions.

To think about where we are now and where we want our trajectory to take us, picture a tug of war, in which one side seems to be winning handily. But when a few key actors switch sides, it suddenly shifts the balance of forces and momentum. In a case of a regime and its challenger, the old regime may suddenly find itself weakened, perhaps beyond recovery, while a challenger alignment finds itself potent, its strength ascending, the "tug of war" moving in its direction. Now, let's complicate our binary metaphor. The problem with the idea of an actor "switching sides" in a tug of war is that such a complete defection from one pole to its opposite is unusual in the real world. While such dramatic conversions are not unheard of, they are quite rare and we cannot rely on such dramatic individual conversions. The good news is this: to win politically you don't have to win over your most ardent opponents.

---

2   Freire, *Pedagogy of Hope*, 115.

The "spectrum of allies" graphic below provides an instructive map of our spectral "tug of war."[3]

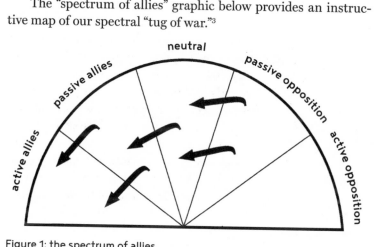

Figure 1: the spectrum of allies

Shifting the spectrum of allies is about moving people and
groups—leaders, influentials, social bases, institutions, polity
members, new and hitherto unmobilized actors, etc.—over just
one notch closer to your position. Groups working on specific campaigns can use the above "spectrum of allies" as a strategy tool, by
identifying (and then writing into the "pie slices") specific social
bases, institutions, and leaders that could potentially shift the balance of power. Perhaps the most crucial category shift is the pulling of *passive allies* into the *active allies* category, as this brings
an influx of volunteers and resources, substantially increasing the
alignment's immediate capacity for collective action. For example,
when pre-movement civil rights leaders and their small nascent
organizations pulled (i.e., activated) black churches, students, bar-
ber shops, etc. from the *passive allies* to the *active allies* category,
suddenly all of the pre-existing infrastructure, resources, and social capacity of those constituencies and institutions went to work
for civil rights, dramatically boosting the burgeoning movement's

---

3   This tool was introduced by Martin Oppenheimer and George Lakey
     in their book, *A Manual for Direct Action* (Chicago: Quadrangle Books,
     1965).

capacity and reach. Probably the next most important shift is in winning over *neutrals*, thereby pulling them into the *passive allies* category. The Freedom Rides were designed precisely with this in mind. SNCC leaders knew that many students in the north were sympathetic but inactive (i.e., they were *passive allies*). By creating a way for hundreds of these students to become actively involved—by riding in integrated buses to segregated southern states, and then lending a hand to voter registration drives—they not only increased the civil rights movement's capacity by bringing in more active participants, they also caught the attention of the families, friends, and broader social networks of those northern students, thereby pulling many thousands of people—including many "politically connected" people—from the *neutral* to the *passive allies* category.

If an emerging movement or alignment succeeds in effecting important shifts in these categories (*passive allies* —> *active allies*; *neutral* —> *passive allies*), it may be approaching a tipping point, where *passive opponents* start losing their conviction—they are "neutralized"—and the *active opposition* eventually loses its base of support. If challengers can keep up their spectrum-shifting trajectory—if they can weather countermoves, counter-attacks, and perhaps repression—their opponents will eventually find themselves isolated and thus weakened to the point of defeat or capitulation.

Of course none of this is easy. There are many obstacles—structural, cultural, social, and psychological—that tend to prevent individuals and institutions from aligning with and adding their energy to a collective effort or challenger movement. Overcoming these obstacles usually takes good planning, hard work, and savvy—and success is still never assured. But however hopeless the present situation may seem, we have to always remind ourselves that our success ultimately depends on a growth trajectory. Progressives will not—we *cannot*—make the kinds of changes we envision with only a small active force. There is a danger of getting stuck on a "low plateau"—where our capacity is limited to that of a small number of "usual suspects." We might even become *comfortable* on this plateau, where all the faces are familiar, and everyone thinks more or less like us. But we have to figure out how to climb higher.

Kinetic and potential force

Let us imagine that a grassroots challenger force like Occupy Wall Street effectively contests cultural meanings and prevailing narratives on a national scale in the United States. This should not be difficult to imagine, as it is a partial description of what actually happened. Following such a symbolic victory, what comes next? Will plutocratic forces simply concede just because challengers have succeeded in debunking their self-legitimizing narratives? Of course not. Here we see an important asymmetry between elites and challengers in hegemonic contests. When forces defending the status quo win a contest over popular ideology—over meanings, understandings, narratives, and common sense—what they then *ask* of the masses is usually simple: "Don't do anything—go about your lives." Status quo forces are like salesmen selling inertia. You do not have to take any novel action; they would prefer it if you did not. The quintessential example of this was in the aftermath of the 9/11 attacks when President George W. Bush called on Americans to "go out and shop."

Political challengers, on the other hand, do not typically have a whole state apparatus at their disposal to carry out their will. Challengers must win a hegemonic contest over meanings—a significant feat unto itself—and they *also* have to breathe life-force into their vision—to arm their vision with "people power"—if they are to change structures, policies, and power relations. For this, challengers have to win more than docility, deference, or uncommitted support from people. They need a sufficiently large base of people to engage in costly collective action if they are to build and wield the institutional power it will take to win meaningful victories. It is incumbent upon the leadership of a challenger movement to provide structures and "on-ramps" that can scale up this broad engagement. In other words, leaders have to provide newcomers with *things to do* that actually add to the capacity of the burgeoning collective force.

Thus the nascent challenger mobilization that succeeds in momentarily captivating popular attention is a threat to the power establishment not for its *kinetic force*, but for its *potential force*. Its kinetic force—the typically small groups that are visibly taking public action at the outset—may very well be a smoke-and-mirrors performance, much smaller in reality than how it appears under the fleeting magnification of the mass media, at least in the early stages of mobilization. This was certainly the case with Occupy Wall Street, as the popular attention that we generated far outpaced the numbers that we actually mobilized in the streets. In this play, a handful of audacious actors hits upon a novel tactic, savvy messaging, a ripe target, and a good measure of luck. Striking a popularly resonant chord, they capture a critical sense of momentum. While it may serve such actors to publicly inflate the momentum they have initially generated, it is indispensable that they privately assess the limits of their capacity at that moment and that they chart a path to expanding their political operation. Relative to the existing power establishment, their operation poses a potential threat not for what it can accomplish on its own, but for how it *might* catalyze aligned action by hitherto fragmented social blocs and institutions—how it might mobilize a critical mass of society. In a word, its *potential force*. These previously disparate forces are the ingredients which, when combined skillfully under ripe conditions, can produce an aligned collective power capable of mounting a viable challenge to the entrenched power of elites. The assembling of such a popular alignment—and, then, the alignment's achievements—is the essential conceptual structure of what we might call an aspiring hegemonic operation.

This activation of potential energy is an essential task of *political organizing*. To *organize*, in the political sense, is not to organize an event, a protest, or even an occupation. It is not just to create an autonomous project. Political organizing may very well involve all of the above activities, but its essence is not itself these activities—all of which can be carried out without necessarily building or being accountable to a substantial social base. *Organizing*, in the political sense, is to organize a social bloc into a political force. It is to name, frame, and narrate the trajectory of a group; to articulate its goals, grievances and targets; to move it into strategic collective action; to inspire other social forces to align in a common direction; and to leverage this force for political ends. Organizing is not a call to action for the already radicalized usual suspects. Organizing entails starting with what already is and engaging with people as they are—not trying to build something pure from scratch. It is not a matter of creating a liberated space that perfectly reflects one's utopian vision. Organizing is a mess, not a refuge.

In different epochs and different contexts different organizational forms have emerged to become predominant, depending both on conditions and on the task at hand. Small-scale community organizations, for example, might emerge on an *ad hoc* basis to redress local grievances, or pre-existing institutions (e.g., religious congregations) might lend their capacity for the same. Labor unions and political parties are among the most important historical forms of people-powered organizations we have observed over the past century and a half. However, with the decline of organized labor in the United States over the past four decades, working people have also lost our foothold within political parties, and it follows that we've lost significant leverage in relation to the state.[4] Part of our historical task right now is to either revitalize the old forms or invent new forms—or likely to find some hybrid—in order to reconstitute the political power we so desperately need.

Whatever the form, *organizing* is important because it puts us on a trajectory towards greater collective power. Given the left's current dearth of power, relative to the formidable power of our opponents, there is realistically no chance of us effecting the changes we imagine, if we do not organize and align larger social bases

---

4   When discussing the *decline* of the power of organized labor, it is important to acknowledge the powerful forces arrayed against unions, and it is also important to acknowledge that union members and organizers are still fighting in the trenches today, holding ground and sometimes gaining ground. Though weakened, labor unions remain one of the most powerful institutions in today's left alignment.

into political forces. To be clear, there are important contemporary campaigns in the United States that have been able to mobilize and organize enough grassroots pressure to win meaningful victories in recent years. The right for same-sex couples to marry anywhere in the nation was just won while I was writing this chapter—through an impressive campaign that mobilized the support of millions over the course of the past decade (and built on decades of earlier grassroots efforts). Many more contemporary campaigns have won important concessions and may be on the verge of bigger victories—from immigration reform to Black Lives Matter.

Occupy Wall Street, importantly, signaled the potential for a broad alignment focused on economic inequality and a rigged political system that serves the "one percent." After a few weeks—but before a few months—into Occupy's novel intervention in the fall of 2011, the amorphous mobilization was recognized by a substantial cross-section of the progressive left "establishment" (e.g., longer-standing institutions including labor unions, community organizations, national organizations, and other membership organizations), as having *de facto* provided the potential for such an alignment. Remarkably, this occurred despite Occupy's ambivalence and self-denial about its own leadership. OWS was widely, if ephemerally, seen as having succeeded where others had failed in articulating a counter-hegemonic public narrative that named an underlying crisis and aligned a hitherto fractured political left. Individuals and groups sensed a major shift in political potential, and many clamored to get involved or to align with the nascent movement. What followed this accomplishment was remarkable. In my two decades of grassroots organizing work, I have never seen such overwhelming deference coming from so many established organizations as during those several weeks in the fall of 2011. Experienced organizers and leaders from a range of notable organizations were asking us how they could best mobilize their members and channel their resources to support the effort.

Occupy succeeded initially in providing opportunities for more people to take action, but we ultimately fell short in providing opportunities at a big enough scale. The first call to action was for *individuals* to join Occupy in Zuccotti Park, and then for people to set up similarly styled occupations in cities across the nation. This was a strategic *ask* at a particular stage in OWS's development.[5] It proved to be effective in attracting self-selecting individuals who we might consider "usual suspects" or "low-hanging fruit"—folks who were waiting for something like this; who were ready to go without too much persuasion. The activation of these usual suspects nonetheless served OWS in its beginning phase. Importantly, it set up new Occupy organizers in other cities to have their efforts become local focal points, by joining—and projecting themselves as part of—a new dynamic national force and story. Some of these local manifestations of Occupy proceeded to invent locally resonant *asks* for constituencies within their reach. The anti-foreclosure campaigns of Occupy Atlanta and Occupy Minnesota are two of the strongest examples. These campaigns succeeded in aligning local social forces to successfully halt many home foreclosures and evictions, and then to change some laws and bank policies.

Yet Occupy failed to cross a critical threshold in overall organizational capacity, at a national level. It was ultimately unable—and to a remarkable extent *unwilling*—to develop the level of strategy and organization that could have provided strategic and scalable asks not just for self-selecting individuals, but also for existing groups and institutions on a nationally coordinated level. An important part of Occupy's problem was that, after its initial success, it tried to continue to grow primarily by way of individual self-selection. Its core attempted to be the whole movement itself, instead of seeing itself as a catalyzing symbol and "special agent" in the service of a far larger unification. Rather than helping to facilitate the activation of existing groups, social blocs, and institutions (e.g., labor unions, religious congregations, identity groups, etc.) into aligned collective action—an opportunity that was available to OWS to a remarkable extent—it too often attempted to build everything from scratch. To join the movement,

---

5   *Ask* is used here as a noun, which is typical in the vernacular of social justice organizing circles in the United States. An *ask* is an opportunity for a person or group to take some form of aligned action, provided by organizers.

one had to come to the park. When natural allies used the frames of "occupy" and "the 99%" to provide action opportunities for their already constituted social bases, they were often denounced as "co-opters." Many of us worked tirelessly to counter this tendency, but we were ultimately unable to stop some of the most self-isolating tendencies from speaking for the movement and repelling the very social forces that we needed to set into motion.

For reasons I have already discussed in earlier chapters, we ultimately lost the initiative. And many of the organizations, some with large constituencies, that had deferred to OWS and our cumbersome processes came to see us as incapable of charting a strategic course to take advantage of the political moment we had initiated. Occupy failed to develop "legs" that could carry forward the vision of the new unification. Trying to keep its *kinetic* force moving (e.g., maintaining the physical occupation of parks), Occupy inadequately engaged the broader *potential* force that it was positioned to activate. It quickly reached its natural plateau, and then unraveled.

Core and base

Of course, high-momentum "movement moments" like Occupy Wall Street are the exception to the norm. Usually, social change groups and organizations have to muster much more meager operations with less energy and attention swirling around them. In these long lulls it is easy to grow accustomed to a low level of capacity, and to neglect to really think strategically about how we might organize in order to grow, in order to win. Instead, we may chug along doing what we can with the little "army we have." The crises we seek to remedy may seem so pressing that we feel morally compelled to throw everything we've got at them—even if we know it will not be enough to actually change the outcome. The thing is, it takes more time at the outset to bring in new people and to orient them to tasks. It's faster, in the short-term, to just have the individuals who already know how to design a flyer, write a press release, or plan the logistics of a protest, to do so. However, if we neglect to prioritize bringing in new folks, orienting them, and developing their skills and leadership, we will tend to stay perpetually at a low operating capacity.

It is easy to become habituated to working in small, low-capacity groups. The ragtag features of such groups may start to feel familiar, even affirming of our values, as if being small and under-resourced were a sign that we are legitimately "grassroots." Such a dynamic, combined with the force of habit, often causes us to think too statically about the size and trajectory of our groups and movements. There is a tendency among people who are very active in social movements to grow too comfortable with ourselves; to look at ourselves and think that *this is it*, that *we are the movement*, that we know all the players. When we think we know all the players, as well as how to talk to them (i.e., to ourselves), then we can become lax in our attempts to reach a broader public or a target constituency. Unconsciously, we compose our flyers, calls-to-action, Tweets, and Facebook posts with *people like us* in mind—folks who are not only already on-board with our values and goals, but who are also acculturated to the idiosyncrasies of our movement spaces and privy to our jargon. This tendency limits our efforts to recruit, activate, or forge alliances with additional players. Again, if we think about a movement only in terms of its kinetic energy—i.e., that which is already in motion—we will look around at the actors currently on the stage and think that it is up to us alone to somehow accomplish large-scale political goals (e.g., transforming the economic system, challenging structural racism, or ending wars). This would require magic. We cannot realize a bold political vision with only our current numbers mobilized. For this we must build a larger social force. Again, we have to activate greater potential energy.

A central task of a challenger movement's leadership *core* is to take responsibility for building up the movement's capacity by activating and facilitating the participation of larger numbers of people. A core has to provide opportunities for everyday people to take meaningful action that is aligned with the aims and strategies of the larger movement. We have to set others up to play helpful ongoing roles that they can sustain. We have to accommodate multiple levels of participation. And we must activate existing social networks and institutions, rather than only building the movement one individual recruit at a time. This facilitative role requires a leadership core to conceptualize itself as such and to understand the nature of its relationship to a broader movement or political alignment.

Core essentially refers to the most active change agents; those individuals who, through whatever combination of circumstance, socio-economic status, experience, effort, biography, and choices, make a social movement or political project a primary commitment.[6] Having a critical number of such committed folks is indispensable to a movement's success. However, a serious impediment to building bigger and broader movements is the tendency among such uniquely positioned individuals to act as if we alone might somehow achieve our ambitious political visions (a variation on the story of the righteous few). Sure, we may be able to have some impact. But if we are talking about posing a potent challenge to entrenched power structures, then we who comprise the dedicated core (a.k.a. the "usual suspects") have to look far past ourselves. If the next iteration of an Occupy-like movement is to succeed politically, it will need to effectively tap hundreds of thousands of people who are willing to give *something*. Millions of such folks are already "out there," but organizers need to attract them and give them some direction and clear ways to participate. If a leadership core cannot effectively activate the next tier of potential movement participants, it will certainly fail to move the broader society. These potential participants are not even the whole base, but rather the *start of the base* needed to challenge entrenched systems of power and privilege. Therefore, the interplay between these tiers of movement participants is of critical importance. If there is an impassable chasm between the core and the potential base, then there can be no popular progressive alignment, and therefore little-to-no capacity for effective political intervention (at least at a national level).

---

6   In discussing a *core* I am, for the moment, putting aside the question of *leadership* within that core—and to what extent it is deliberatively structured and held accountable.

If the kinds of progressive changes we imagine are ever to be realized, it will be through the active participation of large numbers of "ordinary Americans": teachers, nurses, factory workers, artists, service workers, students, religious communities, civic organizations, unions, military servicemembers and veterans, and allies within the existing power establishment. These participants come as they are, and as such we have to welcome them. They give what they are willing to give, and organizers have to affirm the smallest contributions (while also constructing "ladders of engagement" for those who are eager to do more). Social movements that wish to attract everyday folks cannot afford to have a high bar for entry. If we are to build a popular movement, we must accommodate a continuum of levels of involvement, as well as levels of political analysis. Many problems and challenges inevitably accompany such endeavors. But, relative to our current dearth of organized popular power, these would be good problems to have.

Asking people for their time

In his book *Making History: The American Left and the American Mind*, sociologist Richard Flacks discusses how "the left then comes up against a fundamental and profound dilemma. It calls on people to make their history, but finds people making their own lives."[7] People have important social, familial, and professional commitments, not to mention their passions—hobbies, sports, the arts, etc. Thus, a near-constant feature of grassroots organizing is the challenge of getting people to *prioritize* putting time and effort into a collective effort. This can be a big challenge even when people are very sympathetic to the cause.

But if it is generally difficult to get people to devote their limited free time to collective political action, that does not mean that the *manner* in which we approach people has no bearing on our chances of success. One of the most important ingredients to successful mobilization of a person is their belief in the potential

---

7   Richard Flacks, *Making History: The American Left and the American Mind* (New York: Columbia University Press, 1988), 8.

utility of the effort. If you are asking me to spend my Saturday at a rally, is the rally likely to make a difference? If you are asking me to spend my Tuesday evening in an office making phone calls, is this tedious undertaking likely to bear any fruit? Do you have a strategy that guides the activities that you are asking me to spend hours of my life doing? In other words, is any of this likely to make a positive difference? If so, how are you making that clear to me? Because it's one thing to take time away from my family and my busy schedule if I think we can make an impact; it's another thing entirely if we're just shouting at the wind together.

To mobilize beyond the dedicated "usual suspects" we have to articulate not only the reasons *why* an issue is *important*, but also *how* our plan of action is *strategic*—how we have a believable chance of making a difference. The dedicated core of a social change group may get confused about this distinction—because this core may be composed of individuals who will do the work no matter the apparent results (of course hoping that eventually more people will join). I remember leading a strategy workshop for members of a local social justice organization in Boston. In one of the exercises, participants paired up for a two-person role-play in which one partner attempted to convince the other to attend an upcoming rally that was part of an issue campaign they had been working on. The person being "pitched" had specific instructions about their character: they were playing the part of someone who was sympathetic to the cause; they already understood and cared about the issue; they had even participated in related actions in the past. However, they were skeptical about the *effectiveness* of this particular action. Would it make any difference? In other words, they were willing to give their valuable time *if* they could be convinced that the action was part of a larger strategy that had a chance of achieving a political goal—but their instructions in the role-play were to start out with measured skepticism concerning this question of effectiveness. The partners (in the pairs) who were instructed to make the persuasive pitch, on the other hand, essentially had to play themselves: core participants in a campaign they were already active with in real life.

I was fascinated by what ensued. Only a few of the "pitchers" said anything at all about how the action would be effective in a strategic or tactical sense. Disregarding their clear instructions—in a manner that seemed unconscious rather than rebellious—the large majority instead tried to convince the other person of the importance of the issue itself, even though they were explicitly told that the person already agreed with them. Instructed to explain the action's *strategic* utility, they could only explain it in *moral* terms. Is this not a central problem of the dedicated core of today's left? We ask people to join our group, campaign, or action because "they should care about this important issue." Millions of Americans already think the issues are important. Often the problem is not that they do not care. The problem may be that they don't think our actions are effective. And they may be right!

The point here is not that we should replace a moral narrative about our issues with an "inside baseball" conversation about strategy and tactics. Indeed, I can often be found arguing the opposite. However, the rhetorical tools that can win broad sympathy in a public-facing symbolic contest aren't necessarily the same tools needed for persuading individuals to get involved—to give their time—in particular efforts at the local level. We must also be careful to not draw the wrong lessons from those rare and rejuvenating "movement moments" when volunteers seem to be coming out of the woodwork in answer to our moral appeals on an issue; part of the explanation for such rapid influx is that the sense of momentum itself makes it seem more likely that the collective effort could have an impact, and thus be worth joining. Such may be the intuitive judgment—more than the conscious calculation—of new movement participants in these moments. However you slice it, such momentum tends to fade quickly when the moral narrative proceeds without a story about *how* the effort will succeed politically, or absent a believable impression that there exists a leadership with a good plan.

If people see no believable path forward, why should they join our costly adventure? Too often we mistake people's resignation for apathy. In the workshop in Boston, it seemed that many participants really could not grasp the basic concept that a person could

(1) care about an issue but (2) refrain from joining a particular action because (3) they don't see the action's *efficacy*. Take a moment to appreciate the practicality of refraining from joining an action that seems doomed to failure. Is fighting an advantaged opponent without any hope or plan for winning really fighting? If the cause is just, then perhaps fighting with no hope of winning is morally superior to not fighting. However, if taking a righteous stand will only achieve itself, most people will prioritize other things in their lives (e.g., a hobby, or quality time with loved ones). Social justice efforts that rely only on moral suasion—without offering any sense of a believable path to victory—will tend to mobilize only "true believers," martyrs, and saints. Morality must always shape our mobilizing narratives, but we also have to paint a believable picture of what winning will look like. We have to punctuate our struggle with glimpses of victory and credibly foreshadow how we will achieve our big-picture vision in the long term.[8]

---

8   This is one big reason why electoral campaigns are often much more successful at recruiting and plugging in huge numbers of volunteers than issue-focused campaigns or social movement groups. As a campaign, an electoral race has a clear endpoint and you either win or you lose. And, regardless of the platitudes of some radicals, most people intuitively grasp that elections have important consequences. So much so that many people are willing to give significant time or money to throw down for a candidate that they see as a "lesser evil." At the time of this writing, as Bernie Sanders has emerged as, arguably, the first major progressive populist presidential candidate in decades, we are also getting a glimpse of how such a familiar structure (i.e., a presidential campaign) can scale up the involvement of millions of enthusiastic volunteers and donors—who were apparently just "waiting in the wings"—in a way that issue-focused campaigns or movements typically only dream of. Some ultra-leftists see the Bernie campaign as "diverting radical energy" into the electoral realm, but let's be real: most of this energy had been dormant—only *potential* energy—until the Bernie campaign came along to activate it. Hopefully this moment is helping today's radicals to reconsider our relationship to electoral campaigns and political parties— thinking about how we might take advantage of such structures and

To be fair, it is often very difficult for grassroots groups to accomplish such a thing. And that's one reason why we also have to always be on the lookout for new openings and opportunities. Whether we're talking about a local, regional, or national scale, long-haul organizers know that unanticipated events can quickly and dramatically shift the political landscape. From economic downturns to the blunders of powerful politicians—or even the unexpected successes of our own actions—unforeseen factors can suddenly open up new possibilities for challenger movements. When the landscape dramatically shifts and people can intuit potential political openings, the thick fog of popular resignation can evaporate in an instant—and challenger movements may suddenly find themselves inundated with new volunteers and institutions clamoring to join the burgeoning effort. Within such moments and between them, it takes work to plug newcomers into tasks and roles that build our political force.

Plugging people in

In early 2003, during the lead-up to the US military invasion and occupation of Iraq, something big started happening in cities and towns across the United States. Only a year and a half after the 9/11 attacks, the Bush Administration seemed to have spent most of its political capital and was now shamelessly milking the tragedy to lead the nation into an unrelated war of aggression. The lead-up to the invasion provided circumstances that encouraged a lot of people to act on their dispositions to try to stop an unpopular war before it started. People who were generally hesitant or disinclined to participate in street protests did so anyway, hoping that a large showing might make a difference at a critical moment. We certainly did turn out in big numbers. The global antiwar demonstrations on February 15, 2003 marked the largest coordinated protest in world history.

In January of the same year, a small group of folks in my hometown of Lancaster, Pennsylvania advertised for a public meeting to

---

moments as part of a long-term progressive hegemonic operation.

plan for local antiwar action. I had left Lancaster County several years before this, and had been deeply involved in social movements and grassroots organizing in big cities since then. But the idea of bringing the organizing skills I had acquired back home had been growing on me. Frankly, I had little desire to leave the life I had made for myself in radical circles rooted in bigger cities. I had by then built close friendships from my work in social movements, especially in the global justice movement. However, I was becoming increasingly critical of the insularity I saw in the radical left. In clustering into likeminded subcultural enclaves, surrounding ourselves only with each other, we were effectively abandoning areas like Lancaster County—and really most of the state of Pennsylvania between Philadelphia and Pittsburgh. I would often hear liberals jokingly label most of the state "Pennsyltucky," inferring that it was as backward as their idea of Southern Appalachia. Somewhere along the way these areas, once organized by the labor movement, seemed to have been conceded to the right. How would we ever contest the politics of such areas if we gave up on engaging them? Having grown up in rural PA, I started to feel a special burden.

To test the waters, I moved to Philadelphia and started spending time in Lancaster (a distance of about 90 minutes by train or car). I started spending more and more time in Lancaster in the months leading up to the Iraq War, and soon I was involved in helping to mobilize people in the area against the Bush Administration's march to war. To our surprise, the public meeting that we organized drew more than 200 people. I was thrilled to see so many folks come together in this politically conservative area.

We decided that we should start meeting regularly to build something together. While a meeting of over 200 people was inspiring, we would have to structure the next one differently if we were to harness the energy and skills of those in attendance. I volunteered to co-facilitate a follow-up meeting in which we formed working groups to focus on specific tasks and projects. I had prior experience with the working group model, and it seemed a good fit for getting so many people active quickly. The meetings and working groups continued and became the Lancaster Coalition for Peace & Justice (LCPJ), which continued strong for the next decade, growing into a 500-member organization (and also affiliating with the national coalition, United for Peace and Justice). I was excited to help build the LCPJ. No such organization had existed in Lancaster County when I was fumbling through my own politicization process several years before. Now I was helping to build a vehicle that people in the area could plug into, and that could perhaps help to shift local culture and politics. When I had been contemplating my return to Lancaster, I knew that I was interested in building some kind of vehicle that could facilitate progressive collective action, but I didn't have a clear vision about what it would look like. The Bush Administration's march to war in Iraq deeply troubled a lot of people in the area and provided the catalyst for us to organize on the basis of our shared opposition.

It can be quite challenging to get people to take the first step of getting involved in collective political action. Every once in a long while, though, extraordinary circumstances—like the lead-up to the Iraq War—encourage larger numbers of people to take this step all at once. In such situations, organizers may have a hard time just keeping up with the inflow of volunteer energy. But a little bit of effort can go a long way in providing opportunities to new participants, as was our experience in Lancaster. Plugging in new volunteers and getting them to stick around— in a way that adds capacity to a collective effort—is at least as challenging as initially getting folks in the door. In Lancaster we suddenly found ourselves with an abundance of new volunteers. The first wave of leadership in the LCPJ was mostly made up of people who already had important commitments in their lives. A few individuals in particular had taken on a great deal of new responsibilities with the LCPJ. As the organization transitioned to a longer-term existence, many of these individuals were unable to sustain the level of sacrifice that the LCPJ seemed to demand of them. For the most part these folks, while still supportive of the LCPJ, dropped off as active participants.

Over time, I noticed a pattern: those who took on more manageable (but still meaningful) ongoing tasks mostly stayed active, continuing to attend to the same roles or tasks that they originally committed to (e.g., our treasurer, archivist, and graphic designers). Social movement scholars Pamela Oliver and Gerald Marwell shed some light on this pattern:

> ...a lot of the technological knowledge about mobilizing volunteer time is about organizing and dividing labor and structuring events and jobs so that people can be invited to participate in well-defined and limited ways... A technology often used in the charitable sector but only occasionally used in social movements involves creating long-term jobs that involve only a few hours a week such as calling for Jewish charities for three hours every Tuesday night or being on call for the rape crisis center three nights a month. Many people who are unwilling to make the major short-term open-ended commitments that activism entails are quite willing to make a long-term commitment to a well-defined task. They also are aware that failing to keep their commitment will cause a noticeable problem for the event or the organization's mission.[9]

Our mixed success in retaining active members corroborated Oliver and Marwell's findings. We started to intentionally structure our operations accordingly. By the end of the LCPJ's first year, recognizing the limitations and challenges of our all-volunteer organization, we decided to hire a part-time coordinator whose primary job was to maintain regular contact with point people from our multiple working groups. A year later, when the coordinator position became vacant, I took the job and began working to "package" task-sets for volunteers. As an organizer, I sat down with volunteers one-on-one to invite them to take point on specific ongoing tasks that fit their availability, skills, and interests. I aimed to design roles that would not be too overwhelming, so that people could more easily sustain their involvement. With this set-up, new volunteers were able to plug in meaningfully, and they

---

9   Pamela E. Oliver and Gerald Marwell, "Mobilizing Technologies for Collective Action," in *Frontiers in Social Movement Theory*, ed. Aldon D. Morris and Carol McClurg Mueller, (New Haven and London: Yale University Press, 1992), 265.

weren't just another body to add to the mass. They usually found ways to take some creative autonomy in the particulars of their roles. It's good to provide opportunities for volunteers to increase their contribution and to step up to take on greater responsibility. Sometimes it makes sense to explicitly ask and encourage them to do so. On the other hand, it's all too easy to unintentionally over-burden volunteers. An unsustainable workload sets volunteers up to fail or to flee—they may end up flaking on their tasks or burning out and dropping off entirely. Paying attention to such concerns is part of the work of a leadership core of any organization. Leaders can check in with active volunteers about how they're doing with their workload. Counter-intuitively, it's sometimes even necessary to encourage people to do *less*, in order to set them up to do more in the long term. In my role as coordinator, I would sometimes make this explicit to LCPJ volunteers, saying, "You're doing a really great job. I'd love to see you still involved two or three years from now. So I want to make sure the amount of time and energy you're giving is sustainable for you. If you find that you're doing too much, let's talk about it and figure out how to adjust."

These one-on-one meetings eventually became an important organizing tool for us, and several of us became skilled in leading them. But this wasn't how we started out. In the first few months of the LCPJ, when people would ask me how to get involved, I would just invite them to attend our monthly business meet-ing. Sometimes those invited would attend and sometimes they wouldn't. When they did, they often didn't come back. Then one day it suddenly struck me how ludicrous it was that our primary recruitment strategy was "come to a meeting." I had noticed for some time the low retention rate of folks who took this initial step. The thing is, all groups develop some level of internal culture that can be alienating or intimidating to newcomers, and this is always on display in a group's meetings. Certainly, this can be mitigat-ed by groups that make a conscious effort to be more welcoming and to refrain from jargon. Yet, the primary purpose of a meeting is to discuss and make decisions about the group's ongoing work and mission, and this is not always conducive to providing an ac-cessible or appealing first impression to newcomers. I decided to start taking time to sit down one-on-one with individuals who expressed interest in the LCPJ. We would meet for coffee for about an hour. First, I would ask them about themselves—their interests, experiences, talents, and skills, and what had gotten them interested in the LCPJ—and then I would tell them about some of the LCPJ's campaigns and projects. Together we would seek to find a good fit for them. I would also identify capacities that the organization was lacking that I thought they might be interested in working on. I encouraged volunteers to find or invent an ongoing role or task that they could sustain. One woman told me that she never ever wanted to come to a meeting, but that she loved to organize rummage sales and that she would do all the work to organize two of them for us annually. She did so, providing the LCPJ with free publicity and several thousand dollars in funding.

For every new role someone would fill, we increased our collective capacity. We found ourselves capable of accomplishing more, including the capacity for campaigns on local issues. This, in turn, increased our visibility, which attracted even more participation. We also developed a story of many moving parts working together as a whole to build and exercise grassroots power. This narrative gave meaning to even mundane tasks—like organizing our bi-monthly mailing—by putting them in the context of a collective purpose and trajectory.

Jose Vasquez recounted to me his similar working philosophy in building the Iraq Veterans Against the War NYC chapter:

> If a person can give two hours a week, awesome, that's two hours a week. There are so many other people who give zero. So you get the person who gives two, and great... You've got to meet people where they are. If they get passionate about it, they'll reprioritize. They'll figure out what the work requires. I think the more important thing is giving people a feeling that there is a mission here; there is work that needs to be done. It's amazing what some people can get done when they feel a sense of purpose and are all facing in the same direction.[10]

---

10   Jose Vasquez, interviewed by the author in December 2007 as part of

Narrating an organization's mission like this gives people a sense of meaning, purpose, and personal agency, all of which are important if we want new participants to stay involved in our groups, campaigns, and political projects.

Yet there is something else that is perhaps even more important. If we want to inspire people to stick with social justice organizations for the long haul, then we absolutely must make them feel valued and appreciated. It's really basic. People like to be around people who are nice to them and who make them feel like they *belong*. If we want to compete with the myriad options for people's free time, then we have to treat each other well. We have to be good to each other, to take care of each other, to rise above the social elitism that so often infects our society. This work is ultimately about love. Yes, our world is in crisis, and the work of confronting that crisis can be exhausting, but if we are to attract broader participation, we have got to step out of "crisis mode organizing" and take the time to appreciate each other along the way.

Here again, the concept of a *core* is helpful; those active participants who recognize themselves as part of a core have to take additional responsibility for the group culture and make sure that participants feel valued and supported.

Engaging existing infrastructure

When groups like the LCPJ organize actions or events, they have to do so with limited resources. Groups tend to expend what limited resources they have on reaching out to constituencies that seem more likely to attend their events, which often means outreach to other progressive groups. By default, and to some degree necessity, outreach efforts focus on "harvesting" already existing consciousness and networks rather than "planting new seeds." Let's say a group has a budget to make 300 leaflets for an educational event they are organizing, and five folks have volunteered to distribute the leaflets. It makes good sense, with a

the War Resisters League's listening process.

short-term goal of getting good turnout to the particular event, to devote such limited outreach resources to posting flyers at places where likeminded people are likely to see them. However, the short-term goal of using limited resources to get good turnout is in tension with the long-term goal of growing a movement by reaching—and providing opportunities for—new people.[11]

Moreover, if a given group is focusing predominantly on attracting other progressives to attend an event, this is likely to shape the language they use to promote the event. A flyer written to attract people who are already solidly "with you"—i.e., the "usual suspects"—may look substantially different than one written to attract a broader audience. Similarly, the event itself may look drastically different if it is assumed that everyone present is already in agreement. This is yet another reason why many social movement groups fall into the insular patterns discussed in previous chapters. We grow too accustomed to talking to each other. We "preach to the choir." The language we use references commonly held meanings within our progressive or radical groups and networks, and is often alienating or even unintelligible to people who do not share those meanings. Thinking back on the *spectrum of allies* tool outlined earlier in this chapter, our message is aimed only at the far-left "pie slice"—virtually ensuring that we will keep operating at an insufficient capacity.

The problem is not just about where we place flyers and whom we have in mind when we write them. The outreach limitations groups have are real. It may not always be feasible, for example, to distribute flyers to a broader constituency. So we need to think creatively. Posting a flyer—along with posting a Tweet or Facebook event—isn't really a great way of "planting a seed" to reach new folks anyway. *Seed work* requires reaching people where they are, within the spaces and with the references to which they are accustomed. For example, getting an event

---

11   If you think printed leaflets are archaic and you prefer outreach via social media, you'll find the same dynamic of likeminded clustering and self-selection coded into the algorithms. For more on this: Eli Pariser, *The Filter Bubble: What the Internet is Hiding from You* (Penguin UK, 2011).

listed in a church bulletin by finding an ally in the congregation will likely prove more effective than posting a flyer on the wall, because it will feel more familiar or legitimate to congregation members.

We also need to move beyond just promoting *our own* actions and events. It can be far more effective to *bring the event* to existing cultural spaces and institutions; to classrooms, religious congregations, neighborhood groups, and so on. I can easily spend twenty hours planning and promoting an educational forum at which I will feel pleased if even a few unfamiliar faces turn out. Alternatively, I can spend just two hours preparing to talk to a classroom of high school students, presenting a more in-depth critique on a given issue than many of them will have ever previously encountered. This latter option is part of what is meant by *seed-planting work*. It requires finding and maintaining allies within existing cultural spaces and institutions (e.g., the teacher who invites me to speak to their class).

The thing is, a lot of people may hold beliefs compatible with an organization's or movement's goals, but only a small percentage are likely to *act* on those beliefs. And a primary factor for why some people do take action is simply that they encounter opportunities provided by people close to them who are already active. Social proximity to political activity can activate people's dormant beliefs. Social movement scholars Debra Friedman and Doug McAdam cite such proximity as the single biggest factor for why some people become active in grassroots change efforts, while others do not: "Structural proximity to a movement, rather than any individual disposition, produces activism. Although individuals differ in their dispositions, the opportunities afforded by structural location relative to a movement determine whether they are in a position to act on these dispositions. Empirical support for these positions is unimpeachable..."[12]

---

12   Debra Friedman and Doug McAdam, "Collective Identity and Activism," in *Frontiers in Social Movement Theory*, ed. Aldon D. Morris and Carol McClurg Mueller, (New Haven and London: Yale University Press, 1992), 158.

With this in mind, we can see that a primary role of a grassroots organizer is to provide opportunities that turn people's favorable dispositions into collective political action. And this is a big reason why I returned to my hometown of Lancaster to organize: because it's essential that *core* participants (as I have defined *core* throughout this chapter) be embedded in the common social networks and institutions around us. If we perpetually cluster into our own separate spaces—if we surround ourselves only with each other—how many opportunities can we provide for others to get involved? If people join collective action more from proximity to opportunities to become active than from individual dispositions, then we've got to get close enough to people (who are not already active) to be able to effectively provide them with such opportunities.[13]

Along these lines long-time organizer Judith LeBlanc discussed with me how today's movements need to get out there and talk to people:

> Talking and making connections and relationships is the core element to grassroots organizing and we don't have a lot of people doing that. We don't have a lot of people who are willing to go door to door. And when they do, the people who do that, it changes them... I believe the single most debilitating constraint [to contemporary social movements] is that people don't have confidence that you can walk into a church or go to a union local and find a receptive ear who would engage with you in thinking through what it would take to involve a local union or a church or a tenant's organization in any given initiative we're taking on—to just sit down and talk.[14]

---

13   We can think about providing such opportunities for "unusual suspects" at the local campaign level—i.e., individuals and groups around us that we might approach—but we can also think about who are the "unusual suspects" at a national level in terms of demographics and social blocs that have been neglected by progressive political projects over the past decades.

14   Judith LeBlanc, interviewed by the author and Madeline Gardner in August 2007 as part of the War Resisters League's listening process.

Engaging with existing networks and institutions also allows the people within them to consider joining a collective effort without feeling that they would have to lose their existing identity in order to do so. They can take action as teachers, as union members, as students, or as members of a religious community. They do not have to become an "activist"—a distinct identity that many people have misgivings about claiming—in order to take action. Instead they can work for social justice as an expression of who they already are, alongside people they already know.

When we're not intentionally engaging "beyond the choir" like this, we tend to become our own exclusive audience. Distinctly progressive or radical groups tend to orient our meetings, forums, cultural events, and demonstrations toward ourselves—what we feel comfortable with—rather than towards the social bases that we need to be engaging, with consideration for what may or may not be relatable to them. Coming together with like-minded people can fill our spirits, feed, and sustain us, but we cannot afford to lose interest in building a broader-based political force. And we can't neglect to engage already existing cultural spaces. Sometimes we become disinterested in or even hostile toward such spaces because we see them as problematic, as they house the values of the dominant culture. But these spaces also house the people. We can't expect people to meet us where we want them to be. We have to meet them where they are, with the language they use, in the spaces they frequent.

And this isn't just about going into such spaces in order to recruit individuals (even if we do that as well). This is also about what is referred to as *bloc recruitment*: growing a movement by activating whole groups of people at a time. One of the biggest organizing lessons from US social movements in the 1960s is that when movements grow quickly in size and capacity it is usually not by building their own separate infrastructure from scratch, but by organizing within existing social networks and institutions until their members identify with the movement. Then the pre-existing infrastructure and resources of those institutions start to go to work for movement ends. The civil rights movement spread like wildfire and dramatically increased its capacity when black churches and traditionally black schools came to identify as part of a movement. Most people did not have to leave their social networks to become part of the movement. Rather, membership in these existing institutions came to imply movement participation. These institutions and networks then used their resources to further movement goals.[15]

Building our own separate infrastructure from scratch is resource-intensive. And resources for such infrastructure are harder to come by because of the small pool of invested persons. This is not at all to say that specific movement organizations like, in the case of civil rights movement, the Student Nonviolent Coordinating Committee (SNCC) and the Southern Christian Leadership Council (SCLC) are unimportant. Organizations that are constructed explicitly for political purposes often play crucial and irreplaceable roles. However, such organizations do not bring about sweeping changes by "going it alone." Organizers and movement organizations are valuable mostly in their role of organizing and mobilizing social blocs and existing institutions, i.e., by facilitating broader participation.

The tendency to build all our own infrastructure from scratch is related to the tendency to attempt to build something that perfectly and purely reflects our alternative values. Organizations are always, to some extent, a reflection of the values of their members and leaders, but we have to keep in check the tendency towards self-righteous purism. We must not seek such a pure reflection of our values that we become disinterested in effectiveness and lose sight of our instrumental goals. When groups and organizations become overly concerned about their "purity," they cut themselves off from the people they should be working to align with or organize. If such groups seek to grow at all, their recruitment efforts will be impaired by the fact that they are building a righteous, albeit alienating, identity more than a viable vehicle for change.

Radicals cannot afford to focus exclusively on building our

---

15   Doug McAdam, *Political Process and the Development of Black Insurgency, 1930–1970* (Chicago and London: The University of Chicago Press, 1982).

own alternative infrastructure to feed an alternative narrative that distinguishes us from others. As discussed previously, those who maintain this tendency confine themselves to living the *story of the righteous few*, in which they perpetually lack the ability to effect the changes that they long for. The necessary numbers elude them and the necessary resources remain in the hands of others. If, on the other hand, we succeed in connecting with others, then there is no *other*. The walls between others and us start to come down. Resources become available and doors open, not magically, but through effective organizing and alignment that is made possible through relationship; through our orientation towards connecting with others and finding common ground.

In Lancaster County another peace and justice organization, the Lancaster Interchurch Peace Witness (LIPW), emerged to organize local Christian congregations as part of a broader effort for peace and justice. Founded in 2004, one year after the founding of the LCPJ, the LIPW provided a complement to the LCPJ. From the start the two organizations worked collaboratively. Yet the LIPW played a particular role that the LCPJ was not as equipped for. As a group of local leaders and members of Christian churches, the LIPW has been able to work for peace and justice by engaging their own church memberships in ways that no organizer or organization would be able to do were they outside of the Christian faith. LIPW provides opportunities to get involved in peace and justice work that participants experience as an expression and extension of their faith. LIPW's leadership is comprised of people who are active, embedded, and have legitimacy in these particular social networks and institutions. The LIPW leadership strategizes and collaborates together to promote peace and justice within their networks and institutions; to activate already constituted communities—along with their infrastructure and resources—to work for peace and justice in the broader society. They are *insiders* in these communities, genuine and sincere. While some people in their churches disagree with them, they cannot easily dismiss them.

Whether or not we're aiming to engage with religious communities and institutions as the LIPW does, we might appreciate the organization's approach as a model for conceptualizing the relationship between the distinct organizational vehicles we build and the communities and institutions those vehicles engage with. Social movements clearly need to build some of their own goal-oriented organizations, but these organizations have to reach outward, "beyond the choir." Some of these organizations may cast a wide net, as does the LCPJ, while others, like the LIPW, may go deeper into specific networks and social bases. As they say, different strokes for different folks. But all of our organizations—local and national—must learn to see past themselves in order to do their part to grow a larger political alignment.

Leaderful

In this chapter I have outlined a number of things that successful social justice movements and organizations do: develop a core and a broader base; build a culture and a system of plugging new members into meaningful and capacity-building roles; maintain an outward focus so as to avoid insularity; and engage with existing infrastructure rather than constantly starting from scratch.

None of this is possible without good leaders.

That's why we have to reject the "leaderless" ideology that we've seen in certain contemporary social movements. The anti-authoritarian, hyper-democratic spirit of Occupy Wall Street was, in certain ways, a beautiful thing: a call for greater political participation and more horizontal power relations. It was also, practically speaking, a total pain in the ass. Lacking nuance, this culture too often became self-sabotaging: hostile toward needed skills and resources, and toxic for many who stepped up to take initiative. Occupy's anti-leadership bent was of course related to the deeper ambivalence about power (and politics) that I discussed in chapters four and five.

However, leaders did arise out of Occupy who came to explicitly value leadership itself. Among the important concepts that many of these leaders learned was the critical difference between saying *none of us is a leader* and *all of us can be leaders*. At first glance these two sentiments may seem like two ways of saying essentially the same thing: both affirm organizing in ways that are more horizontal than vertical; both attempt to equalize participation and to resist social hierarchies. There is a crucial difference, however, between the idea of *no* leaders and the idea of *all*—or *many*—leaders. If we are part of a group that talks about having no leaders, this phrase can inadvertently make us overly hesitant about stepping up to take initiative. It can create a group culture where individuals are reluctant to be seen as moving something forward—because our peers might see us as "leaders," which would be a bad thing. Such a culture took hold in many pockets of Occupy.[16]

For movements like Occupy Wall Street to scale up, we need a lot more people stepping up to take initiative. The more initiative we each take in our work together—the more political organizing skills we learn and hone—the greater our collective capacity becomes. Building our capacity means increasing what we are capable of achieving together. It means building our *collective power*, which is a central task of a challenger political project.

We need to build a culture where we are all invited to step up—a culture that aspires to shared leadership and a proliferation of leaders. This is not at all to say that horizontal values should not inform our notions of leadership and what it means to "step up." Good leadership includes stepping up in ways that also makes space for others to step up; to help others to feel invited, confident and prepared to take initiative. Stepping up can mean actively listening and learning from others. Stepping up can mean taking time to reflect on how different people can be socialized differently around leadership. For reasons that often have a great deal to do with our different socializations because of gender, race, age, economic class, or other aspects of our identities, opportunities, and social positions, some of us may be predisposed

---

16   While I've seen leadership allergies in all kinds of movements over the years, Occupy was the most extreme. Black Lives Matter, for example, emerging soon after Occupy and using social media as prolifically as Occupy did, has tended to be much less allergic to having leaders and cultivating leadership, even as it has to navigate difficult challenges about how to do so intentionally.

to speak confidently and to take on more visible leadership roles, while others are often predisposed to speak less in the group, or to take on less visible roles. For a conscientious leadership, then, stepping up also means recognizing and valuing many different forms of leadership in the group, and addressing social imbalances around who is taking on more visible forms of leadership. It also means looking for leadership potential; for strengths within the group that are latent or potential, waiting for an opportunity to become active. Stepping up can mean providing the right opportunity at the right time to help activate such latent potential in others, rather than assuming that by simply "stepping back" and leaving "more space," the right people will automatically fill that space, absent intentional leadership development.

However, if we stay in the framework of thinking we should have *no* leaders, why would we be inclined to seek to develop more leadership in our groups and movements? If all leadership is viewed negatively, we may develop a "circular firing squad" group culture, where we tend to cut each other down or we hold back because we are afraid to stick our heads up.

Instead of imagining *leaderless* movements, we have to build *leaderful* ones; movements where we are always encouraging each other to step into our full potential and to shine as individual leaders who are working together collectively for a better world. If we are to climb higher than the low plateau, we need more leaders, and more leaderful movements.

THE INVITATION WE EXTEND

If the previous chapter conceptualized how grassroots organizing efforts and social movements have to expand their numbers and capacity, this chapter looks more specifically at the role of communication in aiding such expansion. Why do some political messages resonate with their intended audiences, while others fall flat?

> "Learn from the people; start their education where they are."
>
> *—Myles Horton[1]*

Pedagogy and ambiguity

Paulo Freire criticized what he called the "banking model" of education. In this model, the student is seen as a passive recipient of knowledge. Knowledge is held by the expert teacher, who attempts to "deposit" it into the empty vessel of the ignorant student's mind. This, Freire argues, is not how human beings learn. People might memorize facts this way, but they do not develop themselves as critical thinkers. In order to really learn, students have to become

---

1   Frank Adams and Myles Horton, *Unearthing Seeds of Fire: The Idea of Highlander* (Winston-Salem, North Carolina: John F. Blair, Publisher, 1975), 206.

actively engaged learners. A student has to feel some sense of *agency* in the learning process. The process itself is more important than the specific content, especially in the earlier stages of the student's development—because once a student has become engaged in a process of critically reflecting upon their own experiences, they are then equipped to keep learning, honing their knowledge, and developing their capacity for critical thinking.

Too often today's left relates to society like the "expert teacher" relates to the "ignorant student" in the banking model of education. We know better than the backward populace. Yet the problem is more complex than a self-righteous or haughty attitude. In fact, leftists can, and often do, functionally use the "banking model" without elitist intentions. Here's how it happens. Let's say we're working on a given issue... let's continue with an example from the previous chapter and say we're organizing a protest against the US military occupation of Iraq. Now, anyone with a developed radical analysis knows that you can't fully understand the Iraq War without understanding the history of US militarism, imperialism, global capitalism, and also Islamophobia and how it is connected to xenophobia and white supremacy. So, wouldn't it be remiss of us to not explicitly spell out this analysis? It can feel as if we would be watering down our radicalism to not make all of this explicit; we feel like we should "call a spade a spade." In such a manner, we may attempt to pack the full depth of our political analysis into everything we do: our flyers, our placards, our speeches, our press releases, our Facebook event pages, and so on. How could we in good conscience produce a flyer about the Iraq War that doesn't mention capitalism or imperialism? How could we leave it out of our speeches?

Here's the thing: the only audience we are reaching by spelling out our full analysis is ourselves. Now, there's a time and a place for deepening the political analysis of the dedicated core. Books like the one you're reading, for example. This is not to argue that you can never deepen the analysis of broader audiences—of course you can. But, at the risk of utilizing a condescending metaphor, you don't drop a college textbook on a kindergarten class. That is what the left too often attempts to do. A good teacher understands that they themselves did not receive their knowledge and analysis overnight. Rather than attempt to force instantaneous understanding, a good teacher creates spaces where students can experiment, experience, reflect, and thereby develop their knowledge and their capacity for critical thinking and learning.

A teaching metaphor is only condescending here if you think of students (or young people, for that matter) as inferior or lacking agency. In Freire's model of experiential education every teacher has something to learn and every student has something to teach. If you've made it this far into the book, you are likely someone who is especially interested in political matters, and if you want to move others to take or support collective political action, then you have to be something of a teacher to the folks who, for many reasons, have not been paying as much attention to political matters as you have been. This doesn't mean that you're better or smarter than other people. Your particular expertise is only one among many kinds of knowledge. But if you want to move and mobilize people politically, then you have to be something of a teacher to the people you want to reach. And if we want to be effective teachers, we have to dispense with the "banking model" of eduction. We have to instead create experiences and processes that foster active learning.

We can design our campaigns with this in mind. Pedagogically, a good campaign shares many things in common with a good lesson plan. A good campaign creatively engages our "students." It intrigues them, sparks their curiosity, connects with the things they are already interested in, builds upon their existing base of knowledge, provides a way for them to meaningfully participate in the learning process, challenges them but doesn't alienate them, and so on.

Such an approach can help us to think about the role of *ideology* in the process of political struggle. It's not that ideology is unimportant. Every course of action is ideologically informed, whether or not the ideology is conscious or explicit. When we talk about ideology, we are talking about an analysis of the world—politics, economics, morality, ecology, etc.—our place in it, how we want the world to look, and how we think we can get there. Ideology informs the goals and strategies of all political projects, from campaigns to social movements, from political parties to revolutions. However, while critically important, leaders cannot simply transfer their ideology to newcomers. Each person entering a political project has to develop their own understanding of ideology through a social process. Ironically, explicit discussions about ideology are often one of the least useful means of assisting newcomers in developing their own ideology.

The reason for this is simple: you cannot transfer your own clarity into someone else's head. I've been using the metaphor of *teaching*. A related metaphor, especially useful for recruitment and alignment, is *courtship*. We have to "court" society— or particular social blocs, groups, and individuals. We have to "win their hand," so to speak. And unfortunately the left often has no charm and no game. To extend the metaphor, it often feels like we're "proposing on the first date": we eagerly put all of our cards on the table at once, inviting the other person to give us their whole life... and then we wonder why we're so alone. On a first date you don't tell the other person everything about yourself. You ask them to tell you something about them. You listen. Then you put a little something out there. Maybe you start with something fun or funny. (And, hey, maybe you even make an effort to dress nice and take a shower for godsake—we could keep running with the metaphor.) The point is, if we only recruit those who fall in love with the left at first sight, we'll stay small. And with the exception of the occasional nerd, analysis is a lousy means of attracting most people.

Ambiguity, on the other hand, can open the door. As long as the meaning of something remains somewhat unclear—or floating—it will be intriguing. When people are intrigued, they are engaged. They have a mystery to figure out. They may even have to re-examine their own assumptions in the process.

The notion that there is positive strategic value in ambiguity may offend some progressive sensibilities. We tend to want clarity. And there are certainly times when clarity is precisely what is called for. It may be important for a group's leaders, organizers, and core participants to have clarity about their campaign goals and about the political terrain that they need to cross in order to reach those goals. We may also want clarity in our own thinking about complex social, economic, and political systems. However, if you want to organize and mobilize people outside of the clubhouse, you have to also befriend ambiguity. If you can't turn off your need for clarity in some moments, you may well succeed in painting a clear analytical picture for yourself, but you're unlikely to attract the social forces we need, if we're to start turning this thing around.

Narrative insurgency

We can't just build a little activist clubhouse and expect people to join us; we have to meet people where they are. In the previous chapter, I discussed how this applies to the physical spaces where people congregate: churches, bars, community events, and so on. But "meeting people where they are" also applies to people's assumptions, belief systems, and the narratives they use to make sense of the world around them. We have to study and savvily engage existing narratives and belief systems.

When you disagree with someone else's views, it can be tempting to engage them in a rational debate. Perhaps there is an inherent democratic value in debate between people who disagree with each other on a topic. But social change work is not debate club. We have political goals and we're attempting to recruit and align the social forces we need to win them. Moreover, attempts at rational persuasion usually quickly turn into something that I call *narrative attack*—that is to directly attack someone else's narrative or worldview from the vantage point, and in the language, of your own worldview.

For example, when someone who denies the existence of climate change wraps their views in the rhetoric of creationism, it's tempting to launch right into an attack on the climate change denier's entire belief system. The problem is that you can't persuade someone to see something your way when that person feels that their whole belief system—the narrative they rely on to make sense of the world—is under attack. A person in such an interaction is more likely to double down on their existing beliefs than to open themselves to considering new ideas.[2]

As an alternative to *narrative attack*, we might consider an approach that I call *narrative insurgency*. This latter approach requires us to examine the other person's narrative framework, learning the component parts, and looking for points of connection—i.e., common ground between their belief system and yours. A "narrative insurgent" starts with and emphasizes that common ground, using it as a base for fomenting "homegrown insurgency" within the larger narrative. Rather than directly attack a creationist's whole belief system, for instance, a "narrative insurgent" looks to overcome or "outmaneuver" the most problematic beliefs by identifying *ally beliefs* that already exist within the belief system, and seeking to reinforce those. When speaking to creationists about environmental issues, for example, an effective point of entry might be to emphasize humanity's Biblical mandate to care for God's creation. You might build upon that ground to win the person's sympathy on the issue, perhaps eventually inspiring them to take action.

Unfettered passionate debate is an important part of politics. But it is only one piece of the puzzle. When it comes to engaging communities and getting them aligned and activated on important issues, we often have to engage in a much more complex dance. Our work is frequently more about asking questions and listening than providing all the answers. It can be helpful to think not in terms of attacking opponents' views head-on, but rather in terms of fomenting homegrown insurgency. The root of the word insurgency means *to rise up*. Insurgencies rise up from within. *Narrative insurgency* rises up from within a cultural narrative, transforming meanings in that culture from the inside out.

At the community level, a well-executed narrative insurgency approach will help to identify and draw out allies in the

---

2   Brendan Nyhan and Jason Reifler, "When Corrections Fail: The Persistence of Political Misperceptions," *Political Behavior* 32, no. 2 (2010): 303–330.

community: in our example, religious people who care about the environment and are uneasy about seeing it ravaged for the sake of private profit. By repeating and positively reinforcing this message in the context of ongoing engagement, the belief that *we should care for the earth* can be strengthened within the given community's complex collective belief system. Narrative insurgents don't reject problematic narratives wholesale, but instead identify and distinguish between those components of a narrative that are *allied, hostile,* or *neutral* to our cause. We embrace as much of a cultural narrative as possible—the allied and neutral components—and use this as a foundation for our organizing efforts with and within the given community.

The *narrative insurgency* approach doesn't mean *always* avoiding direct confrontation with harmful narratives and beliefs. It's more about strategically choosing battles—while finding common ground and utilizing positive reinforcement whenever possible. Ultimately there comes a time when a destructive narrative becomes untenable to a critical mass of people, and when a new *polarization* will be useful (for example, during a crisis of legitimacy in the prevailing order, or a revolutionary moment). The strategy here is to lay the groundwork that necessarily precedes such a moment: to feed the allied components within a narrative until they are strong enough to burst out of the old framework.

At its core, "narrative insurgency" is more or less a fancy way of saying "Listen to people and attempt to understand where they're coming from before you try to persuade them of something." We learn the intricacies of cultural narratives not to deceive people, but to communicate common values in a language that holds meaning for them. While we may often disagree with others, we still value and even empathize with their perspectives. We are forgiving toward shortcomings, always rooting for people, always finding something worthy of praise. Over time, "narrative insurgency" should become second nature: we don't have to feign identification with the allied and neutral components within a community's narrative or culture, because our orientation is to connect with people wherever and whenever possible—because our work for social justice is rooted in our love for real people, in all their complexity.

Inoculation

Sometimes it's difficult to persuade people to join collective action because of the negative stereotypes in their heads about protests and "activists." With such stereotypes, many Americans have been effectively "inoculated" against the very means available to them to effect social and political change. What do I mean by "inoculation"? Think about how a doctor inoculates a person against a virus by introducing a very weak strand of the virus that triggers the body's immune system. This exposure causes the body to build up antibodies against the weak strand. Then when anything comes along resembling that weak strand— BOOM—the antibodies are triggered to defend against the intruder. Immunity. The would-be host has acquired a built-in resistance to the real virus.

We can see an analogous process operating in our political culture. Picture a ridiculous stereotype of a joint-smoking, window-smashing, flag-burning, Kumbaya-singing dirty hippie protester. This exaggerated caricature is the metaphorical weak strand of the virus that conservative opponents of social justice movements have introduced to the public consciousness in order to inoculate it against the real thing. When an opening for powerful collective action comes along, the negative stereotypes are invoked and—BOOM—the public's cultural "immune system" is triggered to react against it. People who could potentially sympathize with or even join the collective effort instead recoil out of an intuitive fear of the negative associations and emotions that are triggered, consciously or unconsciously. They have a built-in resistance. To persuade such a person to join a collective effort, organizers have to identify and overcome this resistance.

Kelly Dougherty, the co-founder and former Executive Director of Iraq Veterans Against the War, discussed with me how, despite popular opinion weighing heavily against the Iraq War, it was very difficult to mobilize many Americans to join any kind of collective action to stop the war. There were many important factors contributing to this difficulty, but one of them was this negative caricature of social movements and "protesters."

"A lot of people have this idea of what an antiwar protester is," Dougherty explained.[3] These negative associations that "a lot of people have" are not random. They're partly the result of a long-term conservative ideological project, whereby history has been carefully revised and progressive movements—especially those associated with "the 60s"—have been caricatured as naïve and irresponsible, at best, and vilified as un-American or even terroristic, at worst. This is neither to give the right full credit for inventing these damning stories "from scratch," nor to argue that pockets of the left have never been guilty of any of the charges against them. In any massive societal shift—like those that unfolded dramatically in the upheavals of "the 60s"—one can find all sorts of excesses and extremities. The right has zoomed in on these, while cropping everything else out of the picture, especially the actual grievances that millions of people mobilized to redress, including social inequality (especially along lines of race, gender, and sexual orientation), economic inequality, and the devastating war of choice in Vietnam. With regard to the war, one of the most damning stories—and potent mental images—told about the left was that antiwar protesters spit on US soldiers when they returned home from Vietnam. No evidence exists that shows this ever happened. Yet, despite it being debunked as fabrication, the story continues to be parroted by politicians and pundits to this day. The story is part of the cognitive backdrop that many Americans hold in their heads, which tints the lens through which they view "protesters."

So, while millions of Americans "don't think that the [Iraq] war is right," Dougherty explained, few would take action because most "wouldn't see themselves as the kind of person that would go to a march or a protest."[4] These stories and stereotypes act as cognitive blocks that deter individuals from joining collective efforts to make change, even on issues that they feel strongly about. The "protester" has been made into an *other*. Not seeing themselves as

---

3   Kelly Dougherty, interviewed by the author in November 2007 as part of the War Resisters League's listening process.

4   Ibid.

such—and lacking a vision for how they might get involved in a way that connects to their own life experiences and the social groups to which they belong—most people do not get involved at all.

Michael McPhearson, the Executive Director of Veterans For Peace, told me something very similar: "The average person doesn't know who the people in the peace movement, in the antiwar movement are. The media and the [George W. Bush] Administration paint us a certain way. And while [people] might not believe it wholeheartedly, they believe it to a certain degree. So they can't really identify with us, *because they don't see themselves as us.*"[5]

Another layer of the caricature about social movements is that people may see movements as being only about *protest*—i.e., about loudly and expressively marching in the streets. They don't see the less visible work that movements do—organizing tasks that are vital for successful campaigns. If people see movements only as self-expressive, they may also miss their potential political utility. To illustrate this point, Dougherty described having attended a play put on by the theater program at Temple University. The play was based on interviews with Iraq War veterans, including Dougherty herself.

> I was one of the characters. It was pretty cool. It was kind of surreal. Afterward, I went backstage to meet the girl who played me and to meet the rest of the cast. And they were all really excited. Being those characters in the play really transformed them—[they became] really concerned about what was going on. Before that most of them probably really didn't understand or have really strong feelings about the war.
>
> Something they said really stuck out to me: "What do you need? We can help you! *We can come into your office and make signs!*"
>
> They had all this energy around this and they had been really transformed by this experience, but then they thought, "Well, I want to become involved. I'll make signs." I wouldn't

---

5   Michael McPhearson, interviewed by the author in December 2007 as part of the War Resisters League's listening process. My emphasis.

belittle them for that because that is what a lot of people think that protesting is. You just make signs and go do a march![6]

The optics of protest can contribute to this confusion. An underdog movement's signature visuals are often a variant of outsider street protest, complete with ragtag aesthetics. By all appearances, protest is a Do-It-Yourself activity. It seems simple: anyone can make their own sign and join a protest—they have only to make the decision to do so—which can give the impression to outsiders and participants alike that there is not much to it—no art or science—other than showing up.

Perhaps anyone can join a protest, but the fact is not everyone does. Who joins a movement, when, and to what effect is not a matter of magic, nor of straightforward structural determinants. There are many important factors that influence a movement's chances of successfully attracting more participants and allies. Gaining an understanding of these factors, and of how to navigate them with savvy, is not child's play. What is needed is an understanding of social action that spans all the way from the macro level of economic and political structures to the micro level of group and individual psychology. The value of such knowledge is priceless for social movements, and one does not obtain it simply by showing up to a protest or making a sign.

"People think that to have a movement against the war, you just have to show up on a day and do something," Dougherty continued,

> And [they] don't really realize all of the work that goes into organizing and planning things. It doesn't get you on the news; it doesn't get you headlines. You know, you can't make a headline every day if you're serious about building a movement. It's hard and it's hard to figure out; and it's a lot harder to actually do the organizing and think about a campaign and think about how your tactics build upon one another. What's your goal? How

6   Kelly Dougherty, interviewed by the author in November 2007 as part of the War Resisters League's listening process. My emphasis.

[are you] going to have an impact? That stuff is all way harder
than just ... showing up at a rally...[7]

Dougherty went on to explain that if more people saw social movements as being capable of achieving "tangible results ...
people would get more energized about it and more people would
join" because "it has a result" that they can see. When it seems
doubtful to people that a demonstration could have an impact,
why would they show up? This can become self-fulfilling, or a
Catch-22, as low turnout tends to also lower a demonstration's
political impact. Marches and rallies are intended as displays
of power—of popular opinion mobilized—but there's always a
danger that they will display the opposite: a *lack* of power. A
feeble turnout or trite rituals that fit into a predictable script
can reinforce negative stereotypes instead of actually pushing
people, including decision-makers, to reconsider their position
in relation to a given issue. Organizer Nathan Paulsen explained
how public demonstrations should, ideally, "create a situation
where there's potential for even more people to step in next time.
That's what scares politicians: maybe this will escalate; they
might have momentum; this might get out of control. If we send
the message that we're ten or twelve individuals, or we organize
a protest with 150 people on a campus of 35,000, the message
we're sending to politicians and the public is that we're isolated
and marginal... A demonstration should be a sign of your power.
That means [it] can also function to signify your weakness too,
if you don't plan strategically."[8]

The point here is not at all to suggest that we should never
hold public demonstrations. This is to say, rather, that demonstrations—if they serve a strategic instrumental purpose—should be
demonstrations of power (or a trajectory of power), and that they
are only one piece of a political struggle—one tool in the toolbox.
If we are to shake up and rewrite the deeply ingrained negative

---

7   Ibid.
8   Nathan Paulsen, interviewed by the author in August 2007 as part of
     the War Resisters League's listening process.

scripts about collective action, we have to do a lot more than march in the streets. We have to enter the spaces where people already congregate—places of worship, workplaces, union halls, community centers, parks, bars, homes, etc.—and have conversations and build relationships with people who are not "the usual suspects" (i.e., the folks who are already perfectly comfortable joining a public demonstration).

On the other hand, we don't have to wait until we can turn out huge numbers to organize strategic public-facing actions, protests, and demonstrations. With smaller numbers, however, we have to make sure that the numbers are not the thing that is emphasized. We can play with the optics, symbols, messages, messengers, backdrops, and props, in order to present ourselves as powerful, and also to avoid playing the parts that so many people—including folks who we need to mobilize—are inoculated against.

An example that comes immediately to mind is when Iraq Veterans Against the War carried out *Operation: First Casualty* in Washington DC, New York City, and several other cities. Veterans put on their uniforms and staged re-enactments of the kinds of combat operations they had carried out in Iraq. In New York City, I helped to organize the "civilian" actors, who would be detained, abducted, or "shot" (with invisible weapons) in the presence of crowds of pedestrians in various public spaces, like Times Square. Dougherty remarked upon how "people were thrown off by and kind of impressed" by the optics of *Operation: First Casualty.* "Where as, if they just saw a march, they probably wouldn't have even seen veterans marching and wouldn't have felt like they could relate to those people."[9] IVAW's action focused the attention on their greatest asset—their credibility and symbolic power as military veterans. Passersby were first jarred by the site of faux military operations in the streets of major American cities, and then they learned that the "actors" were actual combat veterans, re-enacting scenes they had themselves experienced. While people might easily dismiss generic "antiwar protesters," it is not so

---

9   Kelly Dougherty, interviewed by the author in November 2007 as part of the War Resisters League's listening process.

easy to dismiss a veteran who served in Iraq who is now telling you to your face that the war must end. This action profoundly "messed with" the script. Another advantage of this tactic was that IVAW avoided having to invest the enormous resources that it takes to organize large demonstrations, and simultaneously avoided getting caught up in the "numbers game" that is so often used to evaluate (or dismiss) public demonstrations.

Obviously not everyone is in the position to carry out *Operation: First Casualty*. But every group can assess and leverage their particular strengths. Who has credibility or symbolic power—either members of the group, or individuals that the group has access to—and how can a public action put those people front and center? How can props, visuals, messages, messengers, and venues all be aligned to carry a powerful story—one that connects with the positive values of our target audiences, while dodging, or even undermining, the negative stereotypes that so often prevent people from even hearing us?

Branding

In contemplating how to flip negative scripts and shift meanings in the culture, another useful concept is *branding*. In the advertising world, branding is about imbuing a company or product with positive associations inside the consumer's mind. Marlboro, for example, has so successfully associated cowboys and the wild frontier—and popular notions of freedom—with their product, that some of their billboard and magazine ads don't even mention the name *Marlboro*. They don't need to, because their name and product comes to mind automatically at the sight of the now-famous cowboy image.

In the late 1990s Rainforest Action Network (RAN) carried out some very effective *negative branding* campaigns that targeted individual corporations. And powerful people took notice. RAN realized that a positive brand is one of the most important assets of a public-facing corporation.[10] A tarnished brand can repel

---

10   Some corporations do not develop public-facing brands, and are there-

consumers and scare away investors, as Home Depot learned the hard way. RAN effectively painted Home Depot as a reckless de-stroyer of old growth forests, until the company caved and commit-ted to discontinue using old growth forests for lumber. A few other companies followed, like dominoes, just at the threat of a *possible* RAN campaign targeting their good brand name. In recent years, numerous labor campaigns have incorporated brand-tarnishing strategies into their efforts, seeing it as an additional form of lever-age in their fights and negotiations with companies.

My exposure to RAN's successful campaigns got me thinking a lot about branding strategies—and not only about the brands of my political opponents. What about the social justice groups and movements that I was part of? Did they have "brands"? A brand is essentially the memories and associations that come to mind in the popular imagination at the mention of a name. In this sense, individuals can even have brands (though we usually call this a reputation). What associations were coming to mind at the mention of the organizations I was part of? What about at the mention of broader labels such as *activism, environmentalism, unions, feminism, socialism, the peace movement,* and so on? If a tarnished brand hurt a corporation's ability to move product or attract investors, perhaps *our* tarnished brands were part of the reason so many social change groups were having such a difficult time attracting more participants.

So, let's suppose that you're a small business owner who makes very delicious sandwiches. However, despite the deliciousness of your sandwich, your business is in a remote part of town, your storefront display is abysmal, the aesthetic on the inside is kind of weird, and your waitstaff and clerks aren't very good at interact-ing with customers. Are you likely to sell a lot of sandwiches, just because you have a good product? And, to extend the metaphor, it turns out that your sandwiches are *not* delicious after all. You and a few of your friends like your sandwiches a whole lot, but it turns

---

fore far less vulnerable to campaigns that target them on this basis (for example, a weapons manufacturer whose sole client is the United States government and allied states).

out to be an acquired taste. It's as if you sell broccoli sandwiches, which you know and believe to be good for everyone's health and well-being, but why doesn't anyone come to your store? (Maybe it's because everyone but you is being brainwashed! They're all sheeple! ...How I wish that didn't feel familiar.)

Taking political action or getting involved in a social change organization can be about as appealing as a broccoli sandwich. Maybe it's good for the health of the community, but it may be an acquired taste. So what can you do to make what you've got more attractive to more people? Maybe you can remix the ingredients—add a spoonful of sugar to help the medicine go down. Maybe you can move your operation to the city center where there's more foot traffic, and maybe you can make it a fun place that people will want to come back to. And maybe you can find a graphic designer to make a bright sign and a snazzy logo.

All of these things are relevant to organizational branding—anything that affects the memories and emotions and experiences that people associate with our groups and movements. Our organizations and campaigns are vehicles to move agendas forward. Not only do we need to craft our agendas into compelling messages, we also need to recognize that our vehicles are *messengers* and that *the messenger matters to the message*. We have to work to create positive associations in people's minds, so that when they think of our organizations and movements they are attracted, rather than repelled.

This is not to say that substance does not matter—or that we have to win over *everyone*. Some people will inevitably despise some of our organizations, because our interests and theirs are fundamentally in conflict. Those folks are not the target audience that we're aiming to attract with organizational branding efforts. We're trying to reach people who are either on the fence or who are passive allies (i.e., people who are sympathetic, but not presently taking action; think back to the *spectrum of allies* in the previous chapter).

When I started directing the Lancaster Coalition for Peace & Justice (LCPJ), I launched an intentional organizational branding strategy. I started by looking for good graphic designers, and soon we found three—recruited at a local bar—who gracious-ly volunteered their services for the LCPJ.[11] The designers and a few other core members of the LCPJ formed a kind of cadre; we met regularly to strategize and plan and build a compelling and thoroughly *mainstream* brand for the LCPJ. We decided to avoid words like *activist, protest,* and *demonstration,* which we felt were red flags to too many people in our area. We believed we could use other words to connect with people's values. We studied the posters and advertisements of respected local com-munity organizations, and built an aesthetic that fit with what people were used to seeing. Instead of a "teach-in," we organized a Town Hall meeting to discuss the war—for which we reserved city council's chambers. We sought out and met with local ser-vicemembers, veterans, and military families, and some of them became active with the LCPJ. We made sure that their voices and stories were front and center. We even started a sharp-looking bimonthly community newspaper called *The Lancaster Voice.* We were intentional about everything from our spokespeople to our fonts, recognizing that it was all part of our organizational brand, which is to say it all affected our ability to effectively reach mem-bers of the community.

Central to our branding strategy was a projection of ourselves as mainstream and familiar—in order to "cognitively disarm" people. Neuroscientist Gregory Berns explains how "familiarity soothes [the amygdala]," which is the part of the brain related to anxiety and the "fight or flight" response.[12] Recall the earlier discussion of negative stereotypes that have inoculated so many Americans against protest and social movements. When such threatening stereotypes are triggered in their minds, people tend to become anxious and to "look for the exits." These kinds of ste-reotypes are probably much stronger in areas where residents are unaccustomed to actually encountering protest—like Lancaster

---

11   Credit and thanks to Jeff Rummel, Jess Mauger, and Dana Leeper for their stellar design work for the LCPJ.

12   Gregory Berns, 2008. *Iconoclast: A Neuroscientist Reveals How to Think Differently* (Boston: Harvard Business Press, 2008), 140.

was at the time—as people rely more on thirdhand sources, occasional national news stories, and dominant tropes. Yet it seems that we may have successfully alleviated this kind of anxiety by introducing a reassuring familiarity into our actions and messages. This was the intuitive logic at work in the organizational branding strategy of the LCPJ. Everything we did essentially said, "This is a Lancaster community event. Your opposition to the war is a mainstream view, and you can join with other everyday folks in your community to oppose it—without having to become, or even seem like, a hippie." It's not that the negative stereotypes weren't triggered whatsoever. After all, we were in the streets protesting against a war. But our strategic projection of ourselves as mainstream and familiar reassured people and ultimately allowed for new positive associations about protest—and about the LCPJ specifically—to emerge and crystallize in people's minds, which is pretty much the definition of successful "branding."

One especially interesting aspect of this operation was our usurpation of something called the *officialization effect*. This effect, elaborated by sociologist Pierre Bourdieu, is typically wielded by elites to awe the masses. Those who already hold the reins of power also enjoy, as a perk of that position, an aura of presupposed competence. They are assumed to be legitimate, because they display all the signs, adornments, and official seals of legitimacy. The *officialization effect* functions like a wind that blows continuously at the back of the already powerful.[13]

In Lancaster we pulled off a kind of "symbolic coup" by sneakily securing city council chambers for our protest against the Iraq War. Again, we didn't call our protest a protest—we called it a "Town Hall Meeting." The design of our window posters intentionally mimicked the aesthetics of mainstream community events. Everything reeked of the scent of official sanction, rather than marginality and impotence. Importantly, the name of the town and county, *Lancaster*, was the first word of our organizational name. By usurping the "officialization effect" we were able to

---

13   Pierre Bourdieu, *The Logic of Practice* (Palo Alto, CA: Stanford University Press, 1990), 109.

draw a lot of people who were not the "usual suspects"—folks who might have otherwise felt uncomfortable joining a fringe-seeming "protest" (with all that has become associated with this word, especially in a conservative area like Lancaster County). The results were dramatic. We turned out 800 people on the anniversary of the war—the largest per capita turnout of any city in the United States—and this in a conservative area unaccustomed to large protests. The power of this psychological effect was further evidenced by city authorities' reactions during the lead-up to the Town Hall, once they realized we had secured a permit. Some of them were incredulous and attempted (unsuccessfully) to rescind our right to use the public space, whose availability to "the likes of us" had been an oversight that other political outsiders hadn't had the gall or imagination to take advantage of. Our success wasn't a one-off fluke. We turned out the same number the following year. We also developed a circulation of 5,000 copies for our community newspaper, *The Lancaster Voice*. Most importantly, we developed the capacity to organize regular events and to mobilize people to take action on a variety of peace, social justice, and community issues. This level of progressive mobilization was unprecedented in Lancaster County.

Our intentional and disciplined organizational branding strategy was absolutely central to our success. By recognizing the generically negative and marginalized "brand" that some forms of collective action had pinned upon them, we were able to adjust and build an organizational brand that felt familiar and carried positive associations that worked for our local context. Essentially, we took down the (metaphorical) "DIRTY HIPPIES ONLY" sign that some jerk had hung on our storefront, and we replaced it with a sign that said "All Are Welcome."

Good branding can make a big difference. I have yet to encounter a progressive change organization that would not have benefited from developing a conscious branding strategy. There are many components of an effective brand, from your logo to your motto and much more, but what should inform all of it is an underlying goal to meet target constituencies—beyond the usual suspects—where they're at; to connect with the common concerns, common experiences, and common sense that you find in your community, while still pushing forward progressive goals. You create a brand that your target constituents can identify with.

It must be emphasized that LCPJ's branding strategy was one important part of our larger organizing strategy and ground game, part of which I discussed in the previous chapter. Attention to good branding did not replace—but rather complemented—other ways of engaging people. I can imagine many of my community-organizer and union-organizer friends balking at the idea that branding—if narrowly defined by design aesthetics and word choices—could ever accomplish anything on its own without the hard work of face-to-face outreach, leadership development, and organization building. And they would be correct. The concept of branding, like all of the conceptual tools in this book, is a potential aid for engaging communities where they are, not a shortcut that can magically bypass this hard work. And, of course, one of the best ways an organization can improve its "brand" is by showing that it has the strength to win campaigns. On the other hand, I suspect that at least a few of my community organizer and union organizer friends might be surprised if they saw what a difference good branding—including savvy messaging and tight graphic design—can make in helping a campaign's ground game go further faster. Campaigners at staff-driven advocacy organizations tend to rely heavily on branding and PR strategies, while neglecting the time-consuming face-to-face work of organizing a social base into a political force. Organizers at member-driven organizations (e.g., unions or community organizations), however, sometimes make an opposite error: knowing the importance of face-to-face relationships and a persistent ground game, and harboring an often on-point critique of funder-driven, non-membership "bodyless head"[14] advocacy organizations, they

---

14   Marshall Ganz used this term to describe the new kind of non-profit advocacy organization that proliferated in recent decades, in place of the civic organizations with more active memberships of an earlier era. Quoted in: Skocpol, *Diminished Democracy*, 163.

sometimes throw the baby out with the bathwater by dismissing communications strategies as hollow smoke-and-mirrors corporate PR shenanigans.

Some of my other lefty friends have told me they don't like the word *branding* because it sounds like "corporate speak" and evokes the thought of predatory advertising that encourages mindless consumption. I don't care if you call it branding or something else, but it is my view that if corporations put billions of dollars into studying human psychology, it might just be worth examining their findings, as well as the techniques they have developed. While we shouldn't simply mimic corporations' marketing techniques, we do have to navigate the same cognitive universe that they navigate, and it behooves us to study this terrain—we should never be too proud or too pure to learn things from our opponents.

What is commonly referred to as *branding* is a cognitive associational technique useful for navigating the terrain that I have called the *symbolic contest*, which relates to contesting popular meanings, narratives, and common sense. Understanding tools like branding can help us to become more effective contenders in this contest. In this chapter I have used examples mostly at the local level of grassroots organizing. In the next chapter, I dig deeper into how the symbolic contest operates at much larger scales, especially the national level.

THE WE IN POLITICS

*The symbolic contest we have been discussing is over popular res-
onance. A resonant political message appeals to something deep
inside of us: the human longing for belonging and capacity for
solidarity. Solidarity is the lifeblood of politics, but with whom
are we to feel ourselves in solidarity? And against what threat?
Different groups—Democrats and Republicans, socialists and
fascists, and every other sort of political contender—articulate
different premises for group solidarity. Everything depends upon
the question of who is inside or outside of the circle. Who is the us
and who is the them?*

> "Within each such social group, a feeling of solidarity
> prevails, a compelling need to work together and a joy
> in doing so that represent a high moral value."
>
> –Christian Lous Lange[1]

Blinders of individualism

In the previous chapter, I used the idea of "selling product" as
a metaphor for how social change organizations have to "sell

---

1   Christian Lous Lange, "Internationalism: Nobel Lecture, December 13,
1921," in *Nobel Lectures in Peace: 1901–1925*, ed. Frederick W. Haber-
man (Singapore: World Scientific Publishing Co., 1999 [1921]), 338.

themselves" or "attract customers." I must now name an important limit to this metaphor; a limit that many would not see as a limit, because of a profound error that is a cornerstone of the common sense of neoliberal ideology: namely, the assumption of selfish individualism. Codified in the *individual rational actor paradigm*, this is the belief that individuals navigate the world by making individualistic cost/benefit calculations, like consumers looking to satiate their individual desires at the lowest possible cost to themselves.

My objection to this paradigm is not that selfishness does not exist. Of course it does. My objection is threefold:

1. Selfishness is not as central a force in human societies as proponents of the individual rational actor paradigm assume.
2. Group-oriented, solidaristic behavior exists as a significant force in human societies.
3. In the realm of politics, at least, group solidarity is a far more powerful driver of behavior than individual selfishness.

Everyone knows that there are individual careerists in politics. But at its core, political behavior is group-oriented. Intense feelings of group identification, belonging, and solidarity are the fuel of social movements and political involvement. And, as we shall see, this has huge implications for political alignment processes, along with the symbolic contest over meanings, narratives, and common sense that is so fundamental to such alignment. In this final chapter, I will elaborate how collective political subjects come into existence, and their subsequent operations. From local groups to national social movements to much larger and longer-lasting broad alignments like the New Deal Coalition and the Reagan Coalition, if we are to understand the formation, processes, and operations of collective political subjects, we first need to take off the blinders of individualism that prevent so many people today from being able to even see the logic—and the drive—of collective action. As we shall see, using the individual rational actor paradigm to examine collective political action is like using a microscope to map the constellations.

It's a dog-eat-dog world, so we are told. But is this really true, either in a figurative or literal sense? The phrase is of course meant as a metaphor for human society, but let's first ask whether the metaphor itself—as opposed to its human referents—is even true. Do dogs eat dogs? Not very often. Dogs are pack animals; social creatures whose individual survival (in the wild) is highly dependent upon the success of the group. Yes, individual dogs will fight over position and for other reasons, but cooperation is the norm and fighting is the aberration. Ironically, the animals chosen to represent our supposedly selfish inner natures are actually, more often than not, exemplars of an evolved and adaptive cooperation within groups.

More to the point, the same is true for humans. We are thoroughly social creatures, our survival and our thriving dependent upon the groups to which we belong. Even in modern society, sociality is the norm, with anti-social behavior being generally viewed as deviant and subject to sanction from the larger group.

However, there is a trite evolutionary argument against the existence of authentic cooperation and sacrificial behavior in individuals. This argument, highly associated with Social Darwinism, goes something like this: selfish individuals have a clear adaptive advantage over cooperative individuals. Assume evolution started with a "dog-eat-dog" relationship between competing individual organisms. Any genetic mutations that awarded a fitness or reproduction advantage for an individual would win out over time. If, on the other hand, a mutation came along that predisposed individuals to be more cooperative, such individuals would quickly breed themselves out. Selfless individuals who served others who served themselves would be investing their energy into the fitness of their competitors and would have ended up dead fast. If you drop a selfish individual and a cooperative individual on an island with limited resources, the cooperative person is toast, so the argument goes. Evolutionist David Sloan Wilson turns this example on its head by making the *group* the level of analysis: if you have an island full of selfish individuals and another island full of cooperative individuals, which does better? The cooperative island, of course. The crux of Wilson's argument is that we (among other "social species") have been evolving on a between-group level for millions of years, which has given a competitive advantage to highly cooperative groups, thereby making possible the emergence of cooperation, because it is adaptive.

It's not that humans no longer have the capacity for selfishness. Nobody would argue such a thing. But Wilson argues that we humans essentially have a Plan A, which is cooperative behavior, and a Plan B, which is selfish behavior.[2] We are likely happiest as individuals and most efficient as a group when we are set up to lean into Plan A. In other words, humans thrive and are psychologically adapted for giving freely to "the group" while trusting that the group will provide for their individual needs—without having to keep a ledger about who owes what or how much to whom. However, when it becomes apparent that we have to fend for ourselves individually, we still have the capacity to do so. Such a mindset is typically marked by high anxiety—and is related to "fight or flight" mode—because one is fully responsible for one's own survival, and cannot trust others to "have one's back."

Without idealizing a primitive past, we can nonetheless see how modernity and capitalism have profoundly disrupted the highly cooperative and egalitarian traditional small-scale groups that humans for millennia relied upon for their survival.[3] First traditional societies were disrupted, but as neoliberalism's profit

---

2   We're still selecting on both of these levels, among others (e.g., gene level, sperm level), which is why Wilson uses the term Multilevel Selection Theory. A full elaboration of the theory is beyond the scope of this book, but I recommend *The New Fable of the Bees* (citation below) as a starting place. To be clear, this theory doesn't suggest that deep down everything is peace and cherries with humans, but it does open the possibility that solidarity may be its own driver, as opposed to just an adaptive strategy of an ultimately selfish drive. David Sloan Wilson, "The New Fable of the Bees: Multilevel Selection, Adaptive Societies, and the Concept of Self Interest," *Evolutionary Psychology and Economic Theory Advances in Austrian Economics* 7 (2004): 201–220.

3   A far earlier and at least as significant disruption of traditional life was the advent of agriculture.

logic has advanced even in the past 50 years, it has disrupted many of the communitarian features that had carried over into modern societies as well. Today we often have a hard time telling what group we should identify with. We have to "code-switch" between the different spaces that we duck in and out of over the course of our daily routines—home, school, work, church, hobby, neighborhood, etc.—constantly trying to read the values and norms of "the group." It becomes a rare space where we can trust the group to have our back, where we can throw ourselves fully into the arms of the group, and trust that it will provide for our needs. We experience this lack as a longing, and when we find hints of this lost community we may fetishize it—whether it be in a monogamous relationship, a religious congregation, a sports team, or a social movement.

All the while we are barraged with an ideology of selfish individualism. We are constantly told that humans are individualistic benefit-maximizing, cost-minimizing creatures—naturally, evolutionarily, inherently, and thoroughly selfish. Economists, political scientists, and many others subscribe to the individual rational actor paradigm, which assumes such selfishness as the behavioral norm and dresses it up in the language of science, despite volumes of empirical evidence that debunks its merits. Fortunately for humanity, this paradigm prevails in real life only when certain conditions are present—specifically when social relations are structured such that individual selfishness is rewarded rather than sanctioned. Despite popular myths about "human nature," despite the individualistic dogma that masquerades as science in the fields of economics and political science, and despite the increasing penetration of neoliberalism into our most intimate spaces and relationships, it behooves us to take notice of the abundant evidence that most societies and groups throughout known human history have structured their social relations in such a way that encourages group-oriented behavior in individuals. Even today, in most settings—from a church group, to an extended family network, to a board room, to an army unit—the individual's social capital within a given group depends on the group's recognition of their service and sacrifice for the benefit of the group. In a brilliant "design" that is typical of social animals, individual benefit and group benefit are inextricably tied together.

Monetary capital, on the other hand, represents the one "world" in which this interdependence has been almost completely unhinged, freeing the private individual to accumulate his own stockpile without regard for anyone other than himself, without negative social repercussions. Economists, infatuated with this novel world, tend to project it onto all of humanity as the universal norm for behavior. And then they scratch their heads whenever they encounter costly individual sacrifice for the greater good; they clamor to find selfish motives, or they label the behavior "irrational" when no such motive can be found.

Even a great deal of sociological social movement theory tends to emphasize the seemingly autonomous choices of individuals. In the individual rational actor paradigm, the unit of analysis is the generic, atomized, essentially self-serving *individual*. When applied to social movements, the paradigm clumsily attempts to illuminate the supposed "mystery" of *collective* action—"why would selfish individuals sacrifice for the greater good?"—by only examining the peculiar *individuals* who do join collective efforts and their individual incentives for joining, while neglecting to examine the contexts or situations that tend to activate people (which, in reality, tends to occur more often in blocs and clusters than by luring lone individuals).

The common use of the term *entrepreneur* in academic literature to describe social movement innovators betrays this same view of the benefit-maximizing, cost-minimizing individual; a view that is taken for granted as the *modus operandi* of Homo sapiens. In this usage, *entrepreneur* indicates especially active, creative, and ambitious social movement participants who start new projects, organizations, or campaigns. It is, however, in my view, problematic and even grotesque to transpose an individual profit-maximizing logic and terminology onto a thoroughly collective project. Those who are central in facilitating the latter are commonly referred to as *leaders*—not *entrepreneurs*—on account of their savvy or skill in building consensus and solidarity and in articulating values, goals, targets, and strategies that can move whole groups. Their mission is not to maximize private profit. Indeed, for our purposes, their mission may be precisely to challenge, redistribute, or dismantle private profit.

Some sociologists initially used the individual rational actor framework sympathetically to describe social movements, attempting to assert the *rationality* of participants—i.e., the presence of self-interested, rational political goals—and to thereby counter *crowd theory*, which tended to pathologize collective action participants. Despite such good intentions, the individual rational actor paradigm has proven to be a wrongheaded approach to understanding collective action. Among its greatest deficiencies, it misses or at least minimizes the dynamic *life of the group*, which I have been describing throughout this book, as foundational to the motivational drive that fuels collective political action. The life of the group constitutes its own dynamic force that transcends the calculus of selfish individuals. The collectivity itself becomes the *expressive* and *instrumental* and *moral* motivation that drives individuals to lose themselves in the group and make sacrifices that, indeed, make little sense when the profit-maximizing atomized individual is the only unit of analysis. Yet, for such group-oriented behavior to exist, there must exist some process that orients individuals to the interests of a particularly framed group above their own autonomous interests. Such collective alignment processes are at the heart of the inquiry of this chapter.

Freeing our minds of the distortions of the individual rational actor paradigm, we can elaborate a more illuminating definition of politics; one that properly emphasizes *collective subjectivity*. Politics is fundamentally about *groups*. It is about the collective. The whole. The society. The particularly framed premise for solidarity. Politics is all about the *we*. It is a contest over the values, perimeters, and threats to the articulated *we*. Along these lines, political theorist Chantal Mouffe argues that "Liberal thought is also blind to the political because of its individualism, which makes it unable to understand the formation of collective identities. Yet the political is from the outset concerned with collective forms of identification, since in this field we are always dealing with the formation of 'us' as opposed to 'them.'"[4]

While the psychological mechanisms that drive political behavior may be physiologically located in the brains and bio-chemistry of individual human beings, the most potent polit-ical messages do not appeal to individualistic desires or self-ish drives. The most compelling political narratives in history are the ones that appeal to individuals' orientation toward the group, their desire to belong to the group, and even their will-ingness to sacrifice for the greater good of the group. This deep, pre-conscious—perhaps even primal—orientation toward "the group" is what political messages have to tap into, if they are to gain traction. Most people understand on some level how advertisers seek to bypass the mind's rational faculties by ap-pealing directly to the deeper drives of hunger, thirst, and sex, in order to sell a product. Few understand that effective politi-cal appeals do something comparable, only the deep drive they appeal to is our longing for belonging and our faculty for soli-darity. Throughout history, both the left and the right have en-gaged in this terrain. Martin Luther King Jr. and Ronald Rea-gan might have had diametrically opposed visions for America, but both of them excelled at making people feel like part of the *we* of America—even as these two Americas were worlds apart. Thus, the definition of the *we*—the "group" to which we feel a sense of identity, belonging, and allegiance—is among the most important stakes in any political struggle. Who is legitimately part of *we* (e.g., who is included in *"we the people"*?)? Where are its boundaries? Who is outside of the *we*? Who or what are *we* to consider a threat to *us*? What are the values of the *we*? And who gets to define all of the above?[5]

---

4   Mouffe, *Agonistics*, 4.

5   In Beyond the Choir's partnership work with social justice organiza-tions, we examine their narratives and their opponents' narratives through this lens, centered on the *we*: first deconstructing narratives in order to then construct more compelling ones.

The fiction we have to write

Almost overnight, Occupy Wall Street inserted into the popular vernacular the idea of *the 99%*—a *we* that was explicitly framed as a supermajority juxtaposed against a system rigged to serve a wealthy elite, the "one percent." The message resonated popularly and seemed to have opened up possibilities for building a long-term mass movement for social and economic justice in the United States. However, the move from named political grievances to broad-based collective action—at a scale capable of achieving political results—is neither automatic nor guaranteed. Indeed, in the case of Occupy, the initial catalyzing agent seems to have quickly exited the stage, at least for the moment, and with it the prospect of a larger social unification capable of intervening as a political force. At the time of this writing, the Bernie Sanders 2016 campaign showed again—and at a much larger scale—the ripe possibility of such an insurgent political alignment. However, even though the Sanders campaign provided compelling evidence that we are now operating with a backdrop of expanding political possibilities, we also know full well that the odds are still stacked against us. Lacking the political infrastructure and resources of our opponents, we are severely disadvantaged in the present political terrain. If we hope to replicate aspects of Occupy's intervention—especially its popular and politically advantageous framing of political and economic crises—and if we hope to extend the lifespan and momentum of future openings and leverage them politically, then it behooves us to study the processes involved in the kind of political alignment and mobilization of heterogeneous society that Occupy dabbled in—what I will call the process of constructing a *social unification*, or, more colloquially, a *we*.[6]

---

6   The term *social unification* (or simply *unification*) at its highest lev-
      el—as in categories like nation, race, ethnicity, religion, or class—is syn-
      onymous here with Benedict Anderson's term *imagined community*,
      and I use these terms somewhat interchangeably. By *proximate* group,
      I mean an organic social bloc or institution at a size and scale that can
      be directly and interactively experienced by group members.

For this we have to examine aspects of collective identity formation, alignment, and articulation, and the role of subjective political agency—i.e., organized groups with the capacity to intervene effectively—in these processes. By *collective identity*, I mean as it relates both to locally experienced *proximate* groups and to larger abstract "groups"—unifications or "imagined communities"—based on economic class, nation, race, ethnicity, religion, or other categories.[7] How do different social aggregations come to identify with political agendas and emergent social movements, and what factors encourage or constrain such politicization? How do political contenders—both elites and insurgent challengers—engage in hegemonic contests over the meanings and ownership of symbols, language, and narratives, in order to legitimate themselves, delegitimize opponents, and win the loyalty, alignment, or acquiescence of different social forces?

We should be clear that social unification, at least at the scale we will be discussing, is a kind of *fiction*. It requires a compelling story about the world and our place in it, about our friends and our foes, but like all stories, social unification involves imagination and partial representations of reality. This is precisely what is meant by *framing*: attention is drawn to certain details, while other details are cropped out of the frame. And as with all good stories, the protagonists symbolically represent the agendas of their narrators, but must also resonate with the aspirations of their audiences. Though only fiction, social unification is as consequential as it is politically necessary. With or without our conscious intervention, these processes will happen and will shape the world. They always do. Millions of people will align along different lines of cleavage, behind opposite political agendas, depending on the contingencies of these meaning-making processes. For instance, the story of the United States of America that prevails might be the one told by reactionary movements like the Tea Party and the Donald Trump campaign, or it might be one told by progressive movements like Occupy Wall Street, Black Lives Matter, the Dreamers, and the Bernie Sanders campaign.

---

7   Anderson, *Imagined Communities*.

It is clearly in our interest to intervene as effectively as possible in this contest.

This is why an aspiring political challenger must reject post-modernism's wholesale rejection of *metanarratives*—a term which postmodernists themselves coined.[8] A metanarrative is a grand philosophical story that attempts to explain the world for everyone. The Enlightenment and the story of progress are classic examples of metanarratives, but so is Marxism, and the term can be used more broadly to describe any "narrative" or explanatory schema that seeks to provide a universal account of the social world. To be clear, postmodernism's skeptical deconstruction of such metanar-ratives is a worthwhile endeavor, as it can help us to understand how language and symbols often gloss over social divisions and mask the operations of power. Importantly, metanarratives pres-ent *particular* interests as *universal*. For example, the Preamble to the United States Constitution disguised the particular interests of white male property owners by projecting them as the universal will of "We the people." Abolitionists and suffragettes understood this intuitively and resolved themselves to fight to expand who is included in "We the people." But in order to do so effectively, they appealed to the very concept of "We the people" and claimed their rightful share in it. With such contests in mind, we can see that the problem with postmodernism isn't its radical deconstruction, but that it stops there. Rather than fighting to claim "We the peo-ple" and to contest the meanings that elites intend as they wield the phrase, postmodernism posits that *there is no "We the people."* They are analytically correct. "We the people" is a fiction. However, after deflating this and other powerful metanarratives, postmod-ernism then just sits content in its comfy "revolutionary" armchair reveling in the lucidity of its own analytic critique.[9] To deflate a

8   Jean-François Lyotard, *The Postmodern Condition: A Report on Knowl-edge*, trans. Geoff Bennington and Brian Massumi (Minneapolis: Uni-versity of Minnesota Press, 1984).

9   Readers who are unfamiliar with postmodernism might understandably wonder why I am giving it so much attention here. If it kept to itself, I would not, but postmodernism is itself unavoidably—if ironically—a

metanarrative without offering something in its place is to deny people an alternative basis for social unification, which is to functionally deny them the basis for collective mobilization. Such was the "metanarrative vacuum" that Franklin Roosevelt named in his inaugural address when he proclaimed that "when there is no vision the people perish."[10] He proceded to play a key role—as instrumental actor and as popular symbol—in filling that vacuum by articulating a new vision and a new metanarrative: a new "fiction" to align and mobilize society along different lines.

And we should do likewise, understanding that such fictions are highly consequential, with the potential to make, in the words of Bourdieu, "the future that one utters come into being."[11] We cannot simply dismiss metanarratives as mere fictions—we must also recognize them as power moves that shape social and material reality. The residue of past historical fictions is tangible and observable in the present-day structuring of social reality, with all of its lopsided but rationalized distributions and concentrations of wealth and power. If we are serious about engaging *the political*—if we are to build the collective power it will take to win meaningful change—we have to do more than merely deconstruct currently hegemonic metanarratives. We also have to construct our own novel metanarratives with different contents, in the service of a social justice agenda; *construct*, but also claim and contest the meanings of popular symbols and elements of existing narratives. A compelling metanarrative—one that can realign society along different cleavages—is a fiction that we have to write.

But how or in what ways is social unification a *fiction*? In the context of contemporary mass society, many of the large-scale

---

metanarrative that has over the past three decades shaped the thinking of many in academia, which has concurrently shaped the thinking of many radicals and progressives, who have adopted much of postmodernism's language and assumptions, even if the intellectual history is not always known. I think it is worth naming explicitly (and worth picking a fight).

10   Here Roosevelt was quoting scripture verbatim (Proverbs 29:18).

11   Pierre Bourdieu, *Language & Symbolic Power* (Cambridge, MA: Harvard University Press, 1991), 222.

social categories we take for granted are highly abstract, even "imaginary." What does it really mean to be "middle class," to be "an American," to be a "person of color," or to be "white"? To be clear, by calling these different social categories *abstract* or *imaginary*—and to suggest that articulating them is comparable to "writing fiction"—does not mean there is nothing substantive about the category, or that for a social categorization to be *imaginary* means that it is inconsequential. To feel solidarity with people one has never met face-to-face requires a profound exercise of imagination. And this imagined solidarity can operate as the thread that weaves together otherwise dispersed elements into a potent political force capable of consequential intervention in the real world. When we examine the population of a nation like the United States, with more than 300 million people, we find heterogeneity and fragmentation. We find social clustering happening at much smaller and localized levels (geographical or cyber space) than that of "mass society." Mass society is a somewhat unnatural and precarious structure. Left to our own projects and whims, what motivation do we have to entertain the idea of a group at any scale that extends beyond the people we encounter in our immediate lived experience? Larger-scale social unification is hardly organic to the human organism. However, there is tremendous evidence that small-scale solidarity is. Thus any political project of large-scale social unification—e.g., a national public—has to appeal to this latter organic capacity; has to co-opt the locally derived, perhaps even instinctual, capacity for solidarity. Thus, we have to write a "fiction" that helps people to identify at a scale of social unification that is necessary for the corresponding scale of political intervention; e.g., to intervene in national political systems, you need a national social movement or political party.

Hegemonic orders produce and constantly reproduce the fiction of social unification. Just as importantly, they attempt to prevent alternative fictions—i.e., differently framed social unifications—from resonating popularly and ascending politically. If a political challenger wants to mount an actual challenge, it has to articulate a popularly resonant alternative (to the establishment or status quo) basis for unification. The historical task has more to do with "telling a good story" than it does with speaking the "truth." Here again postmodernism has a valid point in its critique of metanarratives. But just as we aim to arm our truth with power, we must also arm it with a good story. As we shall see, a "good story" is essential to constructing, wielding, and exercising power. Here we take to heart Chantal Mouffe's admonition that "the aim of a counter-hegemonic intervention is not to unveil 'true reality' or 'real interests', but to re-articulate a given situation in a new configuration."[12] We intervene as contenders in a contest over how a social unification is framed: who is in it, its parameters, protagonists, enemies and threats, external and internal—essentially a contest over popular meanings and common sense.

To articulate such a narrative is to simultaneously conjure into existence the social unification—and with it the alignment of political forces—that is needed to enter and to win the hegemonic contest. In Antonio Gramsci's concept of *articulation* we are not merely talking about rhetoric, even though there is a significant rhetorical component to it. Following and elaborating on Gramsci's use of the term, I use it to describe the formation of the political alignment itself. Words, narratives, and symbols—but also actions, interventions, campaigns, political developments, and institutional arrangements—can help to form a sense of shared interest, collective identity, and common sense, which can bring a political alignment into being.

I refer to these two interlocking components of articulation as *symbolic* and *institutional*. The *symbolic contest* and the *institutional contest* refer to two fundamental levels of operation of an aspiring hegemonic actor. The symbolic contest is over narratives, symbols, meaning, and common sense. Winning it is necessary but insufficient. When Occupy Wall Street articulated a popular narrative that named Wall Street and the "one percent" as culprits, did the latter hang their heads in shame and hand the reins over to "the 99%"? Of course not. Because Occupy came nowhere close to winning an institutional contest,

---

12   Mouffe, *Agonistics*, 79.

which requires a strong "ground game": strategic capacity to maneuver through the minutia of political terrain to shape structures, laws, policies, distributions of wealth, and relationships of power. The symbolic contest sets the cultural stage, while the institutional contest "gets the goods." An aspiring hegemonic actor gains *moral legitimacy* through the symbolic contest, and it proves its *political legitimacy*—i.e., its ability to deliver on its vision—through the institutional contest. I must stress that these "two" contests are conceptually distinct, but in real life they are inextricable.

The inclusive we

If the definition of *we* is an important stake in political struggle, then political contenders are competing to have their particular framing of *we* win out above alternative frames. In other words, each political contender wants as many people as possible to adopt the contender's definition of the *we*—because this provides the basis for collective mobilization (or acquiescence) along lines favorable to the contender. And this is why a political challenger must, whenever possible, refer to itself using the *inclusive we*. The audience should feel that—or at least wonder if—they are part of the *we*. With the slogan "We are the 99%!" it is possible that the speaker declaring it is referring only to herself and her relatively small band of comrades who are physically occupying Zuccotti Park. But it is also possible—and the television viewer at home might wonder—that the speaker is referring to the larger society; that she is *inviting* the audience member to identify as part of this broad *we*. The boundaries of the *we* are as ambiguous as possible for the intended audience member. However, the political challenger must also frame their political *opponents* as a *they*. In the words of Chantal Mouffe, "the constitution of a 'we'...requires as its very condition of possibility the demarcation of a 'they.'"[13] In the case at hand, "The 99%," with its logical remainder, accomplishes this quite nicely. The "one percent" is a brilliantly framed *they*.

---

13   Ibid., 5.

Elites, on the other hand, whenever possible, will refer to themselves using the *inclusive we*, and will refer to those challenging them as an *otherized they*.

Inclusive we: "As a society, we must have law and order."
Otherized they: "They're a bunch of outside agitators."

At the national level, as long as the economy is running relatively smoothly and other important indicators of stability are roughly up to par, those who sit at the helm of the current hegemonic order will benefit from an association between themselves—particular political actors—and the seat of power that they occupy, as that seat itself is among the most powerful symbols of the broader *we*. However, the economy does not always run "smoothly," let alone for the benefit of most people. And regimes can be destabilized in myriad ways. Costly military adventures seem to be a perpetual temptation for ambitious regimes, and their failure a recurring catalyst for change. These are among the "objective conditions" that can create opportunities for an aspiring political challenger to actually mount a viable political challenge. As the hegemonic order's narrative—i.e., its articulation of a *we*—loses currency, challengers may take advantage of the opening to articulate a different *we* that expands the crisis of legitimacy and that could ultimately result in a transfer of power, reforms, or structural change.

However, as we have seen throughout this book, aspiring political challengers also face "subjective" challenges—obviously in terms of less access to resources than our formidable opponents, but also in the form of dysfunction in our own internal operations, cultures, and approaches. A dispositional problem for many challengers is that we too often refer to ourselves using the *exclusive we*, thereby effectively contributing to our own otherization. This can happen in the most innocent and subtle ways. For example, I was listening to Michael Brune recently on National Public Radio's *The Dianne Reahm Show*. Brune is the executive director of The Sierra Club, and he was discussing climate change on the show. I've known Mike for years, and

I thought he was doing a great job of framing the issue, communicating the threat, naming villains, and so on. And he just sounded good.

But then suddenly he began a sentence with, "We in the environmental community..."

Game over. Listeners who do not identify as part of "the environmental community" will suddenly tune out. In an instant, Michael Brune went from sounding like a protagonist fighting for the future of the whole society to the executive director of a "special interest" group. The difference between "We as a society..." and "We in the environmental community..." is a whole world of difference in the (mostly unconscious) processes of identification and differentiation that are woven into the fabric of everyday symbolic communication.

For this reason it is noteworthy that Students for a Democratic Society's historic *Port Huron Statement* starts with the words, "We are people of this generation..." thereby positioning the authors and the organization as *part of* the broader society; as belonging to the broadest *we*. One might object that people of another generation might not feel like part of that *we*. Technically that may be true. But language is not only a technical thing. Language often taps ambiguity as a strategic device. The listener may not be a person "of *this* generation" but they are a *person* and they do belong to *a* generation, so there is a solid intuitive basis for sympathy and identification. The statement does not start out with "We are student activists..." A lot of "student activists" may proudly identify as such, but what such a label does, functionally, is start out by announcing an *exclusive/exclusionary we*—a *we* that most people do not feel themselves to be part of. Most people have never considered themselves to be "student activists"—and many may well harbor negative stereotypes about the latter that would block them from identifying with authors of a statement who have self-identified as such.

To further complicate this framework, let's consider another example of a distinct identity: military veterans. The military veterans I've been supporting in Iraq Veterans Against the War and more recently the #VetsVsHate campaign (which challenged

2016 Republican presidential candidates' xenophobic rhetoric) do intentionally lead with their distinctive veteran identity. At face value these veterans could be seen as using an "exclusionary we" in the same manner that Michael Brune did when talking about the "environmental community." However, veterans occupy a very different symbolic place in the national narrative than the "environmental community" currently does. Veterans are seen as key protagonists in the story of the United States of America, and as *protagonists*, they symbolize and invoke the broad *inclusive we.*

Radicals often have difficulty appreciating the importance of these subtle linguistic differences, cues, and maneuvers, precisely because they themselves tend to identify so strongly with differentiating labels (e.g., as *radical, activist, revolutionary,* etc.). Indeed, we often use these various forms of an exclusionary *we* to signal identification with each other as members of an exclusive enclave. But if we are aiming to organize, mobilize, and align with broader social bases—beyond the "usual suspects"—then our attention to these subtle linguistic and symbolic cues is of paramount importance. It may only take one stray word to turn off a person or a whole community. Change agents have to take seriously the question of how others are likely to perceive us, and we have to bend accordingly. It is not a matter of "compromising our politics." It's about speaking in a language that people can hear, meeting people where they are.

Anatomy of a political narrative

The symbolic contest is much more than the logistics of public relations or social media amplification. It requires more than "messaging" as an afterthought that's tacked onto an action or a campaign to make it look or sound pretty, after everything else has been decided. A narrative strategy has to be woven into the fabric of everything we do. Narrative is fundamental to how we humans make sense of the world. When we see something, experience something, or hear about something that is unfamiliar to us, we tend to search anxiously for how to assimilate the new information into our operative narrative. By "operative narrative," I mean the accumulation of stories we tell ourselves and each other daily—about ourselves, our roles and responsibilities, and how our lives and routines fit into the bigger picture. Narrative frames our thinking, our actions, and importantly, our social identifications and loyalties. We may "tell stories," but stories also *tell us* how to act and what to do.[14]

The powerful "tell stories" to legitimate themselves—their power, privileges, and the uneven distributions of wealth that are structured under their hegemony. These *dominant narratives* serve to legitimate the status quo and tend to be internalized by many groups in a given society. Indeed, maintaining this kind of "buy-in" by enough groups is essential for the operation of hegemony. As such, ruptures in dominant narratives—triggered, for example, by an economic downturn, war, natural disasters, or visible fissures amongst elites—may portend a *crisis of legitimacy* for the hegemonic order. In such a scenario, ruling elites have to assimilate the rupture into the old hegemonic narrative, while political challengers have the potential opportunity to advance a counter-narrative (i.e., a more convincing story) to mobilize society along different lines. In both cases, "narrative" isn't everything. More raw forms of power are also always at play (e.g., police or military force, or storming the Bastille), but the path to victory for outgunned and out-resourced challengers depends heavily on how we do in the symbolic contest over meanings—i.e., upon compellingly articulating the realignment of political forces.

What, then, does a compelling political narrative look like? Are there elements that we can identify, in order to construct the most effective narratives possible? The basic elements found in most good stories are easy enough to identify. First, you need a

---

14   Here I am paraphrasing my friends from the Center for Story-based Strategy (CSS), whose work on narrative strategy I am indebted to: "Just as we tell ourselves stories about the world we live in, stories also tell us how to live." Patrick Reinsborough and Doyle Canning, *Re:Imagining Change: How to Use Story-based Strategy to Win Campaigns, Build Movements, and Change the World* (Oakland, CA: PM Press, 2010), 17.

protagonist with whom the audience will identify.[15] The protagonist then has to encounter some kind of challenge, obstacle, or threat. "Little Red Riding Hood walked through the forest without incident, arrived at her grandmother's house, and had a nice visit," is not much of a story.[16] Our protagonist has to face adversity and overcome it. A visceral way to embody such a challenge or threat in a story is in the form of a villain—a big bad wolf.

The best political narratives follow this structure and utilize these elements. And these elements are not arbitrary. To understand how to articulate a compelling protagonist and a compelling villain, it helps to understand the social-psychological functions that such "characters" fulfill. In political narratives, protagonists are compelling to the extent that they symbolically represent the aspirations of the audience. In so doing, a protagonist coheres the audience into a group. The best protagonists heroically serve and sacrifice for the greater good. This is precisely why military service members and veterans are quintessential protagonists in national stories, where the nation is "the group" with which the audience is led to identify.[17]

As for villains, they are compellingly villainous inasmuch as

---

15   The question of who counts as a "sympathetic" protagonist is not straightforward. Indeed, central to a given social group's political contention might be popular prejudice against them as members of a category (e.g., queer, black, homeless). As such, presenting a sympathetic protagonist does *not* mean finding someone who is *already* viewed sympathetically. The power of a protagonist is that once audiences identify with her, they may then have to question their prejudice against the category to which she, the protagonist, belongs. And there are techniques that can be used to effectively present a person as a sympathetic protagonist, even to a prejudiced audience.

16   Again, I'm borrowing an example that I've heard used by my friends at the Center for Story-based Strategy. For more information about CSS, see http://www.storybasedstrategy.org/.

17   This is what my colleague Jose Vasquez refers to as the *veteran mystique*, which we at Beyond the Choir simultaneously critique and seek to utilize strategically and conscientiously.

they pose a threat to the framed group. Villains tend to pose one of two types of threats to groups: *external* or *internal*. The most treacherous villains pose both kinds of threat at once. The external enemy tends to be a one-dimensional caricature bent on destruction for no reason other than bitterness or barbarism. Right-wing nationalist stories often appeal to racist and xenophobic stereotypes to invoke a one-dimensional menacing *other* (e.g., the caricatured brown-skinned, Muslim, freedom-hating terrorist motivated by pure hatred and evil). "Inner enemies,"[18] on the other hand, make for compelling villains because of their betrayal of the group's trust. The opposite of the self-sacrificing hero protagonist, such villains are mad with greed; they jeopardize the group by recklessly pursuing their own selfish ambition, willing to throw their own kin under the bus for a buck. Villains, perhaps even more than protagonists, can be conjured to trigger the powerful solidaristic bonding of the framed group, which congeals into a singular body united against a common enemy.

There is a clear "rationality" at work in such stories, but as political persuasion, it is very different from the fully conscious rational argumentation lauded by Enlightenment thinkers. And it is starkly different from the rationality of the individual rational actor paradigm. It is the rationality of morality, which is the rationality of groups.[19] It is no coincidence that we speak of "the moral of the story." Stories serve to reinforce shared ideas of right and wrong—i.e., morality. And the perceived good of the group—though always contested and ever-changing—is what centers moral systems.

The best political speeches in history have used these elements. And groups can intentionally construct these elements—*us, them, protagonist, antagonist,* among others—and embed them into their campaigns and messages.

---

18   Simmel, *On Individuality and Social Forms*, 144.

19   This can help us to understand mass society theorists' mistake in describing individuals who joined crowd actions as "irrational." These theorists were judging group-level rationality through the lens of an individualistic rationality.

Anatomy of a Political Narrative
A worksheet to explore the components of a compelling political narrative.

My organization, Beyond the Choir, uses the worksheet below to support social change organizations and campaigns in understanding the narratives of their opponents, while assessing their own campaign narratives, in order to ultimately reconstruct the latter. In this we are indebted to our long-time allies at Center for Story-based Strategy (CSS), whose Battle of the Story worksheet originally introduced us to some of these "elements of a story."

Gather samples of "discourse" related to your group's mission or campaign: news articles, editorials, interviews, press releases, flyers, web pages, photos, audio and video clips, social media posts, memes, etc. Ideally the mix will include samples that your group has full control over (e.g., your mission statement or a press release), samples that your opponents have full control over, and samples that you and your opponents alike may influence but not fully control (e.g., a news story). Divide into small groups (3–6 people) and examine the different samples, one at a time. In your small groups carefully read, watch, or listen to—depending on the medium—the sample narrative, examining it through the ten prompts below. Review the sample a few times to look for what you might have missed the first time around. Take notes. When all the small groups reconvene, each group will then report back its answers and insights from the small-group discussions. In the discussion, dig into disagreements (e.g., about what is effective and ineffective, etc.).

1. Who is the we?
Who is the we in the narrative? Look at all of the instances in which the words we, us, our, etc. appear. To whom do these words refer? Is the we broad and inclusive (i.e., "we as a society") or is it narrow and exclusive (i.e., "we, members of this activist group"), or is it ambiguous? Is the we compelling to the intended audience? Will they identify as part of the we? What other words refer to—or are imbued with—a sense of we in the minds of the intended audience? Is the we framed strategically (i.e., with intention)?

2. Who is the other?
If the we includes those who are framed as being inside of the circle of solidarity, then who is outside of that circle? Who (or what) is the other in the narrative? Is the other neutral or is it a threat or an enemy? Is the other framed strategically (i.e., with intention)?

3. Who are the protagonists?
Without a protagonist, there isn't much of a story. Instead there are facts, information, and rational arguments. Who in the story is the intended audience supposed to identify with? Is there a compelling protagonist in the story? Why or why not? How could the protagonist be more compelling? What are the characteristics of a good protagonist? How does the protagonist relate to the we? How does the story you're looking at measure up?

4. Who are the villains? What are the threats?
Who or what is to blame for the problem? Does the story have an antagonist or villain? How are threats articulated in the narrative? Do they seem compelling? Are they personified? How do compelling threats relate to the we?

5. What is the conflict?
What is the conflict about, according to the narrative? What is at issue? What is at stake? How is the conflict framed in order to appeal to the audience's values (i.e., to win the audience's sympathy)? Is the conflict presented as a matter of common sense? Is this done effectively? Why or why not?

6. Emotions
What is the narrative's emotional appeal? What emotions and sentiments does the story evoke (e.g., hope, fear, anger, disgust, determination, etc.)? How is this done? To what effect?

7. Symbols and images
What images and symbols are used in the narrative? Remember that stories are different than rational arguments; while the latter aims for clarity, the former often artfully plays with ambiguity, which may include invoking images and popular symbols—e.g., national flags, borders, historical figures, religious icons, scripture, etc.—whose meanings are ambiguous and contested. How and to what effect does the narrative use images and symbols to win the intended audience's sympathy? What other images and symbols could be invoked?

8. Assumptions
What does the audience have to already believe in order for this narrative to be compelling? What are the prior assumptions that must already be accepted?

9. Vulnerabilities
What are the narrative's weakest places? Are there parts of the narrative that are vulnerable to scrutiny? Are there threads that, if 'pulled on', could unravel the whole narrative? What might that look like?

10. Deadwood
What is bland or distracting? What is 'beside the point', extraneous to the main message, or taking up space without doing anything?

Lines of cleavage

Think back to the discussion in chapter three about the "personal becoming political," where problems that had been viewed as isolated incidents, personal problems, or "natural" facts of life are articulated as grievances common to a group of people—grievances whose cause is structural and whose remedy is collective political action. As we have seen in this chapter, the existence of a compelling collective identity itself has to be articulated. Dispersed and fragmented social elements have to come to see themselves as part of a *we*. As this *we* is articulated, so a political alignment is constructed, first to a point where it can even be meaningfully identified as a configuration that holds together, and then to a point where it constitutes a *political force*; i.e., it garners resources and capacity by way of a mobilized social base so as to be able to effectively contend on the political terrain. Such a nascent force inevitably starts out as an underdog who enters into an asymmetrical contest staged upon a ground that moves. The emergent political challenger has to navigate the constraints of a game whose rules and uneven power distributions are rigged against even its emergence as a subjective political actor, let alone that actor's concrete political achievements. Thus, a political challenger's successful formation—as a *we*, and as a vehicle—will not inevitably result in it winning measurable gains, but it does signal a visible threat to elites and the status quo of its potential to do so.

Again, Occupy Wall Street provides a remarkable case study of the rapid formation of such an insurgent *we*. The rallying cry, "We are the 99 percent!" popularly framed a new basis for class solidarity in US society. Heterogeneous and fragmented social elements, whose various struggles may have hitherto seemed disconnected, suddenly shared reference points: a name for their common interests and a name for their common enemy.

Sociologist Pierre Bourdieu described "the evocative power of an utterance," which spoken at the right time can put "things in a different light." Such an utterance "modifies the schemes of perception, shows something else, other properties, previously unnoticed or relegated to the background (such as common interests hitherto masked by ethnic or national differences); a separative power, a distinction ... drawing discrete units out of indivisible continuity, difference out of the undifferentiated."[20]

Here we might describe economic inequality as a property, which for a few decades prior to Occupy had been "unnoticed or

---

20   Bourdieu, *Distinction*, 479.

relegated to the background" in the United States; a common interest "hitherto masked" by differences. It could be argued that the 2008 financial crisis was the initial catalyst for this revived class solidarity, as bankers and Wall Street executives were popularly perceived as villains, along with the politicians who did their bidding. However, until Occupy Wall Street came along, no political challenger arose to narrate the crisis, to name and challenge the culprits, or to frame a popular collective protagonist. One might object that Occupy hardly posed much of a threat to these powers, or that it mobilized insufficiently to even be considered a popular collective protagonist, to which I would answer that Occupy amounted to a fledgling version of the level of operation necessary. Applying the terms I have been using, Occupy was remarkably successful in the *symbolic contest*, but performed poorly in the *institutional contest*, partly because many occupiers objected on principle to key aspects of this contest (as discussed in chapters four and five). If Occupy had (1) not had an allergic reaction to organization, leadership, and power, and (2) had a greater level of organizational resources and political savvy, it might have constituted such a challenge. At that point—in a parallel universe—victory would still not even be close to assured, but the political force (that could potentially deliver that victory) would be far more credible.

Murray Edelman similarly discussed the power of names: how a name highlights particular commonalities that constitute the distinct premises for collective mobilization and alignment. A name:

> ...is presented to our attention and calls for a rsponse. But every name is a metaphor. It specifies some property which a class of objects has in common. It thereby calls attention to that property and by the same token draws attention away from other properties. The name "table" calls attention to a flat, raised surface suitable for eating or writing but ignores other properties of the wood and spaces comprising a table. The term "white supremacy" calls attention to differences in skin color, associated differences in power and status relationships, and all the myths these

concepts evoke. It is in a different universe of discourse from the flesh and blood white and Negro people working and mingling in specific places in all their multifaceted concreteness.[21]

Here a name frames the group itself, the basis of solidarity. Like a picture frame, the name helps to determine what is included in the scene that we (are encouraged to) see and also what is cropped out. The term "white supremacy" may be invoked to frame an exclusionary solidarity among people who apparently have "white" skin (even if *who* gets to be "white" is ever-changing), while shared interests of wage laborers across the color line are cropped out of the picture.[22] Bourdieu specifically mentioned ethnic and national differences as culprits that can mask such shared interests.

We might go a step further to conceptualize nationalism and ethnicity (as well as race, religion, and other categories) not only as things that *mask* common interests, but also as *competing bases* of differently framed social solidarities, each of which invokes a differently framed "common interest." In other words, premises for solidarity such as race and nation—and their corresponding "common interests"—can and often have prevailed over economic class-based solidarity as a basis for political mobilization (or for acquiescence). Alternatively, we could say that *the class-based solidarity of the dominant classes* often wins the day in large part by hiding itself behind other premises for solidarity, grafting the latter onto the former's hegemonic projects. Such was the American scene whence Occupy Wall Street emerged: the race-based solidarity of "whites"—i.e., the wave of veiled race-based appeals for white solidarity that followed the social movements of "the 1960s," (even if effectively disguised in "non-racial" code words)—and the nation-based solidarity, stoked in no small part by the Cold War, had colluded and were wielded as weapons for

---

21　　Murray Edelman, *The Symbolic Uses of Politics* (Urbana & Chicago: University of Illinois Press, 1985 [1964]), 157.

22　　Frederick Douglass, "The Color Line," *The North American Review* 132, no. 295 (1881): 567–577.

decades to mask the class interests of business elites, against the class interests of most Americans.[23] Four decades after business elites launched their devastating counter-offensive against the hard-won gains of organized labor and other social movements in the four decades prior, Occupy arrived and named *the 99%* as a basis for the mobilization and political enfranchisement of ordinary working people, contra Wall Street and *the one percent*.[24]

Occupy Wall Street emerged practically overnight and entered immediately into a symbolic contest—at the level of meaning and "common sense"—against dominant economic and political establishment forces. The next thing we needed to do was to expand our operations in an *institutional contest*. We had to activate our sympathizers, bringing them into an aligned political force. In conceptual terms: we had to win the psychic investments of *proximate groups* into a far larger, particularly framed *social unification*, in order to contest hegemony. The psychic investments of members of such groups are a requirement of political alignment and mobilization. Indeed, such investment is a large part of what is meant here by *political alignment*. For a political project to win this investment and alignment it must translate abstractions into potent messages that resonate within local communities. The sky has to be brought "down to earth." The new "gospel" has to connect to local, already-existing beliefs, narratives, symbols, norms, and rituals (even as nothing it touches is left unchanged). In order to manifest, the frame of a large-scale social unification (like "the 99%") must be internalized at the local group level. And that internalization depends on a felt connection between the organically derived solidarity values and the larger abstraction. Digging into such particulars is how a mass movement takes root at the local, proximate level. What does this look like? To name just one example, consider the

---

23   Ian Haney López, *Dog Whistle Politics: How Coded Racial Appeals Have Reinvented Racism and Wrecked the Middle Class* (New York: Oxford University Press, 2014).

24   Mark S. Mizruchi, *The Fracturing of the American Corporate Elite* (Cambridge, MA: Harvard University Press, 2013).

political moment when the new meme and political claim "Black Lives Matter" went from hashtags and protests in a few cities to a message preached from the pulpit in religious congregations across the nation. One important measure of a movement's capacity is its reach in converting such "spontaneous" expressions of sympathy into coordinated and targeted political action.

Complicating this framework, individuals in modern societies usually identify with multiple groups, framed along different lines of identity, and these fluctuate in precedence for each individual. Most of us juggle multiple roles in the different spheres of our lives, each of which holds a degree of our individual identity and pulls us in different, often conflicting, directions. "We often recognize the lines of cleavage that run through us," asserted sociologist George Mead.[25] It can be tempting, then, to look at identity as a predominantly individual matter, and to conceptualize the modern individual as a kind of consumer who shops for various aspects of their own personal identity. However, each sphere of an individual's fragmented life has its own *group logic* and *group processes* of constructing values and identity. Turning again to Mead: "There are all sorts of different selves answering to all sorts of different social reactions. It is the social process itself that is responsible for the appearance of the self; it is not there as a self apart from this type of experience."[26]

For our purposes here, the term *group* has a range of meanings and scales. A group may be *proximate*: organic, definable, and localized, such as one's neighborhood, workplace, or place of worship. Or "group" may refer to larger *abstract* categories of identification: race, ethnicity, nation, economic class, gender, sexual orientation, religion, or political ideology. People project group-oriented sympathies and behaviors onto a gamut of social aggregations and constructions—proximate and abstract—to a degree that is proportional to their level of identity with the given group.

Restating the anti-individualist framework I have been elaborating: humans do not typically engage the world as lone-wolf

---

25   Mead, *Mind, Self and Society*, 143.

26   Ibid., 142.

individuals; we act as members of groups, with our motivational calculus attuned to the culture and the will of the group. In such a world, proximate groups are always functionally competing with each other for their members' identification and commitment (e.g., workplace versus family versus church), while also interacting with larger abstract group identifications (e.g., working class versus nation versus race versus religion) with their different, though often overlapping, logics, symbols, and narratives. Proximate groups tend to act as intermediaries between the individual and the larger imagined community, as people come together in person (e.g., at church, around the water cooler, at the bar, or at the dinner table) to make meaning of events, experiences, and exposure to mass media. Children discuss with classmates what they watched on television the night before and attune their own opinions to the group's verdicts. Such organic settings can constitute (or be part of) distinct *fields*—in the sense elaborated by Pierre Bourdieu and Loïc Wacquant—each of which "prescribes its particular values and possesses its own regulative principles."[27] And "In the manner of a prism," the group (or the field) "refracts external forces according to its internal structure."[28] In other words, individuals rarely experience cultural developments or political events directly: the impact is mediated by the meaning-making processes of the proximate groups to which individuals belong. And while groups may tend to internalize values of the dominant cultures that they are situated within, there are always important exceptions to this, and such identification is also affected by the group's status or position within the society. For example, a black church in Chicago will likely interpret very differently the collective action coming out of Ferguson, Missouri following the police shooting of 18-year-old Mike Brown than a neighborhood watch association in a predominantly white middle-class suburb of Phoenix, Arizona.

---

27 Loïc J. D. Wacquant, "Toward a Social Praxeology: The Structure and Logic of Bourdieu's Sociology," in *An Invitation to Reflexive Sociology*, by Pierre Bourdieu and Loïc J. D. Wacquant (Chicago: The University of Chicago Press, 1992), 17.

28 Ibid.

The level of a group's or individual's identification with any one type of abstract construction over another (e.g., nationalism over class-consciousness, or religion over both) depends on many factors and may fluctuate from one "political moment" to the next. As already discussed, perceptions of a common enemy or threat can be especially potent in triggering group-oriented behaviors into the service of a particularly framed unification (e.g., a nation or a political party). These motivational feelings of solidarity are the lifeblood of politics. Mead saw such in-group solidarity as being driven by "barbarous impulses," but saw this as necessary to "keep our ordinary institutions running" and to help "enlist the interest of people in public affairs."[29] People who are riled up by a commonly perceived threat may be more likely to turn out to vote or to join a public demonstration. Chantal Mouffe even argues that there can be no politics without a *them*; that in politics "we are always dealing with the formation of 'us' as opposed to 'them.'"[30]

However, serious dangers also lurk in such feelings, as the "threat" that bolsters *in-group* solidarity is often articulated as a personified enemy. This ugly underbelly of group solidarity has manifested severely in the forms of war, xenophobia, and racism. Concerning war, Mead discussed the:

> ...great deal of exhilaration in situations involved in the hostility of other nations ... we all seem at one against a common enemy; the barriers drop, and we have a social sense of comradeship to those standing with us in a common undertaking. The same thing takes place in a political campaign. ...a person does get outside of himself, and by doing so makes himself a definite member of a larger community than that to which he previously belonged. This enlarged experience has a profound influence... It is the sense of belonging to the community, of having an intimate relationship with an indefinite number of individuals who belong to the same group.[31]

---

29   Mead, *Mind, Self and Society*, 220.

30   Mouffe, *Agonistics*, 4.

31   Mead, *Mind, Self and Society*, 218–219.

The Pearl Harbor attack and 9/11 attack are two potent examples of events in US history that triggered a dramatic revitalization of the sense of a particularly framed "larger community." The popular perception of "a common enemy" triggered intense feelings of nationalism—the nation as the "group" with which to identify—stoked and channeled by elite political actors. Along similar lines, nation-based solidarity eclipsed class-based solidarity in most industrialized nations in the lead-up to the First World War. Such patterns can be manipulated by elites to march a nation to war and for myriad other purposes.

It would be a costly mistake, however, to think of this kind of articulation of an *us* and a *them* as the exclusive domain of elites (or of the right). Instead we must conceptualize a contestable symbolic terrain. When a challenger movement emerges, it too has to name a common enemy and simultaneously frame a different kind of solidarity as a basis for political mobilization. A century ago communists, socialists, anarchists, and unionists named bosses, banks, and capitalism as common enemies of a new unification: *workers of the world*. Occupy Wall Street accomplished a conceptually similar maneuver by naming Wall Street and the financial system—and capitalism, if ambiguously—as a common enemy of a new unification: *the 99%*. Such momentous interventions and game-changing events are dramatic flashpoints in much larger and longer processes through which heterogeneous groups align under competing unification frameworks, through epochs of political struggle. The political contest is over the premises of unification (i.e., its meanings, symbols, narratives, parameters, protagonists, and enemies), both *within* particular unification projects and *between* competing unification projects. These aspects of the contest overlap and get mixed up with each other. A project rooted in one premise for solidarity will often graft another premise for solidarity onto itself.

In addition to nation and class, we can see how race, ethnicity, and religion are other common and consequential bases for social unification and division in modern societies, taking particular forms in different contexts around the world. Historically in the United States, through the present moment, the complex tension between an economic class basis and a racial basis for solidarity has been a central challenge to forging a broad progressive political alignment. While all of these different bases of unification and division are in some sense in competition with one another for popular resonance, they also get mixed up with each other in all sorts of complex and messy ways. Nationalism and racism, for example, often go hand-in-hand, operating symbiotically, as we can see today with Donald Trump's repeated calls to build a wall on the US-Mexico border and to ban Muslims from entering the country. But how nation and race get mixed together as premises for solidarity is not always so straightforward or reactionary. While cynical political actors often paint a picture of the nation by using the colors of race, at the same time the concept of *citizenry* (central to the nation's basis of legitimacy) invokes the notion of universal suffrage, which provides a powerful rhetorical premise for those who are excluded and exploited on the margins to claim the symbols of the nation in order to assert their own existence, dignity, inclusion, rights, and rightful share—thereby weakening the basis of racism's potency.[32]

It is also important to note that elites are not the only ones who play at the game of mobilizing along racial and ethnic lines as a basis of solidarity. Social justice-oriented challengers often engage in this terrain too, but—and the importance of this can hardly be overstated—the way that they do so and the ends that they do it for are quite different. The slogans "White Power!" and "Black Lives Matter!" are not remotely equivalent or symmetrical. The former, as a political operation, aims to defend or consolidate privilege and exclusion, while the latter attempts to advance dignity, equality, and inclusion. To reduce these two operations to two equivalent "groups," each seeking to advance its own respective interests in similar fashion is to miss stark power asymmetries and equally stark differences in visions for the organization of the broader society and its distributions of wealth, power, and

---

32   On the other hand, the framework of *citizenry* may pose particular challenges to "non-citizen" immigrants who are attempting to assert comparable political claims.

rights.[33] Yet, it remains important for progressive political challengers to recognize that they and their opponents—however vile the latter's visions may be—both inhabit the same broad symbolic universe and must both navigate the same political terrain, albeit from different positions and in order to achieve antithetical goals.

Historically the left has attempted to mobilize society along lines of class interests, over and above other premises for solidarity. However, mobilizing on the singular basis of economic class is often not easy, or necessarily desirable. Underdog social movements that seek to use class as the basis for solidary mobilization face some unique challenges that other bases of unification, like nation, race, ethnicity, and religion, do not seem as constrained by. For starters, understanding complex social, economic, and political structures can be a lot less intuitive to most people than grasping personified one-dimensional "evil villains." The former tends to take considerably more cognitive work. This is one reason why political challengers often end up mobilizing on the pretext of "corruption" or incompetence, as this allows them to single out especially scorn-worthy *individuals*. (This is how we got the slogan "Anyone but Bush!") While such a move may facilitate popular sympathy or mobilization, it also tends to limit the vision and trajectory of the same. Individual politicians may be successfully dethroned or "thrown under the bus" while the structural basis of the problems that they symbolically represented remains fully intact, and perhaps even unarticulated as a threat.

It is important to note the asymmetry between how the right and the left each tend to personify the enemy or threat. Both sides tend to be relatively unrestrained in their attacks against individual politicians, but that's about as far as parity goes. Historically,

---

33   Even the more similar *seeming* phrases "White Power!" and "Black Power!" despite appearances, are not remotely symmetrical, because of the contextualized meaning of each slogan in relation to the histories and relative positions of the two named "peoples," whites and blacks, in the social structure of the United States, as well as the implied instructions for those individuals who heed the slogans.

and up through the present, the reactionary right tends to scape-goat *kinds of people*, like blacks, Jews, immigrants, or homosexu-als—overtly or by deploying code words, an evolved strategy that seems to be more effective in the United States today[34]—while the left tends to name structures as the basis of grievances. Even when the left names and blames individuals, this is usually in re-lation to the *positions* they occupy within *structures*, rather than essentialized distinguishing features of their bodies, sexualities, or cultures. The moral significance of this difference between how the left and right tend to strategically engage in the symbol-ic contest can hardly be overstated. A related difference, which carries with it a related challenge, is that the left's fight tends to be about articulating a broader and more inclusive *we*, while the right's fight tends to be about articulating a narrower and exclu-sionary *we*.

The difficulty of stoking passions about *structures* is one rea-son why economic class can be hard to mobilize around. Sociolo-gist Immanuel Wallerstein provides additional insights into why class is the odd one out when it comes to premises for political unification and solidary mobilization: "Classes are really quite a different construct from peoples, as both Marx and Weber knew well. Classes are 'objective' categories, that is, analytic categories, statements about contradictions in an historical system, and not descriptions of social communities."[35]

Economic class describes the objective relationships to ma-terial production and of uneven distributions of capital in soci-ety. But it does not describe in a straightforward and intuitive manner routine activities like attending church, going out to the bar with friends, playing a pickup game of basketball, sit-ting around the dinner table, or holding one's hand over one's heart during *The Star Spangled Banner*. These are the everyday spaces, places, and activities through which identity is formed

---

34   López, *Dog Whistle Politics*.

35   Immanuel Wallerstein, "The Construction of Peoplehood: Racism, Na-tionalism, Ethnicity," in *Race, Nation, Class: Ambiguous Identities*, by Étienne Balibar and Immanuel Wallerstein (London and New York: Verso, 1991), 84.

and invested in. To the extent that these spaces are segregated along lines of race, ethnicity, and religion, the group identities produced therein will be imbued with the distinct cultural "essences" of these different and differentiating social constructs. Thus, race, ethnicity, or religion often *feel* like real and compelling categories—and legitimate bases for categorization—while economic class tends to be "a very elusive entity."[36] Objectively, economic class is the *most real* basis of categorization, as it is quantifiable in terms of possession of measurable wealth. But that does not mean that *race* and *nation* can therefore be dismissed as "mere fictions." Even though these categorization schemes are historical inventions and fabrications, their consequences are undeniably objectively real.

Moreover, because economic classes tend to cluster and become spacially segregated from each other, it follows that, in the words of Wallerstein, "constructed 'peoples'—the races, the nations, the ethnic groups—correlate so heavily, albeit imperfectly, with 'objective class.'"[37] So, if groups are spatially segregated by race and there is economic stratification between racially separated groups, then racial identities will be partly defined by class realities and racial conflict will get mixed up with class conflict. "The consequence has been that a very high proportion of class-based political activity in the modern world has taken the form of people-based political activity. The percentage will turn out to be even higher than we usually think if we look closely at so-called 'pure' workers' organizations that quite frequently have had implicit and *de facto* 'people' bases, even while utilizing a non-people, purely class terminology."[38]

This helps to explain why Caesar Chavez and the United Farm Workers succeeded where the Agricultural Workers Organizing Committee of the AFL-CIO failed. Some have attributed Chavez's success to his special charisma, but key to the functioning of Chavez's "charisma" was his savvy in tapping into workers' existing racial-ethnic-religious cultural identities (and

---

36   Ibid.

37   Ibid.

38   Ibid.

corresponding social networks) in order to make shared class interests feel salient. In other words, he didn't try to recruit workers to identify with a brand new (and unfamiliar) "we"; instead, he re-articulated key meanings within a "we" that workers already felt themselves belonging to.[39]

The "we" that we need

The point isn't to just invent a new "we"—a new basis for solidarity—from scratch. Instead we have to tap into the solidarities that people already feel (like Caesar Chavez did). But different possibilities for different bases of solidarity—and different premises for *political alignment*—become possible depending on many kinds of factors and developments: historical, economic, cultural, sociological, and spacial.

We can view political alignment as a process by which heterogeneous individuals or groups that had seen themselves and their situations as separate, even isolated, from each other, come to see important common features in their problems to the point where aligned action amongst hitherto fragmented agents becomes compelling. They may discover that their problems are similar, or that they are caused by the same culprits, structures, enemies, or threats. Georg Simmel discussed: "when circles that are isolated from one another become approximately alike."[40] For example, when equivalent processes of industrialization spread across the globe to nations and regions that were separated by both geographical distance and cultural distinctions, the similar industrializing processes increased "the likelihood that an ever increasing number of structures [would] develop in one group that have equivalents in the other."[41] We can think of the different geographical and cultural locations as "complexes" where "a

---

39   To be clear, this was still no easy task, in part because there was not only one single racial-ethnically defined "we" among the farm workers the UFW was organizing—there were several.

40   Simmel, *On Individuality and Social Forms*, 252.

41   Ibid.

likening...or ideal equivalence" results "between parts of the... complexes."[42] This kind of process, "quite apart from all bonds based on shared substantive interests, will often lead to actual relations between the elements of any two—or of many—groups that have been made alike in this way. One observes this, for example, in the international sympathy that aristocrats hold for one another. ...solidarities also develop at the other end of the social scale, as in the internationalism of social democrats and in the sentiments underlying the earlier journeymen's unions."[43]

This organic solidarity that seems to arise naturally, almost inevitably, from *likeness* is what convinced Karl Marx that a proletariat would imminently emerge in response to industrialization and capitalist property relations, recognize itself, and congeal into a potent historical actor—the premise for the unity of "the people." To an important extent, this did, indeed, happen. However, other premises for unification, other than economic class, persisted and evolved. These premises have time and again been stoked by dominant political actors in order to obfuscate the hegemonic rule of dominant class interests. The "branches" of one premise of solidarity are grafted onto the "trunk" of another.

But here we must pause to acknowledge—and even celebrate—the fact that things do not always work out for elites. While these contests over the premises of the unification and division of society may be stacked to favor the already powerful, history provides plenty of cases where social justice–oriented underdogs have prevailed. The contest is heavily asymmetrical, but the outcome is nevertheless contingent. From the preceding discussion we can formulate three related hypotheses to structure a concept of this contingency: (1) Dominant political actors maintain hegemony in part by projecting their particular interests as universal, i.e., as the common sense for an imagined unification—a *we*—whose components are otherwise fragmented or heterogeneous; (2) Effective political challengers, in order

---

42   Ibid., 253.

43   Ibid., 253

to assemble an insurgent force strong enough to unseat or win substantial concessions from elites, must construct their own universalizing frames of a differently imagined unification—a differently framed *we*; (3) The ensuing *symbolic contest* between elites and challengers over the popular meanings, narratives, and symbols of the imagined unification constitutes an important part of the alignment and activation of various social forces in a given society (e.g., social blocs, institutions, or political parties), which comprise the "ground game" necessary for winning an *institutional contest* that consolidates symbolic victories into policy, law, and structural transformations.

Examining the case of Occupy Wall Street through the lens of this general framework, we find a particular case that seems to fit part of the second conceptual hypothesis, which concerns the articulation and assemblage of a popular political actor out of hitherto fragmented pieces. Occupy may have fallen short in assembling a sufficiently organized political force, but it succeeded in articulating a tentative popular unification. It enjoyed remarkable early successes in the *symbolic contest*, but fell far short—and many core participants lacked the stomach—when it came to the *institutional contest*. In 2016 Bernie Sanders picked up the torch that Occupy lit but stopped running with. And we will see what comes next. This is not to suggest that such an articulation can be conjured out of thin air. The particulars of common conditions and experiences affect the extent to which a given articulation will resonate. Thus, the popular resonance of the message of Occupy Wall Street and of Bernie Sanders may itself be evidence that *likenings* or *ideal equivalences* have been emerging across many fragmented complexes of heterogeneous American society and even traversing nations. We may be seeing "groups that have been made alike" arising in the wake of similar neoliberal policies around the globe—helping to explain why starting circa 2011, in Paul Mason's words, it's been "kicking off everywhere."[44]

---

44   Paul Mason, *Why It's Kicking Off Everywhere: The New Global Revolutions* (London & New York: Verso, 2012).

Recognizing this basic structure of the complex interplay of smaller-scale groups, large-scale unifications, and individuals with fractured loyalties—as well as the importance of underlying structural conditions—we might begin to draw an anatomical map of the process of constructing broad-based challenger alignments capable of effective engagement in asymmetrical hegemonic contests against elite powers. And then we will need to figure out which specific groups, institutions, social blocs, etc. are needed for a contemporary challenger alignment that can win—not only the *symbolic contest* but also the *institutional contest*. The signs are all around us that such a progressive populist alignment is coming into being.

CONCLUSION—THE NEXT LEFT ZEITGEIST

If you are relatively new to political involvement, you didn't arrive "too late to the game." You are right on time.

Today so many "everyday people" are hungry for change—and also for the opportunity to meaningfully participate in a collective effort that can bring about that change. Over the past four decades, the political system and the economy have been rigged to serve the few, over and against the good of the many—reversing the trajectory toward greater equality that earlier struggles had set in motion. Yet, the crisis we face today is not only about unfair economic distribution. The losses we have suffered from abandoning a shared aspirational horizon—e.g., a vision of social equality, the elimination of poverty, an end to racism, a guarantee of health care, and the building of a "great society"—have to be measured in more than just material metrics.

We face a deep moral crisis, which we might also describe as a *crisis of community*. Alongside increasing economic stratification and the continuation of an adaptive racism, a "morality" of individualism has grown more and more severe. With this deadly combination, we have been losing the spirit that's needed to hold any community or any nation together: a *sense of responsibility for each other*. In the long term no community can survive when greed and irresponsibility are incentivized instead of reined in. This crisis points to a decision we must make as a society: Do we want to live in a nation that is defined by inclusionary, solidaristic community values, or one that is defined by the morally bankrupt values of Wall Street and the bigoted, exclusionary "solidarity" of reactionaries?

Our crisis of community exacerbates our crisis of democracy. As neoliberalism, individualism, and social fragmentation have advanced, we have seen a steady erosion of the kind of civic infrastructure that is necessary for effective social change efforts. As a consequence, too many young prospective change agents are "political orphans," unequipped with the basic skills of democratic engagement—e.g., how to organize a meeting, strategically influence a decision-maker, or even talk to one's neighbors about issues of shared concern.

With this backdrop, too many "radical spaces" have followed the organizing logic of neoliberalism, becoming places where self-selecting individuals can retreat into a radical identity enclave. Radicals have been relegated to a righteous corner, while extraordinarily wealthy elites have remade the world according to their designs. They wield the state like a bludgeon against the people, who lack an effective advocate.

American society is in desperate need of an aspirational collective vision. Who will step forward to articulate such a vision? What collective political actor exists today in the United States that is capable of mounting a viable challenge to the consolidated power of elites? Such a collective actor does not yet adequately exist. However, many of its ingredients do exist, and many more are emerging. From immigrant Dreamers to Occupy Wall Street to the climate justice movement, from Black Lives Matter to movements for gender justice and sexual liberation, from the army of Bernie 2016 volunteers to the defiant disrupters of Donald Trump's bigotry, the makings of a new broad and powerful progressive alignment are all around us.

Today a new generation that does not accept the fanciful notion that "there is no alternative" is in motion and on the rise. The "end of history" is over. The 1980s and 1990s are fading points in the rearview mirror, as we awaken to a very different "morning in America" than the one ushered in with Ronald Reagan's inauguration. In 1989 neoliberals and neocons trumpeted the failure of the Marxist historical project. Today in the United States more millennials identify with socialism than with capitalism.[1] And is it any wonder? We have entered adulthood to find our nation's infrastructure crumbling, our government hijacked by a mix of elitist neoliberals and extremist obstructionists, our economic prospects bleak and likely saddled with mountains of debt, our natural world writhing in crisis, our culture's rampant individualism hollow and unfulfilling, the international scene a hot mess, and our society lacking a collective aspirational horizon. Capitalism's platitudes do nothing for us. Call us socialists as an epithet, and it will fall flat.

Something profound has been happening in the subaltern spaces of American culture over the past two decades. The upwardly mobile professional class—which of course includes the punditry—has neglected to glance down to notice the ground shifting beneath its feet. On nearly every major issue, relatively progressive positions have come to enjoy a majority of support. From regulating Wall Street to progressive taxation to single-payer health care, from ending mass incarceration to marijuana legalization to gay marriage, the nation has become progressive.[2] The demographics and the culture have dramatically changed. But because radicals and progressives lack a foothold on today's political machinery, and because our voices are marginalized in the mainstream media, few at the top see what's happening—and what's coming.

Huge changes are afoot. But it is on us to make sure that change moves in a progressive direction—that it brings about a world with more social justice, racial equity, ecological sanity, meaningful democracy, and lasting peace. The current political order is in crisis, which presents us with an enormous political opportunity. However, lacking a progressive vehicle capable of taking advantage of the opportunity, there is no inherent reason

---

1   Pew Research Center, "Little Change in Public's Response to 'Capitalism,' 'Socialism,'" Pew Research Center, December 28, 2011, http://www.people-press.org/2011/12/28/little-change-in-publics-response-to-capitalism-socialism/?src=prc-headline.

2   Peter Beinart, "Why America Is Moving Left," *The Atlantic*, Jan/Feb 2016.

why things can't just keep getting worse indefinitely. In recent US history the political establishment has been trudging along in crisis—unpopular but, to date, hardly threatened by a viable challenger. In this context, a well-organized progressive challenger force would have had ample opportunity to ascend: to articulate compelling progressive premises for society and, rooted in that base of strength, contend in the political terrain. But such a sufficiently organized force does not yet exist.

This current deficiency in progressive political alignment and capacity has many causes and is not the fault of the younger generation. Again, we are at the tail end of a decades-long decline in bottom-up civic, labor, and progressive political infrastructure. In short, there are two sides to this coin (and many more compounding variables). On the one side, the ascendant political right in the 1970s started preparing for its counter-offensive, building up a veritable stockpile of political armaments, from its own media infrastructure to think tanks and cadres of trained political operatives. On the other side, the radical left shrank into the self-righteous shadow of its former self, while various liberal causes and foundations professionalized their work, siloing into a plethora of variegated, and fragmented, advocacy organizations—a lot of "generals without armies."

So even as popular attitudes have changed dramatically in recent years and created a favorable symbolic landscape for progressive mobilization, we are presently lacking in the capacities needed to take political advantage of this cultural shift. It will take time to rebuild such capacities, as these are gained through the course of concrete political struggles and campaigns. Fortunately, such growth often comes in dramatic spurts; we will likely encounter openings and opportunities along the way that, if seized, will help us to grow our political capacity much faster than usual circumstances invite. But there is ultimately no escape from the need to engage in the hard work of building this capacity—i.e., the scale of infrastructure, leadership, and on-the-ground skills that we need to win.

Leadership and organization tend to develop hand in hand. The old organizer's adage goes, "How do you identify leaders?

They have followers." In other words, without a social base, a leader is not a leader. Effective leaders emerge in tandem with effective organizations and movements. In recent years we have seen moments—ephemeral openings—when seemingly "leaderless" movements have quickly garnered enormous attention, broad sympathy, and the start of a volunteer base clamoring to get involved. Occupy Wall Street and Black Lives Matter come immediately to mind. Earlier in this book I have referred to the initial wave of participants in such movement moments as the "low-hanging fruit" and "usual suspects"—those who were ready for something like this to come along and who didn't need much persuasion to join the movement. At the level of society, we might think of this as a kind of initial investment of energy. For every hopeful individual who dives in at the outset, there are many times as many reasonably skeptical sympathizers watching from the sidelines, not yet convinced that the nascent effort can win; not ready to put the time, energy, and risk into something that is more likely than not to fizzle; or simply not seeing how they might meaningfully plug in to the effort or, all too often, not being provided an appealing opportunity to do so. And not just lone individuals, also sympathetic institutions with the potential to lend significant heft to a collective effort.

The long-and-short of it is that amidst the initial core of movement participants who take action at the center of promising political openings, there awaits a much more massive *potential* social force that has to be catalyzed and organized into action. The initial movement is often mistaken for the engine of change—and it often mistakes itself as such—when it is really just the starter motor. The initial eruption might happen with relatively little leadership or organization. But the activation of the larger social force that is needed to win the scale of change desired cannot be activated without a leadership that proves along the way its ability to navigate a winning course.

This is our challenge in the years ahead: to activate the *unusual* suspects. To do so, we have to develop leaders. They will emerge through concrete political struggles and campaigns that show everyday people that an organized collective force can win consequential battles. This is already happening, but we have to scale it up. It's not a matter of winning every campaign, of course, or only choosing battles that we can win. But if we want to attract everyday people into a mass political project, we absolutely have to show that we can sometimes win—and that we can contend within the existing political terrain, even as we are fighting from a position of severe disadvantage.

The establishment is in crisis. Popular opinion is on our side. But we have to step out of our comfortable clubhouse and into the terrain of politics. The little clubhouse called "activism" is moldy and decaying. We no longer fit inside of its self-defeating walls. We have to walk away from the sideshow if we want to seize the main stage. This is not about "selling out" or "watering down" our politics or becoming "less radical." There is nothing "radical" about an attachment to outsiderness and marginality. And what is more radical than believing that everyday people can come together and organize a collective vehicle powerful enough to remake the world?

Our radical project is collective human liberation, and it is the worthiest of goals. When we look at politics, we may feel disgusted by the ugliest of realms. Yet human liberation is only an empty slogan if its advocates are unwilling or unable to navigate political terrain. We cannot be purists. Like a night-light attracts moths, every aspirational social movement will attract its share of moralists and saints. Such persons can potentially play crucial roles, if they can help to articulate a *popular* morality that persuades more people to join or align with a larger movement. But sainthood does not scale up, and the self-righteous moralist is rarely the savvy agent of politics. While there's an important place for morality in political struggle, there is little room for personal purity. The purist becomes locked into particular forms of defiance or abstention and thereby becomes inflexible, unable to navigate the moves and countermoves inherent in a political contest. Movements cannot afford for their leadership to look at political terrain only through the distorting lens of self-righteousness. On the other hand, morality must inform our politics. We have to take up Dr. King's challenge to thread together morality and political power; to refuse to situate ourselves at either end of the false dichotomy we are too often presented, between "immoral power" and "powerless morality."[3]

Our struggle ahead is a contest over popular morality and it is also a contest of political power. For the first part, we have to tell a compelling story; to articulate a broad and inclusive *we* with which many different kinds of people feel a sense of belonging. For the second part we need leadership and organization, and the intentional cultivation of both. If the radical left zeitgeist that followed 1968 can be characterized by fragmentation, insularity, and a "politics of withdrawal," let us imagine future historians looking back on the radical left zeitgeist that followed the global uprisings of 2011 as defined by a politics of contestation. Let us build vehicles that are oriented to claim and contest our culture, our commons, our government, and our future.

The word *hegemony* in the title of this book is not intended as a joke. A left hegemonic project will likely become a realistic possibility in the decades ahead. But it is on us to make it so. It will take time to rebuild the emaciated progressive infrastructure we have inherited. It will take time to build our political analysis, leadership, and on-the-ground skills. But so many of us—more and more each year, it seems—are ready to resume the project of building a society that is based on social justice; a society that is for *all of us*.

---

3   King, "Where Do We Go From Here?"

GLOSSARY

Authors often mean different things with the same terms, or they intro-duce their own idiosyncratic phrases, and I am no exception. In the in-terest of being understood by readers, I offer the following glossary of terms to indicate how I use these terms throughout the book. With these working definitions I make no claims about the "true" meanings of any of these terms.

Activism (and activists)

I studiously avoid this term except when explicitly critiquing it. In chapter one I discuss how *activism* is a relatively new label that tends to unneces-sarily set "activists" apart from the broader society that they need to en-gage (if they hope to get anywhere in the realm of politics). I argue that the term implies a voluntary and self-selecting enterprise, an extracurricular activity, and a realm of subculture. It is a generic differentiating label that adds zero clarity or strategic value, and I encourage people to abandon it.

Articulation

This concept does not just refer to words and rhetoric, even though there is a rhetorical component to it. Following and elaborating on Antonio Gramsci's use of the term, I use it to describe the formation of a *political alignment* itself. Words, narratives, and symbols—but also action, inter-ventions, campaigns, political developments, structures, and material conditions—can help to form a sense of shared interest, common identi-ty, and *common sense*, which can bring a political alignment into being.

Ask

In the vernacular of union and community organizers, an *ask*—used as a noun—is an opportunity that an organizer provides to a person to take some form of aligned action, whether that be attending a community meeting, taking responsibility for a particular task, or stepping into an ongoing leadership role. There are many techniques that different organizers use to make clear and effective asks. A favorite tool is the *one-on-one* meeting, where an organizer gets to know the member, volunteer, or newcomer, and seeks to plug them into some action or role in a way that suits their particular interests, talents, skills, disposition, availability, etc.

Base

See *Core and base.*

Bloc recruitment

This happens when political actors activate whole groups, institutions, or social blocs into aligned action, rather than attempting to grow by recruiting individuals one at a time. When social movements experience rapid and dramatic growth—when they seem to suddenly emerge "from nowhere"—it is often by means of bloc recruitment. When longstanding institutions and social blocs come to identify with a movement, then membership in these pre-existing groups can come to imply activity in the movement—and this dramatically boosts the capacity and "people power" of a movement.

Campaign (+ targets, strategies, and tactics)

Standard elements of an issue *campaign* include a clearly defined political *goal* (e.g., getting a city government to replace lead pipes), at least one clear *target* (e.g., a decision maker who can deliver or concede the goal), and a *timeline*, at the end of which the group can evaluate whether or not it achieved its goal. A campaign also requires an overarching *strategy*, which is a theory and corresponding plan for how to apply political pressure to a target in order to win the goal. *Tactics*, then, are the specific activities (e.g., a protest, lobby day, or town hall meeting) that aim to move the strategy forward. (There are also *electoral campaigns*, where the aim is to get a specific person or party into a political office.)

Challenger alignment

A *political alignment* that is attempting to challenge the political establishment or status quo. See *political alignment.*

Clubhouse

I use this term pejoratively to refer to insular *"activist"* enclaves that, despite their lofty rhetoric, functionally serve as a private retreat for a self-selecting *righteous few.* While there do exist spaces that truly exemplify the "clubhouse," I also use the term as a kind of warning against the tendency toward such insularity.

Common sense

Common sense is what everyone knows so intuitively that it does not even need to be spoken aloud. It is as invisible as the air, as unnoticed as water is to a fish. In the Gramscian sense, common sense refers to dominant political assumptions, including assumptions about what is and what is not politically possible—or even what is or is not seen as "political." Gramsci showed how "common sense" is always a political construction; the current common sense always the outcome of earlier political contests. Elites articulate a "common sense" that validates (and obfuscates) their power and privilege, while a *political challenger* has to redefine the common sense in ways that call the establishment's authority into question. The term—by virtue of its claim to be "common"—infers a universality, but usually hides the particular agendas of particular actors. Throughout this book I advocate that radicals intentionally enter the contest over the contents of common sense (a central aspect of the *hegemonic contest*).

Core and base

Core essentially refers to the most active participants in a political group or social movement: those individuals who, through whatever combination of circumstance, socio-economic status, experience, effort, biography, and choices, make a social movement or political project a primary commitment. Having a critical number of such committed folks is indispensable to any political project. A core can do nothing, however, if it fails to understand that one of its primary roles is to help to activate and facilitate the involvement of a broader social *base.* The base is necessarily much larger than the core, but its members tend to give considerably less time and energy to the group or movement than core members are able to give. A common "repelling mechanism" of social movements happens when core members project their level of commitment onto the base, rather than taking responsibility for accommodating multiple levels of involvement. Core and base overlap, respectively, with the terms "usual suspects" and "unusual suspects" that I also use throughout this book.

Crisis of legitimacy

When the *political alignment* that props of up the current status quo is unraveling because its premises for existence have been significantly undermined by events, developments, disasters, or the actions of a *political challenger*. Those who have been governing are no longer seen as legitimate by a significant portion of the populace. If they cannot regain this legitimacy, they risk losing their power.

Dominant narrative

See *political narrative.*

Ethic of responsibility and Ethic of ultimate ends

Sociologist Max Weber introduced these phrases to describe "two fundamentally differing and irreconcilably opposed" modes of conduct.[1] The adherent to an *ethic of ultimate ends* strives to "do the right thing," no matter how it all turns out—even if a righteous stand seems destined to fail. (This ethic shares much in common with what I call the *story of the righteous few.*) The adherent to the *ethic of responsibility*, on the other hand, thinks about the likely reactions to her action, and adds these likelihoods into her strategic calculus. Neither person has a crystal ball through which they can see the future, but the latter person takes responsibility for making her best educated guess about how her actions are likely to interact with a complex unfolding reality. The former person, on the other hand, feels compelled to take righteous stands as an individual, and let the chips fall where they may.

Floating signifier

Also often referred to as an *empty signifier*, this is a symbol whose

---

1   Weber, *From Max Weber*, 120.

meaning is ambiguous, but that serves to signify, catalyze, or bolster a broad *political alignment.* Floating signifiers are essential for catalyzing broad alignments in a heterogeneous society. The signifier frames and conjures the alignment itself, and is necessarily ambiguous—its meaning is floating, its content "empty"—as all of the groups that comprise the alignment must see their values and aspirations reflected in the symbol. The signifier can be a politician (quintessentially Argentina's Juan Perón), a group (e.g., public school teachers occupying Wisconsin's state capitol), a slogan (e.g., "We are the 99%!"), or a brand (e.g., the "Tea Party"), among other possibilities. Floating signifiers are the "chapter titles" of *metanarratives.*

Framing

To rhetorically *frame* an issue is to present it strategically in a way that aims to win the sympathy of a particular audience. Like a picture frame, a "rhetorical frame" is a partial representation of reality: attention is drawn to certain details, while other details are cropped out of the frame. Also see *political narrative.*

Hardcore

A close relative of the *political identity paradox* is the tendency within highly cohesive political groups to want to "turn up the heat"—to be more *hardcore.* Group members may exaggerate the group's distinctive features as an expression of belonging (and to gain status within the group). This can result in a desire for tactical escalation for its own sake—unhinged from strategic considerations—and can help a group to go "off the rails" in no time (i.e., to lose touch with broader social bases). Good leaders can anticipate this tendency and can help the group to navigate it, by making sure that the hardcore expression is designed to strengthen bonds between the group's core members and its broader political base.

Hegemony

Leadership or predominant influence exercised by one particular group within a given political sphere (e.g., international, national, regional, or local). Key to the concept is that leaders (or government) have to win the consent of those who are led (or governed), as opposed to ruling only by means of coercion and physical force.

Hegemonic alignment

This is simply a *political alignment* that has more-or-less won the *hegemonic contest*. In so doing it has become broadly hegemonic. This alignment then becomes invested in the maintenance of the *hegemonic order* that it has shaped. No longer a *challenger alignment*, it now has to govern or have some political fraction of the alignment (e.g., a political party) take care of governance.

Hegemonic contest

A struggle over which group or political alignment has *hegemony*. For example, a nascent political force may emerge as a *political challenger*, build a broader *political alignment* around itself, and take on the political establishment (or *hegemonic order*). Throughout this book I elaborate on two central aspects of a hegemonic contest: the *symbolic contest* and the *institutional contest*. The symbolic contest is over narratives, symbols, meaning, and *common sense*. The institutional contest has to do with a political actor's "ground game" capacity to maneuver through the minutia of *political terrain* in order to shape structures, laws, policies, distributions of wealth, and relationships of power. While it can be conceptually useful to distinguish between the two (e.g., in order to develop appropriate strategies and tactics), in messy reality the two contests are inextricable, mixing together to constitute the *hegemonic contest*.

Hegemonic order

This is essentially the political establishment—i.e., a somewhat stabilized arrangement of power relations—but the term *hegemonic* emphasizes that this political order has been established not by chance but by the outcome of struggles between competing actors and social forces.

Institutional contest

See *hegemonic contest*.

Life of the group

While the purpose of social change organizations is, ostensibly, to bring about social change, the existence of a group can also become its own motivating force. I use the term *life of the group* to describe groups' dynamic internal motivational structures. I explore how the logic of the *life of the group* often operates in tension with the logic of political instrumentality (i.e., the group's potential accomplishments beyond its own existence).

Lifeworld

Highly related to the *life of the group*, the *lifeworld* is a term that sociologist Jürgen Habermas uses to describe the communal spaces that human beings long for. Habermas discusses how the logics of capitalism and bureaucracy have penetrated and undermined the solidaristic *lifeworld*, and how modern people seek out an intact lifeworld for ourselves. A political problem that I elaborate in chapters three and four is that this desire to create an intact *lifeworld* in social movement spaces can eclipse the motivation for creating political vehicles that can win.

Metanarrative

A grand philosophical story that attempts to explain the world for everyone. The Enlightenment and the story of progress are classic examples of metanarratives, but so is Marxism, and the term can be used more broadly to describe any "narrative" or explanatory schema that seeks to provide a universal account of the social world. Postmodernists tend to deconstruct hegemonic metanarratives and then stop there. In this book I argue that radicals and progressives have to also construct metanarratives that normalize a social justice agenda.

Mobilize

To move individuals and groups into action. Mobilizing is often contrasted with *organizing*, even if the two concepts overlap significantly. In broad strokes, I think of organizing as "planting the seeds" and mobilizing as "harvesting the crop." See *organize.*

Narrative insurgency

This is a conceptual approach to political persuasion (and organizing) that seeks to find points of connection with others, rather than emphasizing differences. *Narrative insurgency* requires an examination of other people's narratives (or worldview), in order to understand the component parts and find common ground. A "narrative insurgent" starts with and emphasizes that common ground, using it as a base for fomenting "homegrown insurgency" within the larger dominant narrative.

Narrative strategy

See *political narrative*.

Organize

Organizing, in the political sense, is to develop disparate social elements—or an existing social bloc—into a unified political force. It is to name, *frame*, and narrate the trajectory of a group; to *articulate* its goals, grievances and targets; to move it into strategic collective action; to inspire other social forces to align in a common direction; and to leverage this force for political ends.

Political alignment

An aligning of different social groups, organizations, and movements into a unified force that intervenes to shape social, economic, and political reality. I use this term to describe both the process of aligning otherwise fragmented groups, and also the force or vehicle that, once aligned, can contend in the *hegemonic contest*. Such an alignment is not necessarily clearly defined, neatly delineated, or formally coordinated; often it is none of these things. A political alignment stays intact to the extent that its component parts identify with or see their interests bound up with it. A political alignment may be a *challenger alignment* or a *hegemonic alignment*, depending on whether it is challenging or maintaining the political establishment and status quo.

Political challenger

A group that is attempting to challenge the status quo. If such a group aligns with broader forces, it can also be called a *challenger alignment*.

Political force

Any social body that has built some degree of capacity to apply political pressure (or contend in the *political terrain*).

Political identity paradox

In order to mobilize members, political groups have to cultivate a strong internal identity; cohesion is essential for motivating the level of commitment that political struggle demands. The paradox, or dilemma, is that strong internal identity can create walls between the group and its potential allies. Too much cohesion can lead down a dead-end path of insularity—and isolated groups are hard-pressed to build the kind of broad-based power needed to achieve the big changes they imagine. I argue that good leaders can help groups to navigate this paradox by fostering a strong internal identity while simultaneously encouraging group members to orient themselves towards allies and others.

Political narrative

I see language, symbols, stories, and narrative as central to how individuals and groups come to understand their own political interests and whether they will identify with one political project or another. *Dominant narratives* are the stories that carry prevailing assumptions (i.e., the *common sense*) which tend to justify "the way things are," including existing power relations. In this book (especially chapters seven and eight) I introduce common narrative elements that *political subjects* use to articulate political interests, visions, and strategies. Engaging with these concepts intentionally is what I mean by *narrative strategy*. Also see *articulation*.

Political subject

This is just a group, at whatever scale, that has the capacity to intervene as a group in the terrain of *politics*.

Political terrain

With this term I use a geographical battlefield metaphor to imagine political struggles. The term implies certain constraints that *political subjects* have to navigate in order to reach their goals. A terrain may be favorable or unfavorable depending on one's position within it. Political terrain is constantly shifting.

Politicization

A process through which individuals come to see their problems not as personal challenges, but as having structural causes, and they begin to identify as part of a particularly framed "we" that shares grievances, interests, and enemies in common, and whose common problems demand collective solutions.

Politics

With the word *politics* I do not only mean *electoral* politics, but any contest between competing interests—usually the collective interests of *groups* (even if these interests themselves have to be *articulated* in order to exist). Borrowing from Gramsci, I judge whether a certain action or group is *political* or not based on its engagement with extant power relations and structures. To be *political* is not merely to hold or to express opinions about issues, but to be engaged with the terrain of power, with an orientation towards changing the broader society and its structures.

Prefigurative politics

In contrast to *strategic politics* (or just *politics*), *prefigurative politics* seeks to demonstrate the better world it envisions for the future in the actions it takes today. Connected to contemporary anarchist movements, *prefigurative politics* represented a major tendency within Occupy Wall Street. Rather than accept this philosophy on its own terms, I position it squarely within the internal *life of the group* (see chapters three and four), and specifically the tendency toward insularity.

Progressive

What an ambiguous label! I embrace it and use it throughout this book partly because of its ambiguity. I use it to refer to people who lean left on *both* social and economic issues—from prison reform and immigration reform, to gay rights and reproductive rights, to taxing the rich and regulating corporations. I mean for it to cast a wide net. Relatedly, I embrace it specifically because, according to polls, the label holds positive associations for a majority of Americans. That may make me sound fickle, but there is a principle at work here: if a word is popular, that usually means it is also powerful. To challenge entrenched power requires us to claim powerful words and symbols and to make them mean the things we need them to mean. My definition of *progressive* encompasses left *radicals*, even if they occupy the left end of the larger spectrum. (The full progressive spectrum—as I've defined it here—points the way to the broad *political alignment* that *radicals* will hopefully play an important role in constructing.)

Radical

Radical literally means to *go to the root*, and I see radicals attempting to get to the root of social problems. The label is unavoidably ambiguous, including in the ways that I use it throughout this book. It can imply an edginess, a willingness to push the envelop with unorthodox tactics, a willingness to take risks, a more active commitment to social change than most people in society are able to maintain, and often a commitment to particular positions on various issues. In popular usage, radical is imbued with ideas of youth, with outsiderness, and it is sometimes used disparagingly as a synonym for *extremist*. I reject the notion that to be radical is to be "extreme"—I see radicals as essential to every major social movement in history. On the other hand, throughout this book I push self-identified "radicals" to not be attached to outsiderness. As I have defined the term *progressive*, all left *radicals* are progressive, but they occupy the left edge of a much larger progressive spectrum. (Clearly, though, not all progressives are radicals).

Social bloc

A group of people, usually at a large scale, who are recognizable as a group because of certain shared characteristics (e.g., blacks, conservative Christians, industrial workers, or peasants). A social bloc's shared features could be the basis of their *politicization* or *political alignment*.

Social movement

I use this term as shorthand because it is common parlance, but I often find its usage unacceptably imprecise. When I use it, I usually mean political action that encompasses a network of groups and individuals engaged in a struggle around a particular social, economic, or political issue, at a relatively large scale over a given period of time. The concept of a *social movement* originated with 18th and 19th century labor, socialist, and abolitionist movements. Among scholarly studies, the US civil rights movement serves as an enduring prototype.

Social unification

The common identification of different, typically heterogeneous, social forces. While a homogeneous group could be said to be "socially unified," this hardly constitutes an accomplishment, so I don't use the term to describe such obvious, already-given unity. For my purposes, I use the term *social unification* to describe both the process and the product of political *articulation*. Social unification is a contingent political accomplishment. It overlaps significantly with *political alignment*.

Story of the righteous few

I use this term to describe a common self-defeating mentality among radicals to prize their own political marginality. Basically if the dominant society is seen as bad, then marginalization within society must be good. Radicals may tell each other stories of how they were ostracized from this or that group, how they were the outcast in their family, how they were the only radical in a group of compromising reformists, and so on. In the story of the righteous few, success itself becomes suspect. This is related to *ultra-leftism* and Max Weber's concept of the *ethic of ultimate ends*.

Strategic politics

Engaging in *politics* with the intention of winning; planning accordingly. Following Wini Breines usage, I use this term to distinguish "regular" politics from *prefigurative politics*. See *politics* and *prefigurative politics*.

Symbolic contest

See *hegemonic contest*.

Terrain of power

Used interchangeably with *political terrain*.

Ultra-leftistm

Ultra-leftists are ideological purists who need to feel, and will claim to be, more radical than you are.

INDEX